D1559001

A volume in the series

MYTH AND POETICS

edited by Gregory Nagy

A full list of titles in the series appears at the end of the book.

BORN OF THE EARTH

Myth and Politics in Athens

NICOLE LORAUX

Translated from the French by Selina Stewart

CORNELL UNIVERSITY PRESS

ITHACA AND LONDON

English translation first published 2000 by Cornell University Press

This work is published with the aid of the French Ministry of Culture.

Originally published under the title *Né de la Terre*. *Mythe et politique à Athènes*. Copyright ©
Editions du Seuil, 1996, in the series "La Librairie du xxe siècle," edited by Maurice Olender.

Printed in the United States of America

Library of Congress Cataloging-in-Publication Data

Loraux, Nicole.
   [Né de la terre. English]
   Born of the earth : myth and politics in Athens / Nicole Loraux ; translated from the
French by Selina Stewart.
      p. cm — (Myth and poetics)
   Includes bibliographical references and index.
   ISBN 0-8014-3419-X (hardcover)
      1. Citizenship—Greece—Athens. 2. Sex role—Greece—Athens. 3. Women—Greece—
Athens. I. Title. II. Series.

JC75.C5 L6713 2000
292.1'3—dc21
                                                                              00-021218

Cornell University Press strives to use environmentally responsible suppliers and materials to
the fullest extent possible in the publishing of its books. Such materials include vegetable-
based, low-VOC inks and acid-free papers that are recycled, totally chlorine-free, or partly
composed of nonwood fibers. Books that bear the logo of the FSC (Forest Stewardship
Council) use paper taken from forests that have been inspected and certified as meeting the
highest standards for environmental and social responsibility. For further information, visit
our website at www.cornellpress.cornell.edu.

Cloth printing   10 9 8 7 6 5 4 3 2 1

FSC Trademark © 1996 Forest Stewardship Council A.C.
SW-COC-098

Contents

nian men are conceived and emerge from the wombs of women. For all other Athenian men, notionally descended as they are from the proto-Athenian man, there are two kinds of *genos* that explain their genesis. Primarily, they are born of the Earth because they belong to the Athenian "race"; secondarily, they are born of wombs because they belong to the human "race."

The problem is that there are people who get left out of this worldview. Only Athenian men can think of themselves as primarily descended from Mother Earth, while other men are descended merely from human wombs. And what about those other men who view themselves as autochthonous, just like the Athenians? Let us take, for example, the natives of the Arcadian city of Tegea, who have a similar autochthonous myth about their own *genos*. In reaction, the Athenians will try to get around this contradiction of their uniqueness by making the Tegeans not unique: they will refer to them not as Tegeans, in specific terms of their local Mother Earth of Tegea, but instead in general terms as Arcadians, since other Arcadians do not lay claim to such a myth of autochthony. It is safer for Athenians to speak of Arcadian autochthony than of Tegean autochthony, since Mother Earth can thus be generalized, stylized, attenuated.

Closer to home, there is a far bigger problem: what if you happen to be an Athenian woman? When you give birth, is the *genos* primary or secondary? What comes first? Is it the birth of a child from a womb or the emergence of a seedling from the earth? In other words, what is modeled on what? When you give birth, are you re-enacting the genesis of the First Man? And what if your child is a daughter? There are other myths about the First Woman, but these will not fit the birth of *your* daughter—unless, that is, you are already thinking of Pandora. These are the questions raised by *Born of the Earth*. To read this book is not only to seek answers: it is to reconfront one's own humanity.

Born of the Earth.

The Athenians were, or at least so they would have others believe, and— perhaps—were convinced by it. Before I sensed it in my body, I questioned it; now I feel it in my heart.

Everything is the same, and nothing is the same.

This I find less questionable. Which gives the texts an extra twist, at least so they say. Each is free to cross or not to cross the boundary, including the difficult boundary of the feminine.

November 1995

I would like to thank Hélène Monsacré, who was kind enough to assume the burdens of manuscript preparation and meticulous proofreading of the French-language edition.

This book was born long ago from a dialogue, never since interrupted, with Maurice Olender. It is also thanks to him that the volume appears today.

N.L.

BORN OF THE EARTH

CHAPTER I

At Last, Born Mortal

There is no Greek Genesis. Nothing to provide the Greeks with, at one stroke, a Creator and a date of birth; nor any Greek poem on the origins of humanity possessing the authority of the *Theogony*, Hesiod's poem on the birth of the gods. All the same, the Greeks had no shortage of myths with which to speak of the first men or to imagine the origin of the human condition: stories of long ago, when the Earth Mother freed humankind from the pressing concerns of the reproduction of the species, when the eternal spring of the Golden Age disguised death in sleep and granted mortal men eternal life.

Man comes from the earth. On this point—ground zero of myth; rarely developed for its own sake, more often alluded to or simply left unstated—poets and philosophers, national traditions of the poleis, and tales of the origins of the Greek race all agree. But humanity has at least two ways of coming from the earth. In certain myths, such as the Platonic myth of the *gêgeneis* (born [root *gen-] of the earth),[1] or the autochthonous Athenian or Theban myths (from *autokhthôn*, born from the earth [*khthôn*] itself [*autos*] of one's homeland), man—mankind, a man, or men—rises up from the earth as a plant emerges from the ground or a child from the womb. According to other myths, such as the Hesiodic story of the creation of women, the human creature (here women and the opposition of the sexes, as we shall see, are not without significance), made of earth and modeled by a god in the role of craftsman, is the product of a fabrication. Earth as field, earth as substance: clod or clay. If at the level of social practices, sowing (or more broadly agriculture) and pottery-making (or more broadly craftsmanship) oppose each other as natural vs. artificial,[2] it is not surprising that between these two versions of creation there should be more dissimilarities than resemblances.

On one side is the earth as field, spontaneously fertile or fertilized by a "sowing," producing men. These are primitive races spontaneously arising from Gê, like the Platonic *gêgeneis*, or deriving from a natural medium through a "mediated chthonic birth"[3] such as men "born of oak and stone," Hesiod's race of bronze sprung from ash trees,[4] and autochthones born from their native soil such as the Theban Spartoi, who sprang up full-grown and ready for combat, the product of a bizarre sowing as indicated by their name ("the Sown"), rising out of the plain on which Kadmos had scattered a dragon's teeth. Likewise the mythical ancestor of the Athenians, Erichthonios or Erechtheus, albeit heir to a family saga of some complexity, was a product of the soil: the virgin Athena having evaded the pressing advances of the craftsman god Hephaistos, the earth received the rejected lover's sperm and gave birth to the miraculous infant who became the king of Athens.

On the other side is the earth as docile matter, fashioned by a divine craftsman, sculptor, or potter. In Hesiod this craftsman is called Hephaistos, and woman is his masterpiece of cunning. A subsequent tradition preferred to have humankind born in the workshop of the intermediary Prometheus, a late invention perhaps, and perhaps also the invention of a philosopher or comic poet; but what is important is that in Greek mythical thought, man could result from a technical act.

Born of the Earth (primordial *Gê* of the cosmogonies, anthropomorphized *Gê* represented in the birth of Erichthonios, a solitary power laboring like a woman giving birth; fertile and nourishing *gê*, universal provider of life, from whom men grow like plants; *gê patris*, a civic homeland whose inhabitants defend it as they would a father and mother), or made of earth (of earth and water in some versions, like Pandora in Hesiod or like the frightened Achaeans whom Menelaus could only bring himself to refer to as women in the *Iliad* [7.99]): man has at his disposal two competing mythical discourses concerning his origin.

Certainly the fertility myths seem largely to prevail over the myths of artifice. The earth is more mother than matter, in Greek thought as in language, where the semantic fields of sexual reproduction and plant growth are inextricably intertwined. Without trying to decide which of the two, the earth or the female, imitates the other, a Greek question

raised by Plato and rehearsed ad nauseam by modern scholars (thus Dieterich in his celebrated *Mutter Erde*),[5] let us note that in marriage as on
the tragic stage, woman is a field to be worked, a furrow to be sown.

Yet we must go further, beyond the opposition of these two models.
The Greeks themselves sometimes blurred the borders between clod and
clay; this happens, as we shall see, with Pandora, the first woman. Above
all, both versions of the creation myth have the same tendency to replace
the question of the beginning with that of what happens afterward.

To explain: humankind exists because there were "first men," yet
the greatest difficulty is not to assign them birth, but to give them posterity. In other words, even if, with Plato, the Greeks were willing to
believe that "men of the preceding age were born from the earth instead
of being engendered one from another,"[6] it was nevertheless required
that one day the endless cycle of reproduction, to which humankind
must be subject in order to perpetuate itself on this earth, begin.[7] Doubtless the process did not proceed without delays and "misfires," since in
order to characterize the beginnings of humanity, myths multiply the
repetition, the reduplication, the discontinuity. Sometimes men are born
from primordial beings who are themselves derived from the earth, and
who, in a sort of dress rehearsal, ensure the transition between the origin and the times of men. Thus the "parents" of Phoroneus, mythical
ancestor of the Argives and "first man," were the river Inachus and the
nymph Melia,[8] daughter of Ocean (according to Apollodorus) or sister
of the *Meliai*, ash-tree nymphs who were born from Gaia fertilized by
the blood of Ouranos.[9] Likewise in the Orphic myths humankind arose
from the ashes of the Titans, who could be seen as a "dramatic prefiguration" of the human race.[10] Sometimes reduplication and discontinuity
dominate, and the myth is prepared to annihilate a first human race in
order to give humanity a new start: the flood removes men from the face
of the earth, but Deucalion and Pyrrha, by throwing stones onto the
ground, produce a new human race that instantly engages in the process
of reproducing itself.

For man *qua* man was born of men, and not of the unknown.

"Tell me your race and your native land, because surely you are not
from the legendary oak tree or from stone."[11] Socrates replies to this
Homeric question a few centuries later: "I too have relatives; since, as
Homer says, I am not 'born from oak or rock,' but from human beings;

consequently I have parents."[12] To codify one's origins in a proverb is, in everyday social life, an elegant way of dismissing them. Greek myths do not make this choice overtly, and with reason: myth is nothing if not the beginnings of things. Yet everything takes place in a manner suggesting that the Greeks were less interested in their origins per se than in this separation from their origins which definitively constituted the human condition.

Whence the delays and new starts, as if the cycle of generations had trouble finding its own rhythm. Between the time of men and that of creation, several human races are intercalated, successively appearing and disappearing forever. So with the four first races of Hesiodic myth: the race of gold, the race of silver, the race of bronze, and the race of heroes.[13] As for the fifth, the race of iron, our own, it does not *descend* strictly speaking from the preceding ones, as Pierre Vidal-Naquet observes: actually it descends only from itself.[14] But, in order for it to exist, there had to be a tale, this strange temporal frame, full of false starts and real endings. The gods "made" the first four races (*poiêsan, poiêse*); to the fifth Hesiod gives neither creator nor origin: it exists, that is the important thing.[15] But it leads its existence via a mode of exclusion, and this is how the myth is to be understood.

Thus genesis flies to the rescue of structure, and when we speak about creation we understand the human condition, *hic et nunc.*

Thus man is born, and dies. Even the language of myth underscores his mortality: men are *mortal (brotoi, thnêtoi anthrôpoi)* before they are characterized as terrestrial, and they are terrestrial only in the sense of "those who live on the earth," *epikhthonioi* (from *epi* [on] and *khthôn* [the earth]).[16] Moreover *khthôn* is not the primordial earth (*gê*) but the earth on which the homes and cities of men are situated, firmly established between the sky of the Olympian gods and the depths of Hades. One might look for a reference to creation in the word *khamaigeneis*; but this rare and obscure word probably means no more than "men who are born on earth."[17] Georges Dumézil observed that for the majority of Indo-European languages, man is "the terrestrial" (thus Latin *homo*, from *humus*) before being "the mortal,"[18] yet the Greek choice of mortality is more than a linguistic preference: a quiet (?) affirmation, and without euphemism. The problem with men, in the end, is not that they exist—

in a way, man is what is there—but rather that they die; or, to put it differently, that they are constituted by death.

In a later tradition man, created by Prometheus and Athena, was made from clay and wind, just as the Babylonian was clay mixed with the blood of a god, and the Jew was dust into which the Creator breathed life.[19] But more generally, Greek myth was little concerned with the duality of mortal body and immortal soul. It was up to the philosophers to associate body with earth and soul with ether,[20] or animate with fire the mixture of earth and water which made the human being![21] Greek myths read death in life, and preferred to tell of the irremediable separation that excluded men from the company of the gods.

Generalizing what Jean-Pierre Vernant wrote concerning the Prometheus myth in Hesiod, one might say that "in some way the story [of this separation] describes the creation of man."[22]

In the Golden Age men were close to the gods, and are so no longer. Hesiod and Pindar go so far to say that they have the same origin, meaning that they both came from Gê.[23] But a rift occurred which destroyed the easy conviviality that certain texts suggest,[24] and in *Iliad* 5.440 Apollo brutally reminds the hero Diomedes that "there will always be two distinct races, that of the immortal gods and that of men who walk the earth."

Let us now turn to the myth of Prometheus in the *Theogony* (535–616), since Hesiod also told the story of this separation. We know that before an assembly of gods and men the Titan Prometheus conducted the first sacrifice, deceiving the gods to man's advantage through a clever ruse; since that time the generations of humankind (*phula anthrôpôn*[25]—and it is not insignificant that henceforth they were so designated) sacrificed to the immortals in order to repair the broken link. But the rupture was consummated when Prometheus repeated his offense and stole for men the fire of which the anger of Zeus had deprived them. With the cooking-fire, man awoke to himself, a social creature who cooked his food: no more nectar and ambrosia, yet at least he no longer ate his food raw, like the beasts. But Zeus was not a god to confess himself beaten, and his anger not likely to tolerate the sight of "the brilliant light of fire glowing among men." Therefore "in the place of fire he created an evil destined for men" (567–579), an evil called woman (*gunê*).

The Creation of Woman

Woman: a beautiful evil, a costly luxury, a poisoned gift to humankind. Fine.

But if there were human beings before woman was created, how could this add-on be a part of the human race? With the formulation of this abrupt question, we see instantly that the humanity of woman is by definition ambiguous.[26] If the issue concerns the extension of the word "humanity," then the whole matter is between two words that French and English (more radical than Greek, which distinguishes the two) translate indifferently as "men": *anthrôpoi*, human beings as opposed to gods, and *andres*, men as opposed to women. In Greek social and political practices only *andres* had the right of speech, and at the horizon of their mythical thought one may discern the regret that women had ever materialized and the dream of living and reproducing without them.[27] Woman is the other, and in the Hesiodic text of the myth she is designated with the neuter gender as long as possible, as if even through the signifier one could hold back the arrival of the feminine. The consequences, it is true, are considerable: as soon as this beautiful evil received a name, "men" ceased to be called *anthrôpoi* and received in their turn a new name, that of *andres*. If the creation of woman is the ultimate consequence of the separation of men and gods, the paradox consists in that "men" are born into the human condition only when they become *andres*, one-half of the human race.

Two halves make a whole; this should (will) make one. But the two halves were strangers to each other from the start, given that the production of the female, carefully distinguished from that of *andres*, derives from an independent account. This is a specifically Greek trait; the creation of woman in Genesis is indissociable from that of man, even within a two-stage process, and the Babylonian creation myth has seven pairs of primordial ancestors. Moreover woman is not born, but produced by a craftsman, Hephaistos, accomplishing the will of Zeus. She is therefore artifice, a living *daidalon*.[28] "Out of earth, the illustrious lame one modeled a being exactly like a chaste virgin."[29] In this is all the truth of the female: woman resembles virgin, woman resembles woman, which is to say that she is entirely and essentially *a semblance*. Woman is certainly the "deceitful feminine form" of Indo-European myth studied by Georges Dumézil, with this basic difference: for the Greeks, the "false woman" is not a disguised man, but woman herself. Unlike the golden maidens of Hephaistos, animated artifices in which the automaton resembles the living, woman lives by being an artifice.[30]

Consequently in and through her, duality is reintroduced into humanity. Not only does the addition of this surplus to the human race have the effect of cutting it in two, but woman herself is a mixture, according to the story in the *Works and Days* (54–105), which parallels that of the *Theogony* without saying exactly the same thing. Made of earth and water, woman combines "the voice and strength of a human being," "the beautiful form of a lovely maiden, in the image of the immortal goddesses" (61–63) and "the mind of a bitch" (67). This before Hesiod, later on in the poem, gives her a womb.

But this womb has from then on the function of reproducing humankind.

Here again we find, even more acute, the tension between origin and the times of men. If it is difficult to proceed from the birth of the *gêgeneis* to human cycles of generation, how can a living artifice assume the function of fertility? Hesiod resolves the difficulty by means of a noun: woman receives the name of *Pandora*, and it is significant that, even if the poet muddied the traces by inventing a new etymology (80–82: "she who is the gift of all"), this was also one of the epithets of Earth ("she who gives all"). But it would be hasty simply to conclude from this that "mortal Pandora is only the transposition of the Earth Mother into the human order":[31] it would be to forget, for example, that in Greek mythical tradition, at least as established in our texts, there is not a single autochthonous woman to be found. Nevertheless, woman had to assume what had been the function of the earth. Reflecting in their own fashion on the strange relationship that is established in Pandora between fertility and artifice, Athenian potters also succumbed to the desire to confound Earth Mother and Earth Clay. A cup in the British Museum shows Athena and Hephaistos occupied with a female figure, statue, or automaton, a stiff doll to whom the sculptor has curiously given the name of Anesidora, another ritual appellation of the Earth Mother. But inversely on an Oxford krater, a splendid *korê* named Pandora rises out of the earth, a bride ready for marriage. . . .[32] Do we have her at last, this autochthonous woman? Those who adhere to the naturist thesis, who recognize a hypostasis of the Earth Mother in every female figure, are of course exultant. Others marvel, or ascribe this contamination between Pandora and Pandora to the double nature of woman.

If everything is nicely arranged in terms of image, things are a bit more complicated in terms of narrative. In the *Theogony* the conclusion of the myth contains a final ambiguity. "From her came the female race of women" (590): thus, far from designating the first woman as the mother of humankind—which, after all, one had every right to expect—the text makes the original woman the mother of a group closed upon itself: the female *genos*, the race of women. As if the same could only produce the same. As if the female sex were reproduced in a closed circuit. As, in the myth of Aristophanes reviewed by Plato, the male is born from the sun (masculine) and the female from the earth (feminine); in order not to complicate things further we will temporarily forget that a third sex, the androgenous, is born from the moon.[33] No doubt this is due to the ambiguity of the word *genos*, in Hesiod as in Plato, which lends itself equally well to designating a sexual gender as to characterizing humankind in its entirety. But there is more here than a question of words. "Are we born from one alone or from two?" "Is the same born from the same or from the other?" With these two variants formulated by Claude Lévi-Strauss,[34] the Greeks set themselves the problem (it does not seem to be easy, allowing the mixing of the sexes): how can men who are truly men and women who are truly women be born from a sexual union? Must one allow that there are male seeds and female seeds? And how can the one emerge from the two? These are questions which philosophers and doctors, comic poets and tragedians, perhaps even legislators have not ceased to raise. But it is the myths that originated them.

Pandora has taken us on a long detour: feminine wiles, no doubt. . . .

Yet one more word before this "cunning heart" is again silenced. The myth of Pandora is perhaps the only creation myth that established itself without contest and without rival in Greek tradition,[35] so imposing was the Greek view of the *genos* of women as the bringer of evil and of the death of men. In a word, of the tragic.[36]

To return to *andres*, this time using the term in its civic sense: *andres*, an assembly of whom constitutes the city (*polis*) according to a Greek adage, are adults, soldier-citizens. Each city has a "first man" as ancestor, founder, and civilizing or political hero, born of the earth like Erichthonios of Athens, of a river like Phoroneus of Argos, from a marsh such as Alalkomeneus of Boeotia, or born from the union of a god and either a mortal woman or nymph; thus Arkas, the eponymous hero of the Arcadians, was the son of Zeus and the nymph Callisto, and Pelasgos the son of Zeus and the mortal Niobe. Moreover, there were multiple instances of contamination between these different origins: the autochthonous Erichthonios could also properly be called "son of the gods," and Athenian tradition was fond of this illustrious title, which was extended to the whole community of *andres Athênaioi*; likewise Pelasgos the son of Zeus was in another version of the myth "like to a god, he whom the black earth bore in the forest heights of the mountains, so that there might be a mortal race."[37] Phoroneus, sometimes son of the river Inachos alone, sometimes son of Inachos and Melia, was the "first man," the "father of mortal men."

Nineteenth-century German scholarship attempted to derive these multiple legends from a single myth, a creation myth common to all Greeks and which each city presented in its own local form: men born of the Earth or the union of the Earth and Sky (Zeus representing the Sky and each of his consorts the Earth Mother, of which she would be merely an individualized hypostasis).[38] But beyond the fact that these wearisome reductions to a single, sempiternal story generally overlook the specific traits of each tradition or each figure, divine or human (Zeus is not the Sky, Deucalion cannot be reduced to Zeus nor Pyrrha to the red Earth; the fire of Phoroneus, a fire of celestial origin like that which Zeus sometimes ignites in the tops of ash trees,[39] should not be confused with that which Prometheus stole for men, nor with that which burns in the forge of Hephaistos, "father" of the Athenians[40]), it is poor method always to seek to reconstitute the singular, as if a primitive, unitary *logos*, lost for all time, continues to be expressed through fragments of discourse, accidental traces of a paradigm that has disappeared.

It is not that each city wishes to tell in its own way the story of the birth of the first man. Every foundation myth is less concerned with providing a version of the beginnings of humankind than with postulating the original nobility of a founder: as Erechtheids, the autochthonous Athenians liked to remember that the palace of Erechtheus was also the temple of Athena;[41] descendants of Pelasgos, the Pelasgians were the true inhabitants of the Peloponnese. No doubt such traditions raised the problem of the passage to the human: if Erichthonios or Phoroneus initiated the time of human history for the Athenian or Argive city, which member of Athena's clan was the first of the *andres Athênaioi*? How could the son of Inachos bring to an end the primordial era in which the first inhabitants of Argos were the Rivers? Zeus is the most frequent "father" of national heroes, which leads some to take the Homeric expression "Zeus father of gods and men" literally, whereas perhaps there is only a classificatory relationship. Yet the problem remains: what makes the son of a god into the first human? In fact the poleis were little occupied with this question. The important thing was that the eponymous ancestor was fully human and of prestigious birth at the same time. Thus the present found its justification in a genealogy that attached it to the earliest times, and poets from the archaic period, the first logographers (and magistrates of cities?), established these "ancient histories"—quasi-histories of the poleis, or even of the Greek people, in which the Pelasgian race attaches itself to Phoroneus or Pelasgos, and the Hellenic to Deucalion.

Between each of these "first men" of miraculous birth or divine origin, and the races of the first men which came from the earth or were created by the gods, a rift develops, the same that separates individual from species, the name from anonymity. In the Greek myths there is no generic ancestor of humankind who receives a name, even that of "Man" like Adam in Genesis. Instead every ancestor of a heroic line or community is characterized by the name which he bears, and which he transmits, in one way or another, to his descendants. Thus in the tragedies all Athenians are Erechtheids, and one of the ten tribes that constituted the civic body of Athens was named *Erekhtheis*; thus also the Argives celebrated the memory of the first city founded by Phoroneus— the *astu Phorônikon*.[42]

Certain texts qualify Pelasgos or Phoroneus as "first man" (*prôtos anthrôpos*). Are we then to conclude that by assigning itself a primordial ancestor every city claimed the honor of having given birth to humankind, like those peoples who name themselves "men, showing by this that in their eyes the essential attribute of humanity disappears when one goes beyond the limits of the group"?[43] Certainly the insularity of the Greek poleis, as well as the rivalry over prestige which set them against one another, pushed them in that direction. Thus Argos made Phoroneus a civilizing hero, who, by gathering men into a city, first ended their dispersion and their solitude;[44] the Argives went so far as to state that it was Phoroneus and not Prometheus who gave fire to humankind. But another model predominates in Athens, where by attributing to themselves collectively the autochthony of Erichthonios, the citizens thought of themselves first and foremost as exemplary *andres*, issuing from a civic soil which, instead of a mother, was the land of their fathers; also the desire to have witnessed the birth of the first human (*anthrôpos*) faded after the proclamation of the exemplary status of the autochthones, and it is not certain that it ever played an important role in the foundation myth of Athens.[45]

Athenian myths, Argive myths: by confronting the two traditions best placed to obtain the prize for excellence in the great contest of antiquity,[46] in which the Greek cities square off through their mythical ancestors, one would like to suggest once more that there is not one possible discourse on origin, but on the contrary a proliferation of rival and parallel tales.

To adjourn these preliminaries, a final myth: that of Deucalion and Pyrrha.

Son of Prometheus and an Oceanid, or of Pandora herself, Deucalion married his sister or cousin Pyrrha, daughter of Epimetheus and Pandora. When the anger of Zeus unleashed the flood against humanity (or, according to some versions, against the race of bronze), Deucalion and Pyrrha took refuge in a *lamax* (chest) and escaped the cataclysm by drifting on the waves for nine days. When they finally landed on solid ground, Zeus granted Deucalion a wish after he had offered him a sacrifice. When Deucalion desires that there be men once more, a new humankind is born from stones which this original couple throw over their shoulders: as they touch the earth, Deucalion's stones become men and those of Pyrrha become women. Later Deucalion and Pyrrha have children, one of whom is Hellen, the ancestor of all the Greeks.

Although this myth occurs in Apollodorus (1.7.2), it is not the late invention of a mythographer, since very ancient sources attest to it, and we will take it as an example.[47] Is it because in this story origin is split in two ad infinitum (origin of humanity and origin of the Greek people; "hard" race born of stone, and heroic lineage of Hellen, born of a man and a woman)? The fact remains that all (or almost all) of the poleis adopted this myth to show a common origin, even while claiming, each for itself alone, the honor of having one day received Deucalion, survivor of the flood and civilizer-hero, founder of cities and temples.[48]

How to disentangle this inextricable confusion of origins? By starting at the beginning, which is actually not a beginning but once again a recommencement: there had been men and there were no longer (or no longer enough). Therefore humanity was born (or reborn): born from death (surely a *larnax*, a Greek Ark, being a chest, would have as much to do with man's birth as with his death?) or from stone, which is the same thing if we accept turning to stone as equivalent to death.[49] Therefore only the generative cycle can (re)commence, with Hellen, heroic founder of an illustrious race. On the one hand, men of stone: an etymological word-game identifies *laoi*, peoples, and *laes*, stones; on the other, at an undetermined later time, men, the children of men. But men who have as ancestors Prometheus the go-between and the first woman. Here the confusion of origins testifies to the fact that myth is always an overdetermination of discourse.

Falling to the ground, the stones become men. By mutation or by fertilization? According to the Latin version of the story in Ovid,[50] stones are the bones of the Earth, the universal Great Mother, and thus the Earth was inseminated by herself, the same by the same. And once more it is true that the same engenders the same: Deucalion produced *andres* and Pyrrha women: without sexual union the separate yet parallel sexes reproduced themselves, each for each, unalloyed.[51] Of course Deucalion and Pyrrha had parents: hence the generative cycle had certainly already begun. But the fragile mechanisms of this process seem to have quickly ground to a halt. It is true that the mother of Pyrrha was called Pandora, and that in her the relation between woman and the earth is not a simple one. Encouraged to recognize no other mother than the earth, Deucalion and Pyrrha appear to indicate that the arrival of woman was all for nothing. Yet the creation of Pandora was not pointless, even if of delayed effect. From now on the existence of woman is irreversible, and at the end of this series of false starts, men and women come together and procreate, just as Deucalion and Pyrrha, also, unite to produce descendants. Here the myth ends: everything begins, nothing more to say. . . .

Encompassing as it does many Greek questions of origin, the myth of Deucalion is exemplary for us. Which does not mean, however, that we are presenting the Greek myth of origins in extremis: in most of the Greek poleis, Deucalion is only a guest, and not the first man.

For each polis, all has already begun.

CHAPTER 2

The Benefits of Autochthony

For Joachim

For a good ending, one needs a good beginning. (It is important to begin well, because of course the main thing is to continue well—this is storytelling.) Such is the implicit but all-powerful rule that a community anxious to edify by telling its story—to itself, to others, to posterity—should follow. More than any other communities, the city-states of ancient Greece respected this rule, because they were out to endow themselves with an exemplary history. There is no city, however minuscule, that does not boast of once having sent an army to the Trojan War. But more than all the others, Athens interiorized this law and further specified it, or rather commented on it: "it is necessary to have begun well" means that what is transmitted from generation to generation is something one has always had.

To those who wish to study the rhetoric developed by a group of people for the idealization of their values transmitted over time, an odyssey through ancient Greece and particularly through Athens should prove instructive. I would like to invite on this odyssey the reader concerned with the present, so that by playing with this distance he or she might return to the present armed with words from the past.

A Rhetoric of Transmission

Here, then, is the Greece of the poleis, a scattered collection of units, each anxious to tell the story of its origin as well as possible. There were cities or regions which took pride in having been founded or civ-

13

ilized by a prestigious foreigner, a king from abroad who was quick to pay his debt to the land that had received him. Thus the Peloponnese took its name from Pelops the Phrygian, and Phoenician Kadmos founded Thebes. In contrast to this foundational alterity, other cities and regions opted for the reassuring celebration of the same by the same. These put forward an autochthonous hero, born from the earth itself (*auto-khthôn*), which he civilized: the Arcadians had Arkas and the Athenians Erichthonios, born from the soil of Attica. So as not to complicate things, we will merely point to one city, Thebes, in which the two origins sit side by side: Kadmos the Phoenician was able to found the city only after his bizarre seeding, which gave rise to fully armed warriors, to whom tradition gave the name Spartoi (the Sown). These, however, immediately set about killing one another, an elegant way of resolving the inevitable conflict between these two overly dissimilar origins.[1]

For the Greeks, undoubtedly, the relation between these two types of beginning is one of reciprocal exclusion, in the edifying discourse of the national imaginary★ of the poleis, as likewise in the more "rational," in any case the more Hellenic, discourse of the historians. Thus in his list of peoples who inhabit the Peloponnese, the historian Herodotus carefully distinguishes those "staying in the same place," meaning those whose ancestor is autochthonous, from the rest who are considered immigrant, or at least displaced populations:

> Seven peoples live in the Peloponnese. Two of them, autochthonous peoples staying in the same place, are established today where they lived in the past: the Arcadians and the Cynurians. One people, the Achaeans, although they have not left the Peloponnese, have left their own country and live in another. The others, four out of seven, are immigrants: Dorians, Aetolians, Dryopians, and Lemnians.
>
> (8.73)

But autochthony must be earned. Etymologically only the first ancestor born from the soil is autochthonous, he whose arrival establishes city life and legitimates the link between the people and their land. One further step, and the autochthony of the ancestor, transmitted by filiation,

---

★For this rendition of *imaginaire*, see Loraux, *The Children of Athena* (Princeton, 1993), 3, translator's note—*Trans.*

extends to all his descendants. Historians take note of this extension, at the same time employing the word subject to two conditions: When it concerns a people, autochthony characterizes the strict relationship which, from the beginning and uninterruptedly, attaches them to their land. Thus Arcadians and Cynurians are called autochthonous because, faithful to their ancestor, they "stayed in the same place." But out of Herodotus' statement a second criterion emerges, implicit but imperative, which adds to the transmission of the soil that of memory. It is well to occupy the land, but even better to maintain the autochthonous tradition, in order to strengthen the ties that bind the present to the time of origin. Herodotus, by mentioning further on that the Cynurians were entirely "transformed into Dorians," discreetly rejects the Cynurian autochthony whose value is, at the very least, relativized by assimilation to the Dorian invader. There remain the Arcadians, who alone merit the title of autochthones (in book two of the *Histories*, they are already the only people characterized as such),[2] and the Greek reader needed no further details in order to understand that the never-ending struggle with Sparta had its immemorial foundation in the opposition between autochthones and immigrant Dorians. In the indissolubly military and political conflicts that endlessly pitted the Greek poleis against one other, foundation myth was an important weapon, and from the point of view of the autochthonous nation, the Dorian myth of the return of the Sons of Heracles, emblematic of Spartan national pride, became the history of an immigration or an invasion.[3]

It was also undoubtedly against Sparta that the Athenians wielded their autochthonous tradition throughout the fifth century. Herodotus, on the other hand, wanted nothing to do with this ideological war preceding military conflict, and in his history of the Persian Wars the Athenians, still faithful allies of the Dorian city, have only the Barbarian as adversary and use autochthony merely to support their claim to be second-in-command of the Greek coalition, which was led by Sparta. Thus they rejected the demands of the tyrant of Syracuse who wanted "their" position: "[We will not yield command of the fleet to the Syracusans], we who represent the oldest people of Greece, and who alone among the Greeks have not moved [. . .]" (7.161).

Arcadians, Athenians, two claimants to the title of the oldest people of Greece: this is one autochthone too many. It is only natural that in book ten of the *Histories* Athenians and Arcadians should vie for the second place of honor before the battle of Plataea. Leaving aside historical conflicts, let us return to tales of origin—while being mindful that, significantly, for a Greek community nothing is more current than origin, for nothing better serves the interests of the present.

Stories of beginning, history of the earliest times of Greece: from the start there is something like a Brownian motion around these two fixed points which are Athens and Arcadia. Let us revisit chapter two of book one of the *History of the Peloponnesian War*: in Thucydides, as in his predecessor Herodotus, the dominant mode of representation for speaking of origins is a disordered hither-and-thither of peoples in search of a land: "What is now called Greece was not formerly inhabited with any stability: there was emigration from the earliest times, and everyone left their homes easily under pressure [of circumstances]" (1.2). In short because, as Thucydides was convinced, in this early period need was the essential mover of peoples, the inhabitants of the best lands shifted continuously amid wars and lesser conflicts. "Thus Thessaly and Boeotia, the greater part of the Peloponnese minus Arcadia, and in general, the most desirable lands [. . .]" (1.2).

Furthermore, there was Athens with its autochthony. The rationalist Thucydides is as little eager to employ a word imbued with the mythical representation of a land giving birth to man for Athens as for Arcadia. Nevertheless, even dissimulated behind the theory of original need, it is in fact the permanence proper to autochthony which one finds in the proposition wherein, just like the Arcadians of Herodotus, the Athenians are defined by permanent occupation of their soil: "At any rate Attica, as far back as one goes, owes its lack of internal rivalry to its aridity, and its inhabitants are always the same" (1.2.5). "Always the same": these are precisely the words Pericles employs at the beginning of his funeral oration at the start of the Peloponnesian War, when he delivers the obligatory eulogy on Athenian autochthony. This is not surprising; it is still Thucydides who is speaking through Pericles, resuscitating (reconstructing) the rhetoric of the prestigious statesman: "Our land, always the same people having lived here generation upon generation, our ancestors handed down to us by their own merit, free until now" (2.36.1).

Once again, in a remarkable displacement, the end tells the story of the beginning; the continuous occupation of Athenian soil, permanence of the same within the same, enhances autochthonous origin even while helping to prove it. Here the reader may ask: if the end justifies the beginning, if continuity of transmission proves legitimacy of possession, what happens to the logical sequence whereby in order to continue, one must first have begun? In fact the circularity of the discourse is complete, and when the city is exalted during public funeral rites, under the guise of celebrating Athenians killed in combat, Athenian state rhetoric successively (when not simultaneously) accredited these two versions of the autochthonous *logos*. In the funeral oration that bears his name, Lysias begins with the beginning: "The origin of our existence is based on right; our ancestors were not, like most nations, an assembly of peoples of every origin, nor did they have to expel others in order to inhabit a foreign land; rather, as autochthones, they acquired in one instant a mother and a fatherland" (17). But often the order was reversed, and as one considers the succession of funeral orations over time, one is convinced that for the city the essential gain from the elaboration of autochthony was the ability to glorify in all serenity the enduring stability of Athens, and its vitality continuously renewed from generation to generation. Besides generalizing the autochthonous birth of the first Athenian to all ancestors, official discourse generously bestowed it upon present-day citizens: through the celebration of autochthony, time is annulled in a perpetual recreation of origin.

For this principle, which is reborn in its entirety in each generation, orators used the word *aiôn*, "force of life [. . .] which continues without end, in the freshness of the ever new."[4] Thus they expressed what was, for the Athenians, played out in the tension between the first time and its repetition: the desire to rescue both origin and the present from the passage of time, through the timeless renewal of generations of autochthonies. Referring to the rotation of public duties, with every year seeing new magistrates presiding over the political life of the polis, the institutional language of the decrees used an "always" (*aei*) in which the perpetual recommencement of the same was expressed, and, with its "magistrates always in office," the city confirmed its own identity, preserved above and beyond the diversity of individuals. Likewise in the realm of the imagination, autochthony gave Athens its *aiôn*.

Perceived as a permanence of the same, autochthony could well have been the Athenian response to a question which was endlessly raised by the Greek poleis, and which at the end of the fourth century the philosopher Aristotle superbly formulated in book three of his *Politics*:

> Is it advantageous for a city to have a single race (*ethnos*), or many? These are the questions which a statesman must not be ignorant of. If we suppose that *the same population inhabits the same territory*, must we say that, as long as the inhabitants are of the same race (*genos*), the city remains the same despite the continual succession of births and deaths, just as [. . .] rivers and springs are the same despite the continual flux of their waters which come and go? Or should we say that, although the population remains the same, the city is different?

Less than convinced by the charms of alterity, the Athenians held to the first formulation of the problem; but the text of Aristotle is a precious resource for us in that it identifies a notion which underlies all patriotic developments of autochthony: *genos* is "birth" but also "lineage," "family," but also "race." Moving beyond traditions, which must be approximate in that they distinguish meanings which the Greek word unifies, we should take a closer look at *genos*.

Variations on the Athenian "Family"

With *genos*, metaphysics disappears, and without further disguise a discourse of exclusion emerges beneath the celebration of origin.

"May none from another house ever reign over the city, except from the stock of the noble Erechtheids [. . .]," wrote Euripides (*Ion* 1058–1060). The stock of the Erechtheids is the *genos sprung from* Erichthonios, the miraculous child of the Athenian soil, and in ascribing this wish to the women of Athens, Euripides transposes a discourse dear to his contemporaries into the remote period of the mythical kings. Merely replacing the *genos* of the Erechtheids by "the autochthonous people of famous Athens," invoked in the very beginning of the same tragedy, gives us the patriotic rhetoric in which Athenians—this was their pride, their honor—constituted a sole and unique *genos*.

All autochthones, the citizens of Athens were according to Plato "all brothers issued from the same mother." A large family. One orator made a show of originality in his eulogy for the dead by refusing to refer to each man's "family," which was in fact a means of glorifying the Athenian *genos*, and moreover of contrasting it with all other peoples:

If one assumes the task of eulogizing other populations which, coming from all over, are collected into a single city, and inhabit it bringing each into the community the characteristic traits of his race (*genos*), in this case it is indeed necessary to relate the genealogy of each, man by man; but when one speaks of Athenians, who, sons of their own soil [autochthones], draw from this communal birth an unequaled nobility, it is to my mind superfluous to celebrate a series of families.

(Hyperides *Funeral Oration 7*)

A single *genos* then, but of pure race. A *genos* commensurate with the polis, all of whose members equally inherit the nobility proper to aristocratic families.

According to the needs of the moment, the discourse of autochthony privileges one theme or the other. That of pure race, for example. Parodying the patriotic prose of the funeral oration, Plato insists in the *Menexenus* on what allows Athens to be Greek, as opposed to all the other Greeks, who are of mixed blood and for whom Hellenism is merely a veneer concealing a barbarian essence:

We have a natural hatred of the Barbarian, because we are purely Greek and without Barbarian admixture. We do not see Pelopses, Kadmoses [. . .] or so many others, Barbarians by nature, Greeks by law, sharing our lives.

So much for the Peloponnesian hero and the founder of Thebes; so much for Peloponnesians and Thebans. Now the orator can return to Athenians:

We are true Greeks, without alliance with Barbarian blood, whence the pure hatred for foreign races which is infused in our city.

(245c–d)

The reader who is perplexed by such a tone should be aware that this declaration, seemingly belligerent, has in fact a strictly internal function, that of reinforcing Athenian narcissism. Furthermore this text is a pastiche, in which Plato allows himself free rein. It follows nevertheless that actual funeral orations would not have employed fundamentally different language, and that more than once autochthones were contrasted with Theban or Peloponnesian "immigrants."[5] Euripides has a foundling, a candidate for naturalization as an Athenian, say in the *Ion*: "They say that the autochthonous and glorious people of Athens are a race (*genos*) which was not imported; but it is here that I have landed, afflicted with a twofold evil, being both the son of an intruder and illegitimate" (589–592). Things will turn out well, since the bastard ends up being a pure Erechtheid. But things might have turned out very badly, because dramatic fiction infuses words with a disquieting efficacy.

Once again it is necessary for the reader to guard against the all-too-easy temptation to assimilate, which grafts doubtful modern ideologies onto Greek discourse. For if Athenian patriotic rhetoric glorifies the *genos* and if the approximate translation of this word is "race," it does not follow necessarily that this glorification accompanied a policy of racial discrimination.[6] Certainly the autochthony theme sounds strange to the modern ear, but historians of Greece know that in the play of similarities the specificity of their object will disappear. Not only was no crusade led by the Athenians in the name of autochthony, but xenophobia was essentially a Spartan practice, little prized in the democracy of Athens, where by all accounts strangers were better treated than in any other city in Greece. Certainly the opposition of pure *genos* vs. the rest was a discourse of exclusion, but an opposition that served to establish citizenship—and Greek citizenship was based on exclusion, keeping the stranger on the margins of the city.

A number of Greek cities in fact knew degrees of citizenship: there were "active" citizens who had access to the magistracies, and those who, doomed to subordination, were citizens in name only. This was a complex distinction which gave Aristotle pause,[7] and which was unknown in Athens, where all citizens participated equally in civil rights which distinguished them *en bloc* from resident foreigners, integrated socially but not politically. Through autochthony, Athenians widened the gulf even further between their system and that of the rest: if only Athenians genuinely had the right to the title of citizens because they were part of the original *genos*, in the final analysis there were no citizens except in Athens: elsewhere foreigners were within the city, and the title of citizen lost all meaning. This reassuring certitude never ceased to be activated in Athenian consciousness by official rhetoric, and even tragedy contributed to this ideological operation. Let us examine an oratorical period, followed by a tragic monologue:

> They alone have inhabited the soil in which they were born and which they have left to their descendants: consequently one is justified in believing that, if other men who came as immigrants to the city and who are recognized as citizens, are comparable to adopted children, they are legitimate citizen-sons of the fatherland.
>
> (Demosthenes Funeral Oration 4)

> Where is there a city greater than ours? Its people are not foreigners from elsewhere: we are autochthones. Other cities, made up of different elements, like haphazard throws of the dice, are peopled by an assortment from everywhere. But whosoever leaves a city to live in another is like a patch in a wooden frame; he is a citizen in name, but not in fact.
>
> (Euripides Erechtheus, quoted in Lycurgus Against Leocrates 100)

Adopted children, extras: other Greeks are quite unfortunate. But once again it is up to Plato, parodying the official rhetoric, to put things in a clear light, by articulating the Athenian word for resident foreigners: everywhere else there are only Metics in the guise of citizens.

> This good birth (*eugeneia*) is in the first place founded in the origin of our ancestors, who, instead of being immigrants and making their descendants Metics in the country to which they themselves came as outsiders, were autochthones; really and truly inhabiting their fatherland, raised not as others by a stepmother, but by the earth, their mother.
>
> (Menexenus 237b)

Through his philosophical wordplay Plato reveals another benefit of autochthony, and not a minor one: by glorifying origin the citizens of Athens were collectively able to assume the nobility that affords a good birth (*eugeneia*). With one word, democratic Athens annexed the values of the aristocracy.

In the classical period the not-too-distant time at the end of the sixth century when the reformer Cleisthenes had organized the democracy through a "fusion of people," through the integration of foreigners and

Metics into the tribes, was well and truly forgotten;[8] the mixture was doubtless well balanced, and there were no long-term concerns over the legitimacy of the new citizens. Also forgotten was the history of the great families, who prided themselves at a time remembered by Herodotus on prestigious foreign origins. At the end of the fifth century, only Thucydides proposed a heterodox history of the constitution of the Athenian *genos*, because he disliked the embellishments of rhetoric: "Driven out of another Greek nation by war or internal rivalry, the wealthiest came to Athens in search of a stable refuge; they became citizens and further increased the population of the city from ancient times" (1.2.6). Attached to the "truth of things," Thucydides thought about the Athenian population in terms of quantity: successive increments increased the number (*plêthos*) of citizens. Official rhetoric wanted nothing to do with this reasoning and rejected quantity in favor of quality; the watchword was the identification of Athens with a unified *genos*, of the Athenian principle with autochthony, and, through autochthony, of democracy with *eugeneia*. This tendency, observable in several funeral orations, is revealed by Plato (yet again) in all its implications:

> Other cities are constituted by populations of every origin and formed of unequal elements [. . .]

So far nothing but the desperately repetitive. But reading further:

> [. . .] whence arises the inequality of their governments, tyranny and oligarchy; men live there with a small number regarding the rest as slaves, and the majority considering the others as masters.

So much for Sparta, for Thebes, for oligarchies and tyrannies (and all the more so for those cities which, without being Athens, imagine themselves to be democracies). Here now is Athens:

> We and our kind, all brothers born of the same mother, believe ourselves to be neither masters nor slaves of each other; rather equality of origin (*isogonia*) established by nature obliges us to seek political equality (*isonomia*) established by law.
>
> (*Menexenus* 238e–239a)

Further on still the philosopher plays at defining Athens as an aristocracy of merit. And there we have it: all authentic nobility takes refuge in democracy because political equality in Athens reinforces the "natural" unity of the *genos*.

Of course this is nothing but fantasy. Or more precisely, the rhetoric of *genos* is a linguistic operation, highly successful insofar as it contributes to naturalizing democracy. In the Greek world of the polis, in which oligarchy—this power of the few—dominates, in which mentalities are permanently imbued with aristocratic values, the Athenian regime is an exception. An exception invented neither in a day nor without struggle, and whose adversaries, numerous inside and outside Athens, would view its fall with immense pleasure. Therefore it is necessary to negotiate, even ideologically, in order to conciliate democratic originality and traditional values. The myth of autochthony serves as a platform for this negotiation. Reference to good character is in ancient Greece the practice of the aristocrat: endowed with good character deriving from noble birth (*eugeneia*), Athenians can forget (while trying at the same time to have it forgotten) that their democratic regime is a historically dated conquest. Democracy? A family affair. . . .

On the *Genos* of Autochthony and of Women

In this attractive setup one point remains obscure. The Athenian *genos* is composed of brothers, all from the same mother. Where then is the place of women in this imagined Athenian family?

To answer this question we will begin with a journey outside Athens in search of the most widespread Greek tradition concerning the other sex. The existence of women is not problematic in Athens alone; it is so in each of the "men's clubs" that were the Greek poleis, where the only citizens were male and where women's status, fundamental and at the same time strictly limited, was purely reproductive. As progenitor of male children, woman provided her husband with sons, perpetuating his family, and the polis with citizens, for its own posterity. Without this other, this woman, there was no polis, because there was no transmission from the same to the same. And yet in the Greek imaginary she was still an extra, and in an authoritative myth Hesiod associated the creation of the first woman with man's (sad) discovery of his mortal condition, his sexuality and separation from the gods. The first woman as mother of humankind? Not exactly, since to take the text literally, she engendered only the "race (*genos*) of women." Yet another meaning of *genos*, to designate gender? No doubt, except that in the Hesiodic poems there is no mention of a "*genos* of males," and Greek tradition as a whole prudently maintained the same silence, as if it were better to abandon the family of women once and for all to their own enclosure. Naturally it was necessary that they bear sons that were like the fathers: such is the definition of good social order in all cities. But at the level of mythical thought Greek males, with a *frisson* of terrified delight, preferred to imprison women in a *genos* always prepared to secede, perhaps even to reproduce in closed circuit. A fruitful operation of the masculine imaginary, liberating the field for the inverted fantasy—surely the true one—of a reproduction which, in the end, would have no need of women.

In this regard the myth of autochthony provided the men of Athens with an admirable imaginative solution in terms of origin. The first Athenian was not born from the union of the sexes, but from their disjunction. The story is quickly told, if bizarre: Hephaistos the craftsman god conceived one day a desire for the virgin Athena, goddess of Athens; barely managing to escape his pursuit, she threw on the ground the bit of wool which she used to wipe the god's semen off her leg. Thus fertilized, the earth produced the infant Erichthonios. I will pass over the multiple implications of this plot for Athenian views of birth, merely pointing out that the Earth Mother relieved Athenians, in the nick of time, from the other sex and its reproductive function.[9]

A single mother, anterior to the union of the sexes, a stranger to the desire that fertilized it. Proclaiming themselves her sons, the descendants of Erichthonios achieved a double goal: their identity as interchangeable citizens, and the symbolic exclusion of Athenian mothers from the model city and from official discourse. A single mother, serving the cause of the fathers: the highest expression of this occultation of maternity is found in the funeral oration of Demosthenes (4), in praise of the dead of Chaeronea in 338:

> Individually their birth and that of their furthest ancestors can be taken back not only to one father, but also collectively to their original fatherland, of whom they are recognized as the autochthonous sons.

One father for each, and for all, collectively, one mother. The problem is that the Earth Mother has disappeared along with the word "mother": Athenians were the sons of their *fatherland* (*patris*). The feminine, the intermediary, retreated a little further, and paternity controled the signifier on all sides. One might object that the reality of civic practice would have predisposed Athenians against such paternal extremism: since the time of Pericles one law defined the citizen as the son of parents who were both Athenian "citizens." Yet it was easy to misappropriate this definition in favor of patrilineal descent: there *were* no female citizens, only Athenian women who were daughters and wives of citizens. To remove women from the discourse, the official orator of the polis required little imagination. Indeed reproduction of the Athenian *genos* had at all costs to be accomplished in the domain of the same. . . .

Perhaps we are now equipped to understand a last avatar of the word "autochthone," this time comic, or at least suggested by comedy. In the *Lysistrata*, which is set in the middle of the Peloponnesian War, Aristophanes has the women of Athens and Sparta resort to strike action, withholding sexual favors in order to force their husbands, Athenian and Spartan, to make peace. The question is why the Athenian representatives at the end of the play are greeted in the name of autochthones when they arrive in great haste to negotiate: "I see our autochthones also arriving. Like wrestlers, their coats are parted over their stomachs. Their illness is apparently 'athletic' (1082–1085).

Officially all Athenians are autochthones; moreover, these particular ones are mandated by the polis. But rarely does Aristophanes explicitly designate Athenians with the stately title of autochthones, and the situation is far from dignified, since, despite all their efforts, the Athenian representatives can barely conceal the fact that, like their "father" Hephaistos, they are prey to the most imperative of erections. This is precisely the force of the comedy: actualizing the ostentatious virility at work in all the discourses on autochthony through the distancing effect of laughter. "Autochthone" appears on another occasion in Aristophanes, charged with the same ironically virile connotations, in a passage in the *Wasps* which illumines the meaning of the comedy. Retired from military affairs, the old men of Athens gleefully indulge in the procedural pettinesses which constitute the civil office of judge; their peevishness and irritability earn them the characterization of wasps. When the waspdotards, suddenly waxing lyrical, sing of the strength that has left them, they dot the i's:

> If one of you spectators, seeing me like this, is surprised to see me dressed as a wasp, and wonders what our "stinger" signifies, I will gladly inform him, however ignorant he be until now. We are, we who wear this appendage on our backsides, the only men of Attica who are truly of pure race and autochthones, a virile race if ever there was one, and rendering this city so many good offices in battle when the Barbarians came.
>
> (1071–1078)

It is hardly necessary to conclude, like the old men, that "nothing is more virile than an Attic wasp"; it is evident that Athenian spectators had long understood this, accustomed as they were to praise of the Athenian principle which associated autochthony with *andreia*, signifying courage as well as virility.

Concluding this voyage through the rhetoric of autochthony on a note of laughter, I would like to suggest that among the advantages of autochthony for Athens, a non-negligeable component was no doubt the pleasure of the discourse, modalized by an acute sense of this pleasure.

This is not to deny the primary benefits of autochthony. To celebrate the Athenian *aiôn* and the transmission of the same, from autochthonous origin down to the present human generation, is to ensure that there will be a sequel, a guarantee of eternity for the polis as against the law of the time of men. The Greeks knew too well that all reproduction has its counterpart in death.[10] Glorifying the immaculate purity of the *genos* yields numerous gains in the area of the political imaginary: the foundation of democracy within origin, the certitude of participating in a polis which of all poleis conforms most to the absolute Greek model, the exclusion of all alterity—that of the stranger, held in check at the heart of other poleis solely by the power of speech, and that of women also, this problematic half of humanity residing amid the citizenry because fathers must reproduce.

Thus the Athenian citizen finds himself alone, contemplating his virility: for the sake of reassurance, and occasionally laughter in the grandstands of the theater. Because even while he has faith in autochthony, he also knows that it is a very Athenian reference point in the discourse on Athens.

A very Greek way of realizing the advantages of ideology in the domain of the imaginary. Or, to use a distinction dear to the Greeks, in the domain of speech as opposed to—fatally aggressive—action (Athenians went to war *and* celebrated their origin, before, during, and after negotiations; they did not go to war in the name of their *genos*).

Perhaps it was to its privileged position within the discourse, in the service of a community which knew how to make allowances for discourse, that autochthony, beyond its rhetoric, owed its status of incontrovertible truth.

CHAPTER 3

The Politics of Myth in Athens

Let us imagine that a polis has just been founded, a group of citizens established on its territory.[1] What is the wise legislator's most urgent task? Drafting the laws, surely? If he follows Plato, he will begin elsewhere: he will create myths.

> [He will persuade the citizens] that in actual fact they were formed and raised in the bosom of the earth, themselves, their weapons and all their equipment; that after they were complete the earth, their mother, gave them birth, and that now they must regard the earth they inhabit as their mother and their nurse, defend it against attack and consider the other citizens as brothers, risen from the earth like themselves.
>
> (*Republic* 414d–e)

To create myths: according to Plato the first concern of the founder of a polis. The sophist Critias, "tyrant" of Athens and kinsman of the philosopher, expressed the same opinion when he grounded political order in the fear of the gods—the clever invention of a sage.[2] We may believe the philosopher of the *Republic*, who hastened to put mythmaking under the omnipotent authority of official censorship (337b–c) as soon as the foundations of the imaginary city were laid. Bad myths needed to be replaced right away by good ones, "noble lies" for the use of the community, for every Greek polis, imaginary or not, lived by myths.

Taking leave of the fiction of the first inventor and the problem of the noble lie, let us return to the "real," to real poleis with their histories and political life. Myth is already here as well: ancient history engraved in civic life, repeated daily and in the most abstruse decisions, telling tales of origin or grounding the present of the polis. It is this multiform presence that we will try to trace within the polis, a prestigious, if not privileged, example of the Greek politics of myth.

A city, then: Athens. A territory (*khôra*), and men (*andres*). At the center of the *khôra*, the urban space, the physical plane of civic life, punctuated by three summits: the Acropolis, the Agora, the Kerameikos—the hill of power and the sacred, the public square, the national cemetery. A community of citizens with their wives (who are entitled to the name of Athenians [*Athênaiai*], but not that of citizens), and two categories of noncitizens, Metics and slaves. An intense civic life, and a dynamic foreign policy dominated by an imperialistic search for power, even more than by a desire to expand.

In Athens as in the other poleis, the myths were concerned with origin, which was necessarily glorious;[3] the legendary cycle of national heroes unrolled a series of exploits or solitary *erga* in which citizens saw a prefiguring of their collective enterprises.

Two myths to start with.

The Confrontation of Athena and Poseidon, and the Myth of Erichthonios

First, the quarreling of the gods and its sequel.[4] A divinity of the polis, Athena ruled over Athens; from the beginning her temple stood on the Acropolis. From the beginning; more precisely from when the Athenians decided in favor of Athena over Poseidon. This took place in the distant period of the partitioning of the *timai* among the immortals; each god expected to receive his or her share of mortal honors, and the cities of men were fiercely disputed. In Athens, then, Poseidon and Athena confront each other. The first to arrive in Attica, Poseidon caused a sea (the *Erekhtheis*) to spring up from a hollow in the Acropolis, while Athena caused an olive tree to shoot up from the sacred rock. A judicial court, established by Zeus or constituted—already!—by Athenians, ruled on the dispute. Kekrops, the first king, half-man, half-serpent, already human but still linked to the monstrous creatures of primordial Earth, was a witness (according to certain versions, the adjudicator). His claims rejected, Poseidon was beaten in Athens as in Troezen, where Athena triumphed, and as in Argos or Delphi where he had to yield to Hera and Apollo. Thus began for the Athenian city-state the era of civilization. And if, at Athens as elsewhere, civilization and the masculine power of the *andres* were synonymous, Athenian myths illustrate this equivalence three times. To choose Athena was to choose a warrior goddess, a virgin without a mother, born of a father who was also the all-powerful father of gods and men: Athena whose "heart was all for men, except in marriage," and who at the trial of Orestes, murderer of his mother Clytemnestra, pronounced herself unreservedly in favor of the rights of the father.[5] Witness or judge, Kekrops was also the inventor of monogamous marriage: he ended the disordered promiscuity of the sexes by instituting patrilineal descent. Finally one variant of the myth based the victory of Athena on the political exclusion of women: guilty of having aroused the anger of Poseidon by voting for the daughter of Zeus while the men voted for the god, who was beaten it is true by a single voice—the women outnumbered the men by one—women were dispossessed for all time from any power in the polis. The city of men was born: the first truly human ancestor of the Athenians could arise.

The myth of Erichthonios tells the story of this birth and ushers the city into the time of men. Erichthonios was born from Attic soil, fertilized by Hephaistos' desire for Athena;[6] his name was glossed by ancient mythographers as *Khthonios*, son of the Earth, and the product of the piece of wool (*erion*) with which the fleeing virgin wiped the god's semen off her leg, unless he was simply the product of the amorous struggle (*eris*) of the two divinities. But this autochthone is first and foremost linked to Athena, and in him repose all the connections between the polis and its guardian. Already in the *Iliad* (2.546–551) the roles were divided between Athena and the fertilized earth (*zeidôros aroura*): to earth, childbearing (*teke*), and to Athena the care of raising the child—here named Erechtheus—whom she made her protégé ("then Athena, daughter of Zeus, established him in Athens in her rich sanctuary"). In the fifth century, Athenian potters represented Gê handing over the newborn to Athena for her to raise—in fact for her to acknowledge.[7] In truth Erichthonios descends from Athena as one may descend from a virgin radically opposed to childbearing: through the mediation of the earth. When he becomes king, Erichthonios repays everything he owes to his protectress, instituting the Panathenaea and thereby associating the name of the goddess with that of her people forever.[8] According to Herodotus (7.44) it is during the reign of Erechtheus that the inhabitants of Attica took the name of Athenians. Thus the autochthonous king inaugurates for Athens the human era of mythic history. Through his birth, he belongs to the original age of Kekrops; on the vases a man-serpent frequently assists at the "birth" of the miraculous child, and Kekrops' daughters, Aglauros, Pandrosos, and Herse, were by the will of Athena made the human nurses of Erichthonios, a weighty task which they discharged badly and which led to their deaths.[9] The end of Erichthonios, or rather of Erechtheus, since the tradition appears to reserve this name for the old king, reconciles Athens and Athena's rival. At the price of two lives: in order to save the city threatened by the expedition of the Thracian Eumolpos, son of Poseidon, Erechtheus has to sacrifice his own daughter before being swallowed up by the ground, struck by the god's trident; his death, however, associates him with the god in perpetuity, and from now on he is worshipped under the name of Poseidon-Erechtheus. From tragedy a new divine protector for the polis is born. With Erichthonios or with Erectheus (whether or not they are distinguished) begins the long line of Athenian kings, as for example on the Berlin vase,[10] which in addition to the usual witnesses of Erichthonius' birth, Kekrops and Hephaistos, depicts Erechtheus the adult king and Aegeus, the father of Theseus.

The "Life" of a Hero: Theseus

The story of Theseus has all the ingredients of heroic saga. From childhood to coming of age, from fortune to disaster, the life of Theseus is a long series of exploits "condensing all the virtues and dangers of human action." The bringing of civilization, dueling with monsters, the transcending of the human condition: Theseus made all such examples of heroic exploit his own.[11] Son of Aegeus, or of Poseidon according to other versions, and Aethra, daughter of the king of Troezen, Theseus grew up in the house of his maternal grandfather, already showing numerous signs of heroism. At sixteen, the age of the ephebe, he lifted the rock under which Aegeus had hidden a sword and a pair of sandals, and armed with these tokens of recognition departed for Athens by the most dangerous route. This was the beginning of a long initiation through which he won the status of legitimate son of Aegeus; on the way he purged the earth of a series of monsters (like the sow of Krommyon) and redoubtable brigands such as Sinis, Kerkyon, and Prokrustes (Proc[r]uste). Recognized by Aegeus, he had still to destroy the terrible bull of Marathon to prove himself a worthy son of the king, and to conquer the band of the fifty Pallantides, his cousins, who disputed Aegeus' power. But doing without rest is the mark of heroic destiny: Theseus embarks immediately for Crete in order to vanquish the Minotaur, who periodically devoured seven young men and seven young women sent by Athens. The rest is well known: his vanquishing of the monster and the Labyrinth thanks to Ariadne, whom he abandons on Naxos, and his forgetting to raise the white sail as a sign of victory, which causes Aegeus' death upon his return. He is now king of Athens. A political king, he embarked on synoecism (from *synoikismos*, cohabitation), which brought together the scattered inhabitants of Attica into one city. A warrior king, he distinguished himself in the expedition against Thebes and the war against the Amazons. The age of adulthood was for him also an age of excess, or at least of the transgression of the forbidden: with his companion Pirithous he stole Helen, daughter of Zeus, and descended to the Underworld to seize Persephone; the affair went sour and earned the hero a long captivity among the dead, waiting for Herakles to descend in his turn to rescue him. Theseus also experienced exile, and violent death on Skyros. Such was the career of the most celebrated of Athenian heroes, the only one given a complete "Life" and a complex character, the only one not completely subsumed in the myth of his birth or his death.

Two myths, one heroic legend. A rigorous selection procedure was necessary to isolate their main features; yet if these three tales were chosen out of the rich Athenian tradition, it was because in them the Athenian polis read (or inserted?) much of itself.[12] These are important, even exemplary, tales, whose position and influence within the life of the polis we will try to elucidate.

Social Functions of Myth: Athenian Autochthony

A discourse on the origin and organization of the human *kosmos*, myth tells the story, for the polis and in the name of the polis, of the advent of culture. In every Athenian it nourished the representation of Athens which it was convenient to create or bestow on others: that of a polis "beloved of the gods" (*theophilês*) and doubly and foundationally anchored in the direct link to the divine attested to by the quarrel of Athena and Poseidon as well as by the circumstances of Erichthonios' birth: "sons of the blessed gods, issued from a sacred and unconquered land, the Erechtheids were ever prosperous."[13] The mythical origins of masculine democracy, the legendary war against the Amazons who would be men and ended as damsels in distress, established the civic order of the *andres* in opposition to women, the passive "half" of the polis.[14] The Amazon story is even doubly exemplary, for it also tells of the victory of civilization over barbarism, of the polis over the foreign: in the *Stoa poikilê* (the Painted Portico), where citizens could contemplate the noble deeds of Athens painted on the walls, legend sidled up to history, and "on the middle wall one saw the Athenians and Theseus fighting the Amazons, then the Greeks after they had taken Ilium [. . .], and, at the end of the tableau, those who fought at Marathon."[15]

Celebrated in word and image, referred to in public speeches, represented on the tragic stage, frequently illustrated on vases or temple pediments, the myth is in serious danger of being worn out through rhetorical commonplaces and conventional scenes. Its polysemy, reinforced in tragedy, comes apart when it penetrates the prosaic *logos* of politics or when potters choose to illustrate one of its sequences—always the same one. But it gains in being, in political terms, a necessary mediation between Athenians and Athens.

One example will suffice to illustrate the numerous functions and multiple levels of social experience assumed by the myth: that of Athenian autochthony. Official religion held to the strictest orthodoxy concerning the birth of Erichthonios, and the history of this prestigious ancestor was an integral part of the *hieros logos* (sacred discourse) of Athena, which occupied such an important position in the mystic watch of the Panathenaea.[16] Tragedy did not choose between the son of the gods and the autochthone, born from the soil of the fatherland, in the representation of Erichthonios, and when the tragedians extended the name of Erechtheids to the whole civic body, they made Athenians both divine offspring and autochthones. But rhetoric went one step further, and, as if the story of Erichthonios was too well known to be evoked yet again, public orators, as for example those who delivered funeral orations (*epitaphioi logoi*) for the glory of citizens fallen in battle, generally avoided mention of the national hero and the divine couple who presided at his birth, in order to attribute the privilege of autochthony to all *andres Athênaioi* collectively. It is not surprising that this generalized autochthony became a central theme of the ideology of Athenian democracy: not only did it serve to justify Athenian militarism—champions of the right (supposedly), Athenians were so by virtue of their status as legitimate sons of the soil of the fatherland[17]—but orators went so far as to deduce democracy from autochthony, or, to put it in Platonic terms, political equality (*isonomia*) from equality of origin (*isogonia*).[18] Thus law (*nomos*) was founded in nature (*phusis*), and the power of the *dêmos* achieved its title therewith: endowed collectively with high birth (*eugeneia*), autochthonous citizens were all equal because they were all noble. One step further, and the speeches contrasted Athens with all other poleis, heteroclitic assortments of intruders established like Metics on foreign soil. Have we lost the myth along the way? We must not forget that in the religious calendar as well as in civic terms, in daily life as well as festivals, each Athenian encountered the myth of Erichthonios on numerous occasions: at the Acropolis and the celebration of the Panathenaea, on the Agora, illustrated implicitly by the presence of Athena next to Hephaistos in the the temple of the Craftsman,[19] on the tragic or comic stage, in the potter's workshop where vases, kitchenware, or *objets d'art* endlessly repeated the gesture of Gê handing the infant to Athena, and in the works of art with which their city was embellished.[20] And if the myth was weakened by the rhetoric, we may still assume that Athenian audiences were prepared to refer the general propositions of the speeches to the living context of the myth. Unless Athenians really heard something else in the speeches on autochthony: the *muthos* of Athens. . . .

Myths, then, do not die from politicization. How could they, when they endow the polis with its own identity, establishing the eponymy of Athens or watching over the *paideia* of the defenders of the fatherland? For this reason the oath taken by the Athenian ephebes invoked Aglauros, child-rearing maiden of bloody destiny, at the head of the list of religious powers called to witness the irreversible engagement of the citizens. For this reason also Cleisthenes, establishing in 508 the ten tribes that would constitute the politico-military framework of Athenian life, put them under the patronage of ten national heroes—the ten *Epônumoi*, among whom are found unsurprisingly Kekrops, Erechtheus, and

Aegeus, and whose deeds the citizens were invited to repeat in an end-lessly renewed *mimêsis.*[21]

Between gods and heroes, between the original kinship that linked them collectively with Athena and the classificatory kinship that sepa-rated them into ten tribes, Athenians had no lack of models, inscribed in the civic and temporal space of the polis, to incite them to found their actions in myth.

Myth: In the Space and Time of the Polis

Myths are present everywhere, punctuating the space of the polis where they indicate pathways and form constellations, complex knots of tensions and relationships.

In the second century of our era Pausanias Periegetes, the indefatiga-ble wanderer and even more indefatigable collector of mythical tradi-tions, visited Athens, inaugurating a series of scholarly promenades through the Greek poleis: entering through the Gate of Dipylon, which gave access to the Agora from the cemetery of the Kerameikos, he crossed the Agora, climbed the Acropolis, returned to the Agora, and left the city by way of the Kerameikos. This touristic as well as scholarly tour provided opportunity for his antiquarian skills; but Athens was already merely a museum of the past.[22] Let us imagine for a moment what an Athenian of the fifth or fourth century would have seen or described, following the same itinerary (here simplified). From the Kerameikos to the Acropolis and from the Agora to the Kerameikos two processions in-tersect—assigned different portions of the year by the calendar, but along whose routes a timeless impression still lingered: that of the Panathenaea, rising toward the sacred hill where Athena's olive tree grew, where the goddess received Erechtheus in her ancient temple, where the virgin daughters of Kekrops danced at night, "trampling the green ways before the temples of Pallas";[23] and that of public funerals, which passed from the Agora, where the national heroes stood guard, to the official burial site of those fallen in combat, worthy imitators of the *Epônumoi.* On the Agora, the center of political life, dominated to the southeast by the Acropolis, to the south by the hill of the Areopagus where Athena one day convened the first tribunal, and to the northwest by the temple of Hephaistos, the twelve Olympian gods rubbed elbows with Athenian heroes: to be brief we will mention only the ten *Epônumoi*, whose monument played an essential role in the military and political life of the polis, and Theseus, whose exploits were pictured on the interior freize of the Hephaisteion and the *Stoa poikilê*—in the Hephaisteion, *sub specie aeternitatis*; in the Stoa, in the context of Athenian history, from the war with the Amazons to the battle of Marathon, when the hero intervened accompanied by Athena and Herakles. At every step stood heroic figures, in every corner tales of myth; in fact going for a relaxing stroll was probably not a city thing to do, because no space is less neutral than that of the city. Perhaps it is necessary for the person wishing to take a walk without encountering the polis, omnipresent in its myths, to leave the city walls?[24] A naive hope: beside the river Ilissos, Boreus carried off Oreithuia, the daughter of Erechtheus; at Marathon the memory of Theseus lingered, as well as by the banks of the Cephisos; at Eleusis one saw the tomb of Eumolpos, killed by Erechtheus, and so on.[25] In the country as in the city, myths spoke to the citizens of the polis.

Let us return to the Agora, or rather to the hill of the Pnyx where the assembly met, where Athenian policy was decided all year long. Here more than anywhere else, myths spoke of the present and the past of the polis. Or at least politicians and orators were engaged in making them speak.

Myths and heroic legends were part of the fabric of Greek historical consciousness; this is a given which needs no emphasis.[26] We will concentrate instead on the relationship established within the political sphere between repetition and event, when event took account of myth. This "very ancient history" was history that was used and reworked. History, also, that informed the actions of the present.

Each polis brandished its myths and heroes in the faces of the others. No doubt Theseus owed his great good fortune to what the tyranny of the Peisistratids needed to oppose: the tales the Peloponnesians told of their hero, Herakles. The hero's story gave a prefiguration and a legitimacy to all territorial expansion. Theseus chose the most dangerous route from Troezen to Athens, passing through Megara and Eleusis, because it enabled him to vanquish the enemies of civilization, and because Athens desired to legitimize the conquest of these cities, before or after the fact, whether such conquest was uneasily maintained or merely wished for. When the hero stopped off to dance at Delos en route to Athens from Crete, the dance was certainly a celebration of victory over the Minotaur, yet it also had its function in the polis of the Peisistratids: a below-the-surface justification for its designs on the Aegean. As for Ion, eponymous ancestor of the Ionians and minister of war under Erechtheus (or the king's successor), his appearance in Athens and in Athenian myths was only to make the polis of the olive into the metropolis of Ionia. A maritime empire, too, has need of myths. What about autochthony then, major weapon in the rivalry of the city-states, brandished by Argives against Athenians, by Athenians against Tegeans?[27]

More complex but just as real is the effect of myth and heroic legend on internal political life: here the give-and-take between former and present time is constant. The present remodels the legendary past, and at the beginning of the fifth century, in the polis which had been definitively freed from tyrants, representations of Theseus on Attic vases suddenly began to reproduce the attitudes of the Tyrannoktones (murderers of the tyrant), as two famous sculptors had immortalized them for the edification of the *dêmos*. Likewise Pericles' law of citizenship may have given renewed authority to the myth of autochthony around 450. But inversely, the present may imitate the legendary past: when Kimon brought the "ashes of Theseus" back from Skyros, in order to install them ceremoniously at the heart of the polis, at the foot of the Acropolis and near the Agora, it was an opportunity for the politician who saw himself as a new Theseus to slip into the figure of the hero.

Theseus' was a strange destiny within the democratic city. A story whose peaks and troughs correspond to fluctuations of Athenian policy from the sixth to the fourth century. The tyrants glorified him; Cleisthenian reform downplayed him, which set him apart from the *Epônumoi* his father Aegeus belonged to.[28] The aristocratic reaction that followed the Persian Wars made him a dominant figure once again, the very incarnation of Athenian pride; did he not fight on the Athenian side at Marathon? Thus Theseus occupied a prominent place on the monument to the *Epônumoi*, erected by Athens in the Panhellenic sanctuary of Delphi to commemorate the victory of Marathon (and its own glory): an aberrant *epônumos* who ousted Ajax, whose principal failing was to have reigned at Salamis. In the civic space of Athens, such a substitution was impossible; here he was honored everywhere, in his own sanctuaries and the temple friezes of the Olympian gods. No doubt he again suffered an eclipse when democracy returned, although his links to Peisistratus and Kimon were themselves sufficient to make him suspect. But starting from the fifth century he is no longer contested, and bit by bit he takes on a new and final appearance, on the tragic stage and under the influence of political moderates: that of the democratic king, of the ancestor who in the beginning gave power to the people, or, less compromisingly, that of founder of the ancestral constitution (*patrios politeia*). Henceforth, who will be able to tell legend from history?

Thus in perpetual reactualization, the tale of distant *erga* weighs on the actions of the present, whether it inspires them directly or whether it plays for the agents of history, for their own use or that of others, the role of an interpretive model to be projected onto the action.

In order to characterize this overlapping of repetition and event, perhaps we might say, parodying Claude Lévi-Strauss, that nothing resembles ideology more than myth when it becomes political.[29] Perhaps also, refusing to start down the slippery path of resemblances, one might observe that there are no "noble lies" in which the liar is not himself implicated, particularly when the storyteller merges with the audience, when the polis tells stories to its citizens.

CHAPTER 4

An Arcadian in Athens

A jamming of indicators, a loss of meaning, an abolition of signs: these signal the presence of the god Pan. Snow falls: tracks disappear before the straying shepherd, who recognizes too late the power of the god. So when a sudden, fair-weather squall arose, scattering flocks of oligarchs in 403 B.C., it was to Pan that the Athenian democratic resistance, holed up in the fortress of Phyle, owed their rescue. Pan rescues and leads astray; sometimes he prefers to lead astray; other times he brings safety, at the price, always, of derangement.[1]

Madness and fear, derangement is panic. The faltering of the solitary pedestrian who loses his footing at the edge of a cliff, the collective disarray of the army that precipitously raises a siege, assayed by a disastrous confusion of signals indecipherable in the night. On the mountain as on the battlefield, Pan is always elsewhere, ungraspable, never next to those with whom he allies himself by inciting disorder in the enemy camp. God of the inexplicable (p. 143), master of the echo—that disarticulated sound, that bodiless voice, that distant music, absent yet irremediably there—this is Pan, who "makes nothing seem like something" (p. 181), and who introduces inextricable confusions between the same and the other. For example the "error" of the Gauls who, defeated before Delphi and prey to sudden panic, lost all sense of common identity to the point of massacring one another, over-full of a desire whose erotic object was fragmented and dissolved by violence. Whether he acts at a distance or takes possession of a body, Pan manifests himself in disquieting epiphanies, outbreaks of the supernatural, and moments of discontinuity which overturn the times of men.

And yet at the same time this divine trickster, part he-goat and barely humanized, has his place in the cities of men. He acts as mediator, restoring peace at the end of a conflict, showing a marked preference for democrats and democracy and, confronted by barbarian invaders, showing himself to be a staunchly faithful ally of the Greeks. Of course with Pan the historian of religion must be ever on the alert, and not the least of the paradoxes of this strange and familiar god is that while he is without an individual saga in mythological discourse (pp. 85–90), he is nevertheless inversely linked to the *historical* history of the Greeks. At the beginning of the fifth century Pan erupted into history; he left his native Peloponnese, the site of his cult, for Athens, whence he was introduced into Boeotia and then into the rest of Greece. Abandoning his place of origin, he established himself in the polis in the midst of an expansion whose goal proved to be the mastery of the human era of history.

That the intervention of Pan in the world of the poleis took the form of an *event* narrated in Herodotus is not unexpected,[2] except by historians of Greek religion, disturbed by a periodization which they have not the satisfaction of having constructed themselves, and which, as if to reinforce their resistance, comes from a Greek historian whom it is fashionable not to take seriously. It is just the audacity of Philippe Borgeaud to have adopted this event, in the search for the muddied traces of the elusive god of goatherds, as an operator of intelligibility.[3] Behind the voice with neither body nor meaning, beneath the inarticulate cry or the illusory echo which dogs the search for the god throughout the book, like so many other signs of his presence, there remains the encounter of Pan and the historical discourse of the Greeks, where the intervention of the gods assures the victory of men, and where in turn men may contribute to the glory of a god.

Thus Pan encounters the world of the poleis, or rather he encounters the polis which like a good ferryman must conduct him from his Arcadian "conservatory" into the space and time of politics. There is no doubt that the characteristic traits of the god of shepherds were "reinvented" in the course of this displacement, which Borgeaud does not dispute. But it is through this reinvention that Pan can be understood, and one must take this into account. One might of course retain a certain nostalgia for Pan without Athenian coloration; but it is better to take account of the fact that for the writing of this chapter of Greek religion, the example of Athens is yet again "informationally and historically privileged" (p. 263). Resigned to making the best of this encumbering Athenian domination, one may follow Borgeaud without a second thought and with pleasure and profit. In doing so the historian who is anxious to broaden the narrow framework of the history of religions will find several opportunities to reflect on the articulation of events and the duration of religious artifacts, or on the obvious tension between the local character of a divinity and his relationship to the symbolic system common to the Greek poleis.

The study of Pan necessitates holding two apparently contradictory propositions simultaneously: although a naturalized Athenian, Pan is first and foremost an Arcadian, even an Arcadian par excellence. "Pan emerges [. . .] at the moment he is uprooted from Arcadia" (p. 10); let us say for greater clarity the *real* Arcadia, since the imaginary one continued to accompany him as his quintessential property. Let us try to resolve the apparent contradiction.

Pan is inseparable from the mountainous landscape of Arcadia, which is why he was accorded a wild locale even within the city: in the civic space of Athens as in the other Greek poleis, the cult of the god of pastoral regions was located in a grotto. We must also understand why, conversely, the Arcadians only dedicated formal temples to him. The answer is clear and convincing: in Arcadia a grotto is a grotto, but outside Arcadia the grotto shelters Pan because it "signifies Arcadia." In other words, Arcadia is indissolubly a reality and a *representation*. The "real" region is itself immovable in the autochthonous foundation which binds it to the soil, but imaginary Arcadia is easily exported beyond the borders of the Peloponnese, because it is a model. Pan is a true Arcadian because he is so in both senses of the term; yet there is no doubt that his Panhellenic image privileges within him Arcadia as symbol.

Idyllic region or inhospitable landscape,[4] the rural territory of Arcadia locates within itself the primordial era of the most distant origins: older than the moon, were not its inhabitants fed on acorns from their oak trees, ancestral oak trees from which they were born? Or so it was said in the Greek imaginary, wherein Arcadia incarnated the ever-possible regression toward original savagery. In short Arcadia was a Greek *topos* (p. 18), and perhaps, Borgeaud suggests, even an Arcadian one, in which Arcadians "portrayed their humanity to themselves," thereby clarifying "their specificity as Greeks."[5] For those who would invent themselves, Arcadia was an affirmation of difference and therefore an effective operator, and "by adopting the cult of Pan, the Athenians recognized that they possessed something of the Arcadian" (p. 81). Nevertheless, Pan was an "outsider" god (p. 281), whom the Athenians set up after Marathon (Athenian victory if there ever was one), at the foot of the Acropolis.

An outsider god among Athenian autochthones. But also the representative of another autochthony, as venerable as the Athenian: "alone of humanity, you and they are autochthones," Demosthenes reminded his fellow citizens.[6] But Herodotus already knew that, from this perspective, there was a certain homology between Athens and Arcadia. Perhaps a reader more Athenian than Arcadian in imagination may be permitted to ask: in welcoming the Arcadian, was it really an "outsider" that the Athenians were introducing into their midst? It is a *topos* of Athenian rhetoric to present the inhabitants of the Peloponnese as so many intruders in their own poleis, because they occupied a territory they did not originate from; only Arcadia, immutably entrenched in its own soil, could escape this condemnation, always supposing that among two traditions of autochthony there isn't always one too many. Is it the autochthone, then, that the Athenians saw in Pan? Or must we conclude that, others' autochthony being wrong by definition, Pan the imported god preserved for Athenians his radical foreignness? A difficult question. Knowing that it is unanswerable, we will yet pursue it a little further.

By establishing the Arcadian in his own grotto on the flanks of the Acropolis, the Athenian polis was not content to stay the wandering course of the divinity, suddenly immobilized: it integrated Pan into the sacred precinct of Athenian origins. It was on the Acropolis that the infant Erichthonios was born, miraculous son of the civic earth, fertilized in ancient times by the desire of Hephaistos for the maiden Athena, and more than any other myth the legend of this first Athenian marked the soil of the goddess's hill. In his obscure cave Pan was a neighbor of Aglauros, daughter of the primordial hero Kekrops, nurse to the child autochthone, and virgin protectress of ephebes, to whom official piety had likewise dedicated a rock-hollow; the grotto also sheltered the love-making—violent, as with all "Panic" unions—of Apollo *Patrôos* (the Ancestral) and an Erechtheid princess, as well as the birth of the infant Ion, born of this secret union and destined for Athenian royalty. There is no doubt that Athens integrated the Arcadian into the civic space of autochthonous myth.

But is it Arcadian *autochthony* which is honored through Pan? One hesitates to agree, while recognizing with Borgeaud (pp. 220–225) that the Arcadian has a rightful place in a space concerned with origins. Certain indications viewed from an Athenian angle, isolated yet significant, suggest something resembling a rivalry based on autochthony between Athens and Arcadia and, on the part of the Erichthonian city, a barely concealed reticence concerning the Arcadian myth. No doubt it is this rivalry or this reticence that lies beneath the dispute in Herodotus' book nine between Athenians and Tegeans as to who will occupy the left flank against the Persians at the battle of Plataea. The right flank, a position of honor, went to the Spartans along with the command of the Greek forces united against the invader. The left flank was for the taking, and Tegeans and Athenians made their respective claims to second position alleging "past and present deeds": a "historic" episode no doubt, but certainly symbolic in the account of Herodotus, whose pro-Athenian bias would be denounced much later in Plutarch. Nevertheless, the Athenians won on the basis of having claimed both Marathon and mythological exploits, and it is significant that, by proclaiming "their ancestral (*patrôon*) right to the first rank over the Arcadians, being eternally courageous," they wiped out Tegean specificity, dissolved in the generality of Arcadian nationality. No longer Tegeans—Arcadians. Herodotus' Athenians knowingly gave their rivals their proper name, that of Peloponnesian autochthones (8.73), and this is certainly how the Lacedaemonian army understood it when they were said to have proclaimed that "the Athenians merited the left flank more than the Arcadians."[7] After the heroic period of the Persian Wars, time to laugh: Athenians could also neutralize through comedy various representations of Arcadian autochthony—military values, for example. At the end of a lengthy enumeration of provisions (spices, papyrus, incense, ivory . . .) which Athens imported from all over the world, the comic poet Hermippos lists Arcadian mercenaries between Phrygian and Thessalian slaves,[8] which is surely a roundabout way of devaluing autochthones who make their military force available to others? But in the end, it is explicitly and unreservedly between one autochthonous myth and another that the rivalry of Athens and Arcadia is played out via mythological tradition. According to Pausanias, Lykaon, son of the autochthonous Pelasgos, was much less wise than his Athenian contemporary Kekrops.

Pan's Twin

Let us compare the two myths more explicitly, even at the risk of seeming to have forgotten Pan altogether. Patience—he is not far off.

An autochthony of acorn-eaters. Arcadian tradition, to which Borgeaud devotes the first part of his enquiry, establishes a "proto-humanity" (p. 43) whose beginnings are no less than magical: regression, transgression, flood—this somber myth has everything, in keeping with the Greek view of primitivism in general.[9] Indelibly marked by this immemorial origin, Arcadians inherited a fundamental ambiguity, an anchorage in time which is problematic to say the least—something like a lack of historicity; and the redoubtable honor of being the most ancient of the Greeks made them "ambiguous entities." Athenian autochthony on the other hand was basically political, proclaiming for internal Athenian use the original singularity of the polis: with the birth of Erichthonios Athens instantly became a part of history, civilized from the start.[10] In order to measure the gap between these two traditions, we need only closely compare the temporality of the two myths of origin.

On the Arcadian side an autochthone immediately appears: Pelasgos. The region named after him, however, is still inhabited only by Pelasgians. Next Lykaon, son of the autochthone, institutes the cult of the gods; but after having offended Zeus with the monstrous sacrifice of a human child, he falls back into a pre-human, savage, or bestial state: he becomes a wolf. A false start, or at least a regression in the second generation. During this period, if we accept the fiction of a Panhellenic chronology of myth, Athens (though not yet known by this name) is familiar with civilization and is learning to honor the gods satisfactorily, under the authority of the primordial Kekrops whose body is both man and serpent, and who perhaps owes to this well-balanced double nature his ability to respect the double frontier separating humanity from the divine and from the animal. With Lykaon and his male descendants wiped out by the will of Zeus, it was Lykaon's daughter Kallisto who perpetuated the autochthonous line: lying with Zeus and metamorphosed into a bear, she paid dearly for her dangerous liaison (with her human form, even her life), but she gave birth to Arkas, the first Arcadian to finally civilize the region to which he gave his name. Arcadia had finally begun. . . . But from the rise of Pelasgos to the reign of Arkas a long crisis testifies to the difficulty of arriving at a clear distinction between man, animal, and god (p. 61). Meanwhile on the Acropolis Erichthonios is born; a child of the gods but fully human, he invents politics and also gives the polis a name—not his own, but the prestigious name of the goddess of the polis, Athens. This comparison is instructive: Athens might have taken its time to produce an autochthone, but it appears to have produced one at the right moment: just when all was in readiness for a human history to begin. The delay reverses into an advance, that which in the civic world of the Greeks a polis must achieve over a region with an overburdened past. A side-by-side comparison of the two traditions is not unwarranted, for Pausanias also suggests one in his introduction to Arcadia; it is authorized by the Greek system of shared representations, in which Athens and Arcadia present two divergent models of autochthonous origin and political life.

And where is Pan in all this? The son of Zeus and Kallisto, according to Aeschylus: Arkas' brother, then. To be sure this is only one of his numerous genealogies (fourteen altogether), and we know that the most widespread tradition makes him the son of Hermes and a nymph. But Borgeaud seems to give sustained attention to this singular version of the birth of the goat god which gives him the first Arcadian as his twin brother (in a sense his double), and it is perhaps not accidental that this version was formulated by an Athenian. Of autochthonous descent, yet marked by an animality his brother manages to avoid, Pan is the irreducibly distant neighbor whose presence at the foot of the Acropolis signifies the familiar strangeness of the savage within the city: welcomed, yet established, even annexed to the greater good of Athenian autochthones.

We must interrupt this promenade on the border between two autochthonies, to which we have been led by the very beautiful and very dense pages in which Borgeaud, in the guise of an introduction to Pan, assays a "Greek representation of Arcadia." Undoubtedly there are other approaches to such a subtle and accomplished book, and other readers, attracted by shortcuts, will skirt Athens in favor of a more integrally "Panic" journey, among the convulsive beauties of eroticism and possession evoked in the second, central part of the book. We may at least agree that it was important for Borgeaud to establish the Arcadian within the polis, since before concluding with the timelessness of the festival he once again solicited Pan, and his accomplice Artemis, in aid of the Athenian democrats who rose up against the oligarchs of the Thirty in 403.

As authentic representatives of the polis yet exiled outside Athens, faithful to the hoplite spirit of the oath they had only just sworn as ephebes in the sanctuary of Aglauros, yet also mercenaries of fortune, combatants in a civil war but eager to establish peace, these men certainly merited the assistance of Pan. Of the god of last chances. Of the god who intervened in war only for the sake of peace. Of the god of the grotto, where secession becomes return.

An Arcadian in Athens: a good opportunity for weaving together the immemorial—that of Arcadia, and that also which presides over the history of religions—with a political history which is able to hear what the Greeks had to say about those moments of crisis when, in the face of silence from the great gods of Olympus and abandonment by all human allies, the hope of men who live in the polis takes on the incongruous form of Pan.

CHAPTER 5

Glory of the Same,
Prestige of the Other

Greek Variations on Origin

Under the heading of "autochthonous languages," I would have liked to be able to write about the Greek language.[1] But I am not a linguist, and although the Greeks may have numbered language—after blood and before cults—among the relevant criteria for Hellenism,[2] it is not certain that they credited their language with an autochthony.

According to Plato, the opposite would appear to be true. In the *Cratylos* Socrates insists on the barbarian origin of certain Greek words—let's suppose that a declaration of Socrates is not always ironic in principle—which suggests that the idea of an autochthony of language should perhaps be viewed as Greek fantasy.

"It seems to me that the Greeks have taken a large number of words from the Barbarians," says Socrates (409e). It is "not easy" then to connect these words with the Greek language (literally "the Greek voice"), which under the circumstances would amount to "doing them violence" (410a). Careful! Etymology is a Greek practice, as in the search for truth (*etumon*) in a word.[3] It would be better to admit that there is something of the Barbarian in Greek, and that this Barbarian kernel will always remain obscure, compact, unintelligible. However great the philosopher's desire to elucidate a word like *sophia* in Greek terms, one is forced to recognize, a propos of this word in particular, that it is "somewhat obscure and foreign (*xenikon*) in form" (412b). Here Plato's voice can be heard unmistakably beneath the Socratic irony, with his constant preoccupation with puncturing the vast pretensions of Greek self-satisfaction.

The word for "wisdom" is confidently identified as foreign, while in reference to the word for evil (*kakon*), for which a Greek would be perfectly content with a non-Greek origin, a word equally "bizarre" (more precisely "without place," *atopon*—therefore without a Greek foundation?), the hypothesis of Barbarian origin is denounced as pure expediency (416a). Until the veil is lifted in turn from this expedient, "which consists of attributing a Barbarian character to what we do not know" (421c–d). The Barbarian hypothesis was only a fiction, but at the same time it must be admitted that in the Greek language there are words that are opaque, for which the search for origin is destined to fail. So long, primitive words. So long, dream of the Same! In these words of unknown origin, the Other has taken the place of the True.

We assume then that Plato aims to discredit all research into an autochthonous foundation for language; but herewith he also suggests the existence of such an idea. What is most striking is that this philosopher of the Same and the Other proposes that there is otherness in Greek, even if in ambiguous vein (the truly other, since this irreducible opacity was at one point assimilated to Barbarian origin).

"Barbarian": a means of designating, through his unintelligible idiom, someone who speaks no Greek. A babbler.

But among themselves, Greeks, naturally, speak Greek, and to "speak Greek" (*hellénizesthai*) means to "side with Greece," as for example during the Persian Wars. Likewise in the Peloponnesian War, *attikizesthai* designates a pro-Athenian bias in Thucydides. Thus language is absorbed in the generality of "Greekness," and becomes, as always, a means for political ends. Dissolved into Greek discourse.

Therefore I now turn my attention to discourse, hoping to surprise the Same and the Other—many Others, actually—at work there.

The word "stranger": from language to discourse, the going is rough.

What is a stranger, for a Greek speaker? The language has a ready-made response, to be sure: the stranger (*xenos*) is one who, for having been born elsewhere, is a priori an enemy, and therefore one better turned into a guest (*xenos*) without delay.[4] But actions speak differently: every stranger does not, even in thought, turn into a guest, and to give a stranger his full measure of alterity, one is strongly recommended to keep him at a certain distance. The risk is that the gulf may be too wide, as in the ill-conceived divisions Plato assigns to the crane in the *Statesman*, a bird supposedly endowed with reason but whose first act of categorization is to isolate the crane "race" in opposition to all other animals, which are tossed indiscriminately into the ignoble category of beasts (*thêria*).[5] Faulty categorization? No doubt, yet at the same time a necessarily *Greek* categorization, such as a postulates a good and a bad side—one's own and that of the rest of the world. There is a tendency, just as Plato says, to divide the entire human race into "Greeks" and "Barbarians," as if it were sufficient to impose a single term upon a multiplicity of races in order to make them one; and once the category "Greece" has been created, it becomes evident that for each polis, the stranger is also one's neighbor.

Faulty categorization? Imaginary operations, operations of the imaginary. It is this terrain of the imagination I wish to explore: the tables of polarity thus arrived at are certainly corrupt by definition (logically, at least), yet through them the historian learns much about what a society gains (or imagines it gains) in terms of identity when it assigns to the stranger the place of the Other. How can we acquire a coherent grasp of the Athenian ideology of citizenship without taking the time to add up the "benefits of autochthony" in the "Same" column?[6] And, in order to discover what is said about the other, why not once again adopt those arguments that within the city serve to deny from the outset the existence of any external contribution?

Since imaginary operations are more radical in the domain of origin (as if one must always begin with a process of severing, in order to speak of the earliest beginnings), it is instructive to put the question of the stranger in terms—for a Greek, mythical, mythico-historical, historic, it is all one—of origin, and more specifically of autochthonous origin. Thus I pursue discourse, modalities of reasoning, without systematically investigating the reality of their foundation. It has to do with what poleis say about their very first citizens, whether they are born from the soil of the fatherland, or whether they are foreign. Resisting the arguments of Aristotle, for whom questions concerning the citizenship of primordial ancestors were pointless because aporetic, we will take these variations seriously, for they are very Greek.[7]

Autochthonous discourse, then, is our "anchorage," to be closely examined by opposing the Same and the Other. To judge by some of its developments, the danger might be that of losing all reference to the other, because one would find only the same. A clever orator in Xenophon fills Arcadians with pride by "telling them that to them alone was the Peloponnese a true fatherland, because they were the only autochthonous inhabitants, and that of all the Greek races, the Arcadian was the most numerous and the most robust" (*Hellenica* 7.1.23).

Such is (to deduce the exemplary from the exceptional) the imperialism of the Same, which, by a series of equivalences, tends to make autochthones more than they are: the Arcadians are the only true Peloponnesians, and from there it is but a short step to being the only true Greeks—certainly the first ones. As for the Athenians, it seems that they did not hesitate to take the step from autochthony to paradigmatic Greekness. This occurred between Herodotus, who merely attributed to them the claim of being "the only (Greek) people to have not emigrated" (*mounoi* [. . .] *eontes ou metanastai*), and Plato, who in the *Menexenus* ironically derived the isolation of the Athenians from their unique status as Greeks of pure stock.[8]

And the rest? What happens, in the logic of autochthony, to the "other Greeks," an empty generalization that could minimally serve as a backdrop to the auto-exaltation of the Same? The usual thing is to exile them, as they are invoked, to the frontiers of Greekness. In the *Menexenus* the "others," because the primordial ancestors they worship are foreign—Pelops, Kadmos, Aegyptos, or Danaos—have receded as far as possible, to where the Greek world adjoins the Barbarian. Designated as "semi-Barbarian" (*meixobarbaroi*), they are no longer Greeks, and the way lies clear for exclusive Athenian occupancy. We must guard against the assumption that the others have disappeared, however: Platonic irony, it is true, indulges in this sort of play on limits, but the real risk is less the loss of the other than the dissolution of the self. To such an extent does the Same need others, even if only to affirm its own identity.

Once again we come back to autochthony, which each time necessitates a new reading of the official prose of the Athenian *epitaphioi*.[9] But how to avoid it? For inasmuch as we have access to the Greek imaginary of the classical period, the dominance of Athenian discourse within it is such that it is worth trying, yet again, to evaluate the prestige of autochthony and the effectiveness of its discourse, as well as the contours of the mirage.

The Fatherland of the Same

The utterances of autochthonous discourse privilege Athenians as the only true Greeks; on an everyday level, however, they are content to maintain that they alone are true citizens. All others then are "displaced" in their poleis, like "patches in a wooden frame," which is to say that they are citizens only in name and never in fact.[10] Or that in contrast to Athenians, "legitimate citizen-sons of the fatherland" (*gnêsioi gonoi tês patridos politai*), other Greeks, because their ancestors arrived from elsewhere one day long ago, have no status in their own cities other than that of "adopted children" (*eispoiêtoi*).[11]

This makes sense only with reference to the Athenian definition of citizenship. The reference is complicated, however, by the fact that the definition is both practical, supported as it is by practice, and perfectly ideological: the practice sheds light on the discourse of autochthony, while the ideology is nourished by it. Hence the following, rather circular, reasoning: in order that there be true citizens in Athens and only in Athens, it is necessary that other Greek poleis have only a semblance of citizens, in other words mere *inhabitants*, naturalized as citizens: therefore Athenians are true citizens. From this reasoning it follows that, in Athenian thought, the rights of citizenship automatically entail a basic lack. Given how parsimoniously citizenship was awarded in Greece, this is hardly surprising.[12] But it is the business of representations to virtually autonomize themselves, and the fact is that the discourse goes well beyond practical requirements. Treating the "other Greeks" as citizens of lesser quality because their earliest ancestors were not born from city soil is to forget that even in Athens a generation is sufficient for the sons of naturalized Athenians to rise to the higher magistracies.[13] The discourse is clearly excessive; it is true that to speak of autochthony is to have already forgotten the real, so that all reservation is transformed into exclusivity: he whom chance rather than birth has made a citizen is so only by default, having been "manufactured" rather than engendered—the former an almost craftsmanlike act, as when Gorgias says that magistrates in Larissa "manufacture" Larissans.[14]

Adopted children, newly minted citizens: assimilation is spontaneously generated out of a system of thought in which naturalization and adoption appear to be interchangeable,[15] so that an orator speaking for the defense may make a pretense of believing that all adopted sons in

Athens are foreigners in search of authentic citizenship.[16] If there is legitimacy only through birth, if *gnêsioi politai* (legitimate citizens) are by
definition *genei politai* (citizens born as such), if birth must characterize
the citizen of Athens, then there is only one possible pronouncement
concerning citizens of all other cities: the others are not "born."[17] No
doubt I could end here, and emphasize the extent to which autochthonous discourse in its circularity is fragile, because it requires others by definition, even if only to throw them back into nonbeing. But this would
be to close the chapter on birth, so elaborated in Athenian rhetoric,
rather abruptly.[18] Let us take the time to examine the word *phulon*.

An autochthonous term, certainly (*phulon Arkadikon* in Xenophon
helped to bolster Arcadian pride), *phulon* meant "stock," and hence regularly served to bring the same into opposition with itself and others, as
the very existence of the derivatives *homophulos* ("of the same stock")
and *allophulos* ("of other stock") confirms. A *phulon*—"that which develops as a group"—generally presupposes others, to which it is opposed
in order to isolate itself more effectively in its own enclosure.[19] Characterizing the group then in its homogeneity, *homophulos* suggests trans-
parency and facility of relations between those who are made equal by
their belonging to the same stock. This is the case with *philia homophulos* in the *Menexenus*: familial friendship among citizens, based on kinship
derived from common birth. *Allophulos*, on the other hand, means foreign birth, converted into hostility in an instant.[20]

I said that *phulon* was an autochtonous term. Given the frequency of
-phulos derivatives in Thucydides, which characterize the relations that
every city, including colonies, maintains with those within and without,
do I still stand by this statement? If so, I must advance the hypothesis
(taking full responsibility for it) that there was no polis able to imagine
itself without some identification with the Same.[21] Witness the recurrent
idea that citizens are equal and interchangeable by definition, an idea in
which the Greeks enshrined their representation of the polis, and which
we hasten to adopt wholesale as the very expression of Greek political
philosophy. Such an idea is necessarily fictitious, but we must suppose
that this fiction was necessary for life in the polis. At least it was thought
to be, as we find in Aristotle. When the philosopher whose every effort
was aimed at arguing against Plato that a polis is built upon the dissimilar,[22] when he too comes to recognize that troubles arise more easily in
a polis whose unity is not cemented by a common stock (*to homophu-

lon),[23] one begins to suspect that no Greek could do without the fiction of the *phulon*, which I will maintain is a minimal form of autochthony.

If we accept this hypothesis, we will find it easier to understand how the argument that derives democracy from autochthony, reasoning from purity of origin to perfection of the system, could have authenticated the idea that the Greek model of the polis was ultimately realized in Athens, for the Greeks, and now for us as well. Every polis—Aristotle again, and this time the concession is important—"wants to be composed of the same and the equal as much as possible."[24] What interests us here is not whether the political instrument of this desire should or should not be the middle class, as Aristotle imagines; rather it is the idea that the dysfunctional polis is, as he suggests, made up "of masters and slaves," which takes us back to the heart of the opposition between autochthones and others. Not only does the common birth of Athenian citizens imply equality in and of itself, because it renders all individual genealogical pride obsolete;[25] political equality also is easily derived from birth under the banner of equality. In the *Menexenus* democratic Athens can be contrasted with "other cities," made up "of masters and slaves"—here we are—because they are composed of disparate elements, and are ignorant of the beautiful homogeneity of the Same from the start.[26]

We could continue down this edifying path by stating with Isocrates that autochthony protected the Athenians from the great familial crimes which are represented in tragedy, and which flourished in earlier times "in other cities."[27] However, as inventive as they are, the different versions of autochthonous discourse are nevertheless characterized by repetition, and without developing Isocrates' argument, I will uphold its conclusion (that of every argument concerning autochthony): Having never known anything but the Same, Athens was, in nature and in origin, the polis at peace with itself. In other words the Polis.

What remains for the others? Claiming their alterity, perhaps.

Under the Sign of Movement

Once again we would need free access to what others say about themselves. This is not of course easy, and we must be resigned to the screen of autochthonous discourse intervening between us and them on more than one occasion.

Even in the prose of the great historians, albeit animated by a "Hellenic" (hence global) view, we find the antitheses of the rhetoric of the Same. In opposition to the native sons, "others" find themselves frozen in the status of "arrivals," once the status of their ancestors. Arrivals, immigrants, intruders: all are encapsulated in the word *epêlus*, whose meaning was occasionally fortified with a verb of motion.[28] We find the clearest formulation of the word *epêlus* as reduced to a basic meaning of "not autochthonous" in Herodotus, always so careful not to betray the multiplicity of the "*logoi* of others."[29] His subject is Libya: "Four nations occupy it and no more, two of which are autochthonous and two not (*ta men duo autochthona tôn ethneôn, ta de duo ou*). The Libyans and Egyptians are autochthonous [. . .] the Phoenicians and Greeks are immigrants (*epêludes*)" (4.197).

It is clear that here the positive criterion is autochthony. The condition of the *epêlus*, on the other hand, is negative by definition, even when the reference to autochthony is only implicit, as it is in Thucydides, who avoids the word *autokhthôn* presumably because it is too rhetorical. Reconstructing early Greek history, Thucydides must make Pelops, the eponymous mythical ancestor of the Peloponnese, sufficiently wealthy to explain how a "stranger" (*epêlun onta*) could have given his name to the region.[30]

Incidence of the rhetoric of autochthony in historiographic prose is generally limited to use of the word *epêlus*. In neither Thucydides nor Herodotus does the term induce an automatic swerve toward the very negative series of words for foreigner. Greek historiography seems to have resisted the suggestions of a language in which *epêlus* gave way to *epeiselthôn* ("the arrival") or *epaktos* and *epeisaktos* ("the intruder"), or even *polemios* ("the enemy").[31] But no precautions of historical reasoning could prevent the word from occupying a precarious position, and it took little—a slight change of register, an exegetical interpretation of prophecy, for example, for the foreigner to become once again the enemy.[32] Oracular speech pierces through the indirect narrative style; it has tragic overtones, and, like tragedy, associates *polemios* with *epêlus*.[33]

The arrival, then: virtually the enemy. Or at best, one whose foreign birth (*epêlus genesis*) made his descendants, as in the *Menexenus*, "Metics" (*metoikountas*): mere residents in the place in which he had one day appeared from elsewhere (*allothen*).[34] Could immobility be so precious that movement must always be so despised? That only those who have never

moved are citizens by nature, while the rest are condemned to an infe-
rior status? Aristotle, for example, retranslates as *metoikos* ("Metic") the
Homeric term *metanastês*, employed by Achilles when he complains that
Agamemnon has treated him as a "wanderer" (a refugee, an emigrant),
unworthy of honors. Between Homer and Aristotle the word may have
been officially absorbed into the sphere of autochthony, on the negative
side of the domiciled foreigner. So we might suppose when the Athenians employ it in Herodotus as proof of their great worth: "Alone of all
the Greeks, we are not *metanastai* [. . .]."[35]

"We are not emigrants . . . " Likewise, in order to identify the Arcadians as autochthones, Herodotus states in book two that they "remained
in the same place and did not emigrate." Or at least, to translate somewhat literally the verbal form *hupoleiphthentes*, that they "were left behind" when the population of the Peloponnese had to emigrate in order
to escape the Dorians, "and therefore did not emigrate."[36] As if for the
Father of History the norm was displacement, as if the dynamic was on
the side of movement. The tables are turned when autochthonous immobility is expressed as negation of movement, when it is the same that
must be defined negatively, through the absence of emigration. Should
we conclude that there are, perceptible in Herodotus but doubtless prior
to all historical writing, two opposing, and warring, traditions?

It is also in Herodotus that we find indications of a more precise response to this question. In book eight he lists seven races which "inhabit" the Peloponnese.[37] Two of them, being autochthonous, are established (*hidrutai*) where they were already living previously: the
Arcadians and the Cynurians. At the other end of the list, there are four
"foreign" races (*epêludes*): Dorians, Aetolians, Dryopians, and Lemnians.
And between them the Achaean race, which was not displaced, at least
beyond the Peloponnese, because it was within these limits that it aban-
doned its own territory for another. In fact as far as the Peloponnese is
concerned, it seems that in terms of expression, movement is quick to
reclaim its rights: the Achaeans were not said to be "staying in the same
place"; Herodotus merely says that they never moved. However, even
in terms of movement, it seems that there exists an autonomous formulation of immobility of the same; in this case, in opposition to everything
which suggests displacement or the coming and going of peoples over
territories that do not belong to them, autochthonous relationship to the
soil is expressed vertically: *hidrutai* denotes taking root, establishing, lay-

ing foundations, as well as the action of erecting a building, a stele, or a statue.

Two ways of occupying the soil, and perhaps two competing models; in Herodotus this polarity begins in book one when Croesus, courting friendship with the most powerful of the Greeks, discovers that these are the Lacedaemonians and the Athenians, and that of the two, "one had never moved and the other had wandered everywhere." The historian then lists the successive migrations of the Dorians.[38]

The two models are in place: it is time to advance.

Yet it is just here that I must digress. To escape from the logic of the two—in other words from the Herodotean framework, which often amounts to a too-pregnant opposition between Athens and Sparta—we must examine a third discourse. This is the moment to introduce, if briefly, the complication of the Theban myth of origin. I have two reasons for doing so: because it poses a difficult problem for a strictly orthodox autochthonous conscience, in that it resembles a successful grafting of a history of the *epêlus* onto autochthony;[39] and because in grafting the other onto the same it frees us from the naive expectation of finding an alternative to the opposition of the two models.

We know that Kadmos was a Phoenician—a Tyrian, specifies Euripides—who arrived one day in what was not yet Boeotia, in order to found, colony-like, the city that will take the name of Thebes.[40] Thus he belongs, like the Lydian Pelops,[41] to the category of great hero-founders who were both primordial ancestors and foreigners, those whom Plato will accuse in the *Menexenus* of reducing their descendants to the condition of "semi-Barbarians." But this, needless to say, is the autochthonous point of view, and we can be sure that in the classical period the citizens of Thebes or the peoples of the Peloponnese saw in the foreign origin of their ancestor only a matter for pride.[42]

Likewise there are two possible discourses with which to describe the reign of Kadmos and his relationship to the descendants of the autochthonous Spartoi (the Sown), according to whether one is Theban or Athenian: the former will glorify, like Pindar, "Kadmos and the sainted race of sown warriors," and the latter, like the *Menexenus*, will treat Kadmos as a simple "associate," *living with* Greeks of pure stock.[43]

As for these autochthones, chance—or was it?—saw that in the classical era they figured mostly in Athenian texts. And how could these

Spartoi, whose autochthony was derived from their having been "sown" by Kadmos and who set about killing one another immediately after birth, appear otherwise than as oxymora in Athenian tragedy?[44]

To make the Theban tradition speak, I should embark on a thorough and detailed enterprise of reconstruction. But not yet. Let it suffice for the moment to suggest that, when a discourse resists the opposition of two models, even if by combining them, access to it is difficult for this very reason.

End of digression. Back on track, I will adhere to the two competing poles which so clearly inform Herodotus' account.

What then do those whose origin belongs to the alterity of movement say about themselves?

There are places, such as Asia Minor, where the opposing discourses of the Same and the Other seem to enjoy equal favor. The Carians, island-dwellers turned continental, claimed to be autochthonous, and the Caunians, whom Herodotus considers autochthones, believed they came from elsewhere.[45] But once having acknowledged the unreliability of everything that is said in Asia Minor, what can we conclude about a system in which each discourse has nothing to recommend it, except in the eyes of those whose origin it falsifies? Leaving Asia Minor and returning to the Peloponnese, we find among the Lacedaemonians what we are looking for: a perfectly serene assertion of the movement that presides over their destiny.

As far as concerns their remotest past, they are in disagreement with the poets only on a single point, according to Herodotus: "that it was Aristodemos himself, great-grandson of Hyllos, who when he was king brought them to the region they presently occupy, rather than his children."[46] In other words, the only problem is chronological, while the fact of the migration is never questioned. In fact just the opposite: the Heraclids are said to have embarked on the migration with eager enthusiasm, not only in Pindar, who is speaking as a Theban, but also in Lacedaemonian terms.[47] Moreover a Lacedaemonian has no trouble acknowledging that he is only Dorian in name. To claim to be Achaean, like King Cleomenes on the Athenian Acropolis, is to go back in memory to the time before the migration—in other words, to something like a prehistory.[48]

But the moment we venture outside Sparta, certainties begin to unravel. Because the desire (the regret? the need?) for the same inevitably comes to trouble those who see themselves as other, foundation myths find numerous ways to reduce the foreign element in any origin.

The first, the simplest, is to start at the point of origin itself, in other words the place which is the point of departure for movement. It does not matter that the other is displaced; viewed from the same by those who weren't displaced, it remains in the realm of the same. Pindar calls the Aegeids, who went from Thebes to Sparta, from Sparta to Thera, and from Thera to Cyrene, "my fathers." The displacement is canceled out since nothing of the Theban principle is considered to have been lost over the course of the migrations.[49] There is no doubt that such reasoning on the part of a mother-city (this term extends beyond the great colonizing metropolises) often has to do with pure strategy, and must be linked to the intent to "establish or maintain dependence-relations."[50] But because there is no discourse of origin which does not engage the essential—I believe that there is always more to it than simply interests that are ultimately circumstantial,—the aim of these arguments, which is that of erasing from a story all its alterity, be it mythical or no, must be restored.

And there are many other ways of reducing the foreignness of origin. When the foundation myth does not end with the expulsion of the other (e.g., Kadmos the Phoenician, no doubt a poorly naturalized Theban, eventually goes into exile, leaving Thebes for Illyria whence he directs Barbarian hordes against Greece[51]), the temptation to convert that other back into the ranks of the same is powerful. There exists the option of transforming the invader into legitimate heir and the invasion into expedition of reconquest. Hence we speak of the "return of the Dorians"[52] and the "history of peregrination (which) becomes that of a circular migration."[53] Sometimes too the beginning divides in two, so that foreign origin becomes secondary, and the first point of departure Greek. But the operation does not always occur naturally, and sometimes raises more difficulties than it resolves. An example is Danaos the Egyptian, mentioned as such (disdainfully) in the *Menexenus*, but styled as a descendant of Argive Io by Aeschylus in the *Suppliants*, and hence a close relation of the Argives. Egyptian by accident, Greek by blood: thus Danaos escapes alterity. This is not so, however, in the actual plot, where on the contrary he belongs to the problematic category of the "citizen-strangers" (*astoxenoi*).[54] His reintegration proceeds with great uncertainty: King Pelasgos, the son of an autochthone, oscillates a long time between the recognition of the Argive origin of Danaos and his daughters and their maintenance in the status of *epêludes*, until the matter is determined by a people's decree, which awards them the title of Metics. As in the *Menexenus*, Danaos becomes nothing more than a resident alien.[55]

But any ideological operation spawns multiple versions, and the neutralization of the other is no exception. The Aegeids once again furnish an example: a Spartan "tribe" or "phratry" whose origin was traced to Thebes, to the point that some derived the name of Sparta from that of the Theban Spartoi.[56] But as we might expect, with the Aegeids, as with anything that has to do with Greece, the attempt to neutralize the other works both ways, and we get two opposing versions: one which assigns the main role to Thebes (put forward, naturally, by the Thebans, as I mentioned above, and it is also the version of Pindar, who mentions the "Dorian colony" of the Lacedaemonians among the national glories of his city),[57] and the other which offers the Lacedaemonian interpretation of the myth (the Aegeids have only a secondary role in the formation of the Spartan polis, where incidentally their ancestor was born, a descendant of exiled Thebans, to be sure, yet already Lacedaemonian).[58]

Thus the conflict of origins rages, wherein the Other is offered up to all annexations. This does not mean however that we must conclude in extremis that the victory of the Same is inevitable. Better to observe—a less grandiloquent but more accurate attitude—to what point each of the two rival discourses, that of the motionless same and that of the moving other, labors to preserve an autonomy, ever claimed, yet threatened at every turn by the arguments of its neighbor.

Of Impossible Autarchy

Now it is the turn of the Other to tackle the Same, which is only fair. Once again, then, I take up autochthony, but this time resolutely paying attention to the reflections of the historians, in which permanence in the same is only one of two poles on a scale of intelligibility where all the figures of movement are deployed.

Neither Herodotus nor Thucydides is particularly forthcoming when it comes to autochthony; at least reservations are never more apparent than when the historian leaves Greece proper. Herodotus is more critical in Asia Minor than in the Peloponnese,[59] and Thucydidean irony is more explicit concerning Sicily than Athens.

Thucydides reserves the term *autochthones* for the Sicani; this is his only use of the word, which betokens a certain lack of enthusiasm. Thus the historian divests the word of all its Athenian connotations, while at the same time allowing himself the authority to doubt the sincerity of those who employ it. Like the Carians in Herodotus, the Sicani *call* themselves autochthones, yet they are among the peoples listed as Barbarians. (In reality they were displaced Iberians.)[60] Here, then, we have the word singularly modalized by this one occurrence. But to have read closely the few sentences in book one of the *Peloponnesian War* devoted to Athenian autochthony (without its being mentioned by name) is to understand that on this patriotic theme the reticence of the historian is equaled only by his irony. Permanence of the same men on the same soil, without conflict because the aridity of the soil was not a drawing factor, followed by, during the period of the migrations, the influx of powerful men from other cities in search of stability, and finally integration of these foreigners "turned citizens":[61] this is all that Thucydides says. But it is sufficient to undermine Athenian pride, which loved to boast of the fecundity of the soil and the "unmixed" character of the race.

Indeed, for a Greek historian anxious to reconstruct the earliest period of the Greek fact (and on this point, Thucydides does not depart significantly from Herodotus), movement suggests a much more intellectually satisfying operator than the permanence of the "fixed abode." In the beginning everything suggests movement, starting with the inevitable statement that nations kept changing names[62] because they kept changing locations. Whence the necessity, for those who would identify the spark that first sets a group on the migratory path and commits it to permanent alterity, of always going further back, from migration to migration, from name to name.[63] An example in Herodotus is the particularly thorny case of the Pelasgians. To answer the question "what language did they originally speak?" (the eventual answer is a Barbarian language), it is necessary to proceed by conjecture, based on the three remaining contemporary groups of Pelasgians: those who live in the city of Crotona, those who colonized the Hellespont, and "other cities" which were Pelasgian. The difficulty is that none of these groups has been preserved intact: the cities have changed their names, the colonizers cohabited earlier with the Athenians, and finally the description of the first group leads one to deduce the irresistible movement which

elides names and nations in the same location. Thus Pelasgians who inhabited the city of Crotona "were once neighbors (*but they are no longer*)
of those who today are called Dorians (*but they didn't always have that
name*) and who lived then (*but they have since moved*) in the territory now
called Thessaliotis (*but which then had another name*)" (Herodotus 1.57).[64]

To recapitulate: no nation is where it was, the names of groups and
locations have all changed, and yet the historian expects his readers to
keep up. Thucydides' reasoning is similar in regard to the settlement of
Sicily,[65] but even more relevant here to my thesis is the *prooimion* of book
one of the *Peloponnesian War*, where the historian develops a plausible
discourse on origins in terms of movement.

I will pause at this *prooimion*, known as the Archaeology, to examine
two series of signifiers which serve to structure the account: one that
consists of all forms of inhabiting (the noun *oikos*, the verb *oikeô*, and
their derivatives,) and another that is built around the verb *histêmi*.[66]

We begin with *histêmi*, or rather its derivatives. Although the verb
histêmi expresses stability,[67] which might lead to its being used to denote
a taking root in the soil—but it is precisely in the beginning that there
is no durable taking root,—its derivatives, through the vast number of
prefixes which can attach to it, all suggest movement in action. In other
words the compounds of *histêmi* unmake its sense. Thucydides, who uses
the simple verb not once in the Archaeology,[68] makes systematic use of
these derivatives, as if to irremediably destabilize the expression of being
at rest.[69] There is no taking root, and even in the signifier the turbulence
of beginnings comes to subvert immobility.

What should not, above all, be immobilized is origin, according to
the law that runs as follows: if A inhabits a territory, B will arrive to
chase him off it, to be chased off in his turn by C, until an order is established, which is that of the present.[70] In this *perpetuum mobile* of prehistory, where people take up residence only in places they will have to
leave, living somewhere (as provisionary as it is threatened) is one of the
obligatory reference points of narrative, in Thucydides as in Herodotus.
But we recall the insistence with which the official rhetoric of autochthony credits Athenians with an *oikein* (with a way of "inhabiting")
that distinguishes them from the rest of humanity. Is this merely a way
of reversing the discourse of others to proclaim that, decidedly, one is
not like them?[71] Or were the orators, when they maintained that Athenians (in contrast to other Greeks) inhabited their own territory or in-

habited that territory successively and were always the same people, arguing for more a pertinent usage, a properly Athenian one, of the verb
oikeô? The question deserves attention, because the language of the
Same, and the degree of autonomy with which one can credit autochthonous discourse, depend upon it.

Living somewhere cannot define the citizen, according to Aristotle,
since one can also speak of the *oikêsis* of the Metic or slave.[72] A reminder
that in Athens itself, institutionally, the language of legality sees in the
act of inhabiting (*oikêsis*) only "being domiciled" or "residing," which is
just what defines the Metic, whose relationship to the territory is not
controled by nature.[73] Already we are far from autochthony. Suspicion
crystallizes when we note that the historians used the verb *oikeô* to characterize the occupation of territory by a non-Greek people, at the time
of a migration and at a very early period, and, also, the first colonization
of a nation:[74] it is from the logic of alterity—from this way that others
have of occupying the soil which, by definition, does not belong to
them[75]—that Athenian orators derived their variations on autochthonous
occupation of territory.

Let us recapitulate the evidence for autochthony. The verb *oikeô* was,
in fact, appropriated by the Athenians; the expression is used to emphasize the identity or uniqueness of autochthones, the exceptional "inhabitants," established from the beginning on their own soil: "they were the
same people, generation after generation" (*hoi autoi aiei oikountes*), "alone
of all humankind they inhabited the land in which they were born"
(*monoi pantôn anthrôpôn [. . .] ôikêsan*).[76] But more often than not force
of habit assigned *oikein* to others, strangers, imperfect citizens who one
day took over someone else's land, a hodgepodge, ragtag crowd from all
points of the compass, and autochthones had to be content with "inhabiting" their land differently from the rest.[77] Decidedly there may not
be much to say about the same, except to invert what is said about the
other. Which comes back to not being able to define oneself other than
negatively.

There may be nothing to say about the same when one puts oneself
in the position of others. When one tries to see oneself in terms of
movement, ready to claim to be its starting point, without even inventing to this end a language of taking root[78] (but would it have many
words? Probably not). When one censures that which constitutes the

true Athenian core of autochthonous thought: the family saga of Erichthonios, a story that speaks of the division of the sexes and reproduction.[79] In other words when, within the myth of autochthony, it is the myth that one censures.

Autochthony without myth: a rhetorical device for denying movement, where one anticipates that, from the repetition that Athenians are not like others, the same will really arise. But it would be necessary to shift everything. . . .

Perhaps we might find the seed of such shifting in the way in which certain Athenian writers operate on the signifier when they try to resemanticize autochthonous *oikein* in the sphere of *oikeion*, in other words from the "own" conceived as essentially familial.[80] In these passages one may look for the mark of familialism which characterizes the Athenian fourth century;[81] I see here largely an attempt to deal once again with the family history of the Acropolis which democratic discourse, in its desire to generalize the birth of the ancestor to all citizens, tries to erase, at the risk of condemning itself to speak the language of others.

Such is the paradox of an autochthonous discourse: it is hopelessly afflicted by instability, caught as it is between the ineffable Same and the verbal suggestions of alterity, as between two inevitable reefs. On one side tautology threatens, and the motionless repetition of a statement without the history of event (Athenians are Athenians); on the other side, the risk is that of never reaching the uniqueness of Athens, because the same is made with the other, because movement is more powerful than anything that denies it.

Perhaps at heart I have simply tried throughout this roundabout journey to demonstrate what happens when one puts oneself in the domain of the Same and the Other in order to imagine civic identity: one thinks one has chosen one's side, as if the same could conceive of itself without the other, or as if inversely one could claim a pure position of alterity. Doubtless it would be sufficient to reread the *Sophist* in order to be convinced of this; but there is a civic usage of these philosophizing polarities (the Same and the Other, Rest and Movement) whose impasses and ever-renascent appeal Plato likes to demonstrate, and it is this civic usage that interests me. Therefore I must insist on the discourse of autochthony, in order to try to elucidate what is untenable as a conceptualization of the Same in a statement of the type: "Alone of all the Greeks, we are *not* immigrants." For in the element of movement, where one must put oneself as soon as one wishes to jettison the other there, the all-powerful principle of alterity reigns.

I began with the crane in the *Statesman*, and I would like to return to Plato to finish this chapter, in order to attempt to answer the question, embarrassing to say the least, of the Platonic treatment of autochthony. Why is it that when he introduces a myth of autochthony better known under the rubric of the "noble lie" in book three of the *Republic*, Plato turns to the Theban model, rather than to the Athenian which he developed in the *Menexenus* (whose echo reverberates—and more than once—in the *Republic*)? It is Kadmos the Stranger who may well provide the key to the enigma. In designating the autochthony of the citizens of the *Republic* as a "Phoenician story"—a Sidonian tale according to the *Laws*[82]—does Plato, for whom the Phoenicians have no positive reference,[83] intend to suggest to what point the other informs the same? In the complete invention by the city-founders (*oikistai*) of a myth which is a useful lie, certainly.[84] But also and chiefly in the project of autochthony itself; that of Athens, which Plato does not treat kindly,[85] and that of Thebes, integrated into a whole both composite and on this occasion completely obscured behind the figure of the stranger-founder. "Nothing new, a Phoenician tale . . . ": a story that comes from elsewhere, for an autochthonous *phusis* in the form of pedagogical artifice.

What is a stranger? One whom a Greek cannot dispose of, by classifying him for all time under the heading of other.

CHAPTER 6

Inquiry into the Historical
Construction of a Murder

To deny a people the man whom it praises as the greatest of its sons is not a deed to be undertaken lightheartedly—especially by one belonging to that people. No consideration, however, will move me to set aside truth in favor of supposed national interests. Moreover, the elucidation of the mere facts of the problem may be expected to deepen our insight into the situation with which they are concerned.

—Sigmund Freud, *Moses and Monotheism*

We begin with the story of a political murder.[1] The scene is Athens in 514 B.C., some thirteen years after the death of the tyrant Peisistratos, who was succeeded by his sons. On the day of the Panathenaea, Hipparchus, the son of Peisistratos, was killed by Harmodios and Aristogeiton. This was not the end of the tyranny of the Peisistratids, since the tyrant who was overthrown in 510, through the intervention of the Lacedaemonians and the active hostility of the great family of the Alcmeonidae, was Hippias. It was an Alcmeonid, Cleisthenes, who gave Athens the regime of liberty which later would be termed democracy.[2] Harmodios and Aristogeiton killed Hippias' brother, not tyranny itself, yet the Athenians, as long as democracy endured, considered them worthy of the title "Tyrannoktones," "killers of the tyrant." The Tyrannoktones were less champions of democracy than a couple of aristocratic *hetairoi* ("companions"), as their names indicate: *Harmodios* is "the assembler," and *Aristogeitôn* "the best neighbor" or "the best associate."[3] But in search of heroic founders, Athenian democracy lets this go by. Error, perhaps, but who would dare accuse a people of being mistaken about its national heroes?

Freud and Thucydides

Thucydides was the Athenian who dared accuse Athenians of being singularly mistaken about those they called the tyrant-killers. Not that the historian was at pains to correct this error; in his eyes there were too many other errors surrounding Harmodios and Aristogeiton—and graver ones—to impute to the people of Athens, for him to be concerned with the one that made heroes of democracy out of a couple of *hetairoi*. But because he would reveal the secret that the collective memory of the Athenians had obscured, Thucydides could have written the opening lines of *Moses and Monotheism*, in which Freud takes on the duty of divesting the Jewish people of the man whom they consider a "liberator" in the name of truth. In the case of the Tyrannoktones, however, I will examine what Thucydides actually wrote. Which supposes that one sticks to the text, and to the text alone: that, renouncing the endlessly revived discussions in the philological tradition, one does not seek to establish, with or against the text, either what really happened on that day of the Panathenaea in the year 514, or the exact moment of this fundamental deception by means of which an astute politician—Cleisthenes perhaps, or Themistocles—gave the democracy such debatable heroes.[4]

Therefore it is not the legitimacy of the celebration of the Tyrannoktones which interests me—it is enough for me that the celebration was meaningful for Athenians,—but the reasons that led Thucydides thus to deny all relevance to Athenian tradition. Particularly forceful reasons, apparently, since the historian tackled the question twice:[5] first, briefly, in book one of the *Peloponnesian War*, before devoting a detailed analysis to it in the form of a digression in book six. Particularly complicated reasons, as is apparent to those who pursue the complexities of his reasoning in book six.

Here, then, in outline is the long digression on the murder of Hipparchus. The account of the Peloponnesian War has reached the year 415. Irreversibly, Athens has embarked on the Sicilian expedition. But the fleet has yet to leave Piraeus when two religious—i.e., political— scandals erupt: the mutilation of the Herms and the profanation of the Mysteries. Alcibiades, having been denounced, is recalled to defend himself, because the people, who love and hate him in the same breath, suspect him of aspiring to the tyranny. Meanwhile the inquiry is pursued relentlessly, "because the Athenian people knew through tradition that the tyranny of Peisistratos and his sons became oppressive toward the end, and that moreover it had been not he [Aristogeiton] and Harmodios who overthrew him, but rather the Lacedaemonians; hence they lived in fear and were suspicious of everything." Thucydides embarks on a long account of the plot of Harmodios and Aristogeiton in order to make it clear, he says, that no one, not even the Athenians, has anything accurate to say about this event. Shorn of the fear of Lacedaemonian intervention—and with this fear, the only correct assumption with which the historian credits the people,—all that remains is the story of a daring coup, arisen out of a sentimental imbroglio. Simply put, a love story with an unhappy ending. Aristogeiton loves the beautiful ephebe Harmodios, of whom Hipparchus is also enamored. The ephebe rejects the advances of the son of Peisistratos and confides in his lover, whence the conspiracy is born. Here Thucydides interrupts the narrative to present evidence for what he has already maintained in book one: that the tyrant was not Hipparchus, but his older brother Hippias. The story resumes: the rejected Hipparchus revenges himself on Harmodios by humiliating his younger sister, and the plot to bring down the tyranny, therefore Hippias, takes shape. On the appointed day the lovers, believing that the plot has been betrayed, shun the tyrant and descend upon Hipparchus. They kill him, and are killed. Fearing for his life, Hippias disarms the Athenians, and the city is paralyzed. Conclusion and return to the point of departure: haunted by the memory of tyranny, Athenian democracy lives, in 415, in fear of conspiracy.

The affair is obscure, to say the least, and generations of readers have remarked that neither the point of the digression nor the conclusion to be derived from its arguments is evident. One could, of course, restrict oneself merely to listing the elements of the tradition which Thucydides submits to historical scrutiny. These are four, according to the authors of an authoritative English commentary:

—Hipparchus was not the tyrant when he was killed;
—the murder arose out of a love affair, not an uprising of the people of Athens;
—the murder did not put an end to the tyranny;
—up to the time of the murder, the tyranny had been tolerated by the Athenians.[6]

To these four points I would add a fifth, less consequential in appearance and hence less attended to, but significant perhaps nonetheless: contrary to the predilection evinced by the Athenian *dêmos* for Harmodios—predilection recognized, moreover, by the historian—it is not the younger of the two conspirators, but the mature adult Aristogeiton who takes the initiative in what Thucydides, reversing the usual order, calls "the bold deed of Aristogeiton and Harmodios."[7] Systematic adoption of the opposite position to that of the *dêmos*? No doubt. Substitution of the less excusable intemperance of an adult for the ardors of youth,[8] and hence denial of any lyricism to the enterprise? Perhaps.

In fact, and to return to the basics of the story, what is most obscure in all this is still the aims of Thucydides. Rehabilitation of tyranny? It might look that way (but what has this to do with the account of the Peloponnesian War?). Explanation of the climate of Athens in 415, by way of analogy? The analogy would have to be operative, or at least remotely decipherable, observes Philology, caustically. And why is Thucydides so clearly concerned to correct the erroneous opinions of the Athenian *dêmos* about its own past? This leads certain commentators to propose as "the most plausible explanation" that he succumbed on this occasion to the irrepressible "temptation of all historians to correct error wherever they find it," at the risk of compromising the overall relevance of the account.[9]

The desire for truth as the historian's weak point? Since we must end by finding a beginning, this proposition—ultimate explanation or minimal hypothesis—will serve as a point of departure.

Truth as Rectification

To begin at the beginning: the beginning of the story (which is also the beginning of chapter 54):

> In fact the bold deed of Aristogeiton and Harmodios arose out of an amorous coincidence. In recounting this story in detail, I will demonstrate (*apophanô*) that [. . .] the Athenians [. . .] are inaccurate.

Turning immediately to the first sentence of chapter 55 (i.e., to the "digression" concerning Hippias):

That it was Hippias, as the elder of the two, who was in charge, I have—
even from the point of view of the oral tradition—a more accurate
knowledge than others, and on this point I am certain (*iskhurizomai*).

Apophanô, iskhurizomai: I can demonstrate the truth, therefore I am certain. Viewed as the model historian, Thucydides is he who rectifies what
has been distorted. Warning to the reader who may have forgotten it
along the way: because he fights for the truth, the historian rectifies all
distortions.

Now apropos the Tyrannoktones, it is decidedly important to recover
the truth. Thucydides had already attempted it, briefly, at a strategic
point in book one. In the guise of a conclusion to the reconstruction of
the distant past of Greece which is known as the Archaeology, and also
to introduce the description of his methodology, he rectifies two errors
or series of errors: the error of the Athenians concerning their past, and
those of his predecessor Herodotus (whom he is careful not to name) on
certain points relevant to the contemporary history of the Lacedaemonians. An elegant way of clearing the way for the epiphany of truth in history.

Recovery of the truth, in the particular case of the Tyrannoktones but
also in general, proceeds counter to memory. We should not be misled:
if Herodotus is more than once the anonymous target of criticism, the
most serious adversary of the historian is still *akoê*. *Akoê*: listening, with
the immediate pleasure it brings to the auditor; but also what one most
often listens to if one is Greek: the oral tradition, with its immediate link
to the past; but also, memory. *Akoê*: a Greek dimension of memory,
rooted in hearsay.

From his outline of methodology in book one, it is clear that Thucydides is wary of all modalities of hearing. Hearing is deceiving for whoever aims at full recollection of the speeches given in effect by the actors
of history: even hearing them oneself, one is no closer to the truth. In
terms of actions, the problem drops back a pace: one can give a clear account of those one has witnessed; the rest is oral testimony, invalid because always distorted, either through the partiality of the informant in
favor of one side or the other, or by his memory (*mnêmê*). Information:
deformation. Here we find memory in bad company, associated with
partiality—hardly more reliable and likewise producing deformation.[10] It
follows that Thucydides does not relate the past, or hardly, since for his-

torical facts there is no source other than *akoê*; therefore better rid our-selves of the account of the past as quickly as possible. This produces, in the opening pages of the book, the eighteen chapters of the Archaeol-ogy. And when despite everything one must return to the past, the his-torian relies only on his own intelligence, brought to bear, like that of a judge, on those indices (*tekmêria*) which he is able to collect.[11]

Now, in one of those dramatic turns in which Thucydides is a spe-cialist, it may happen that once his intelligence has honed itself on the decipherment of the evidence, the historian permits himself an *akoê*.[12] This is exactly what occurs concerning the tyranny of Hippias in book six: "I have—even from the point of view of the oral tradition—a more accurate knowledge than others. . . . " Why the *akoê* all of a sudden? The inclusion of the parenthetical clause is overdetermined. *Akoê* is like a luxury in which the historian can indulge, because he accompanies it with a display of methodology (like a display of force): the rest of the Hippias episode piles on the evidence, as if to counterbalance this in-congruous resort to hearsay. But claiming *akoê* also allows Thucydides to acquire an important benefit in passing, assuring him the unconditional allegiance of the reader toward his desire for truth: because he desires the truth, we have to accept his word, even in a minefield (explicitly iden-tified by him as such), and do without the slightest verification since we will never know where this *akoê* comes from, yet we will have to accept that the deeply held conviction of the historian is sufficient to validate the tradition *ex machina*.[13] Finally, and this is probably the most com-pelling reason for resorting to *akoê*, it is a question of combating the tra-dition on its own terrain, of wielding, against the tradition of the Athe-nians, a greater tradition. In the guise of memory, the Athenians possess an *akoê*?[14] Fine: Thucydides the Athenian knows a better one.

Here the goal of rectification becomes obvious. When they glorify the Tyrannoktones, Athenians are in a way historians, albeit atrocious ones. This is evident from book one, where Athenian tradition concerning the murder of Hipparchus is cited as the very example of the unforgiveable negligence which "the majority brings to the search for truth (*zêtêsis tês alêtheias*)": "even when it concerns their own nation, people will no less readily accept, and without examination (*abasanistôs*), the traditions (*akoas*) which are transmitted about the past. Thus the Athenians [. . .]." And likewise the succinct rectification of the traditional version of the murder of Hipparchus.[15] Book six goes further: no more than others (other

Greeks? other historians? to the reader to respond, if he/she desires) the Athenians themselves are inaccurate with regard to these tyrants, although they are part of their own past. But it is on this memory—or rather this error—that in 415 the people of Athens thought they could base their zealous pursuit of the recently uncovered scandals, and "subject the affair to examination (*basanisai to pragma*)."[16] To seek, to find the truth: these are the key words of the historical method; based on inaccurate premises, the Athenian enquiry becomes a parody of history. The zeal to "examine" a contemporary deed onto which one projects an *akoê* which itself has never been examined: this too is parodic.[17] In short, as far as Thucydides is concerned, Athenians are lousy historians, capable of parodying historical inquiry by actualizing, in the form of a legal proceeding, what in the outline of methodology was judicial metaphor. In Platonic language, one might say that they remain at the imitation stage, because they are thinking in false terms when they relate their ancient history.

To return to Thucydides: if the historian must rectify any historical error, the Athenian owes the truth to his fellow citizens. Just as it was up to Freud to enlighten the Jews about Moses, belonging himself to the Jewish people, so Thucydides must enlighten the Athenians about their national heroes, being the author of a Greek History with no other determinative than "the Athenian."[18] "The irrepressible temptation of the historian" unites with the critical duties of citizenship: establishing the truth about the murder of Hipparchus comes down to elucidating what, in the collective conscience of Athens, constituted a "permanent trauma."[19]

To force Athenians to hear, even once, the truth about their history. Or, more exactly, to *read* it, far from the seductions of hearing. Then perhaps they will learn to uphold the truth, and be forced to admit that the enterprise of the tyrant-killers was anything but political.

An Unpolitical Act

A heroic cult celebrated by the polemarch, a tomb in the official Athenian cemetery, statues in the Agora, an injunction against blaspheming the killers of the tyrant, privileges awarded their descendants: the celebration of Harmodios and Aristogeiton was an official affair for Athenian democracy. Whether or not this highly effective symbol, useful for sealing the cohesion of the *dêmos*, was instituted by Cleisthenes, this question so preoccupying to modern scholarship meant little to Thucydides; it was sufficient that in 415, the memory of its origin having long since disappeared, this celebration contributed to the structuring of the Athenian representation of the past, like a memorandum which served at the same time as a framework of memory. Engraved in the memory of the democracy, Harmodios and Aristogeiton had a share in the future of the constitution which was like a second nature to the Athenian polis. In 410, after a moment of oligarchy following the anxieties of 415 and the disarray provoked in 413 by the disaster in Sicily, it appears that the restored democracy engaged in a solemn reaffirmation of the glory of these benefactors of the fatherland, who were proposed by decree as a model for the democrat in action.[20]

Thucydides was well aware that the celebration of the Tyrannoktones was democratic before it was Athenian, attributing the erroneous tradition to the "mass" of Athenians (*plêthos*: "crowd," but also the majority and the regime that represented it), and carefully distinguishing what was known and what was believed by the people, in other words by the democracy (*dêmos tôn Athênaiôn*). It is possible that the desire to rectify tradition does not derive solely from a historian's project, but also from political interpretation.

Why was it necessary to establish that Hippias, rather than Hipparchus, was the tyrant in 514, unless to suggest that Harmodios and Aristogeiton, who did not kill the tyrant, did not merit the title of Tyrannoktones? In other words that they were not political heroes, since in order to liberate Athens, they would have had to kill Hippias. Thucydides describes how the two conspirators, not content with killing Hipparchus alone, killed him adventitiously: thinking that they had been betrayed they lost their heads, and "wished, before being arrested, to accomplish a deed which justified the risk they had taken."[21]

—But if it wasn't Hipparchus they wanted to kill in the first place; if it was in fact Hippias, and their plan becomes entirely political again?

—Patience, Reader; what is not learned in book one will be revealed in book six: in mounting the conspiracy against Hippias, Harmodios and Aristogeiton still had very private motives. . . . Strange, you say? Again, patience, even if you find contradictions in the story, even if the causality of the murder strikes you as somewhat overdetermined.[22]

Harmodios and Aristogeiton were not, then, the political heroes the democracy liked to make of them. This means that they were not the liberators celebrated in speeches and glorified in song at fifth-century Athenian banquets.[23] The citizens did not owe them the equal participation in the city (*isonomia*) which the orators were wont to extol. Moreover, according to Thucydides the people knew perfectly well that the Tyrannoktones had not overthrown the tyranny. At any rate in 415 they were supposed to "know it through tradition." An unwarranted reputation, rapidly dissolving.

—Perhaps, if one has decided once and for all that political memory feeds on error. But the opposite is true: there is knowledge in tradition. The banquet-hymn cited above is only one version of the story, the one which derives the all-new *isonomia* of Athens from the Tyrannoktones; yet another version of the same hymn exists, which accords them the single merit of having killed *a* tyrant—a Peisistratid—and not *the* tyrant. Therefore the people were well aware that Harmodios and Aristogeiton had not in fact liberated Athens. But they were grateful to them nonetheless, because they also knew that they had given their lives in an attempted opening-of-the-way toward liberation. They knew this in 415; they knew this in 410 when they revived the cult of these heroes.[24]

—But there is still a difficulty: how could the people recognize the Lacedaemonians as their sole liberators,[25] yet continue to honor Harmodios and Aristogeiton?

—If this knowledge were sufficient to destroy the image of the Tyrannoktones, would Thucydides have spent so long reconstructing the story? Of course the Tyrannoktones were dead, and had not liberated Athens. But nothing is so heroizing as death, and this death made them the symbol of Athenian resistance to tyranny. What price the glory of a living Jean Moulin?*

*French hero of the Resistance who died at the hands of the Gestapo—*Trans.*

—But Harmodios and Aristogeiton succeeded above all in exasperating
the tyrant. What an advantage for the Athenians!

The people knew, according to Thucydides, that "the tyranny had
become oppressive toward the end," since they also acknowledged, un-
enthusiastically, that the Athenians were no more successful than Harmodios in dislodging the yoke. From here it is only one step to attributing to the people the conviction that, in failing in their attempt,
the tyrant-killers simply increased the burden of the tyranny, which
Thucydides does not, however, broach explicitly, even though this is
clearly his view. Here he follows Herodotus (the exception makes the
rule) who, it is true, would extenuate the glory of the Tyrannoktones in
order to exalt that of the Alcmeonids, whom he promotes as the liberators of Athens; but he follows him with the certainty of someone for
whom only action, effectual action, exists.[26]

—All right: in the eyes of Thucydides, history knows nothing of attempts
and mistakes, and all power which stays in power is legitimate. . . . By this
reasoning, why not call those who resisted in 1940 dangerous terrorists?

—Pure anachronism! Back to the Athens of Thucydides. In any case, the
historian still has one argument, which is decisive: it was strictly private
vengeance that Harmodios and Aristogeiton pursued.

Here I will end the dialogue—imaginary, but by no means false—between a politically minded reader, more preoccupied with the memory
of the Resistance than with the Tyrannoktones, and a champion of
Thucydides, convinced that in all cases the historian of reason can but be
right. I end the dialogue because it is becoming increasingly evident that
in trying to prove too much, Thucydides' reasoning invites suspicion,
when he does not provide himself the counterarguments that will invalidate it. This is often remarked: after all, how important is the real motivation of Harmodios and Aristogeiton, if it was truly the overthrow of
the tyranny which they envisaged from the beginning? What about the
organization of the plot, as presented in Thucydides? The historian is at
pains to point out that the conspirators were few, yet the very existence
of a conspiracy and the expectation that, at the first sign of insurrection,
the Athenians of the Panathenaic procession would use their weapons

"to participate in their own liberation," all these indications, which we owe to Thucydides, suggest that this story is much more political than he would like to acknowledge.

But this is exactly what Thucydides does not want: to condone through his authority as a historian a political interpretation which a close reading of the text more than once suggests, to admit that in forming a conspiracy against the Peisistratids, the assassins were truly seditious (insurgents; others might say *résistants*).[27] Seditious in a good cause, according to the democracy, which never ceased to uphold this opinion. But such a notion is unacceptable to Thucydides, who prefers to credit the Athenians with an "error" rather than with a way of thinking in which he clearly saw a crime against the idea of the polis.

By taking as pure patriotic courage behavior that Thucydides considers mere "reckless undertaking" (*alogistos tolma*), the people of Athens reasoned like the instigators of the civil war whose fallacious rhetoric was exposed by the historian in book three.[28] By exalting the heroism of the Tyrannoktones, Athenian democracy recognizes as its founding act one of *stasis* (sedition, a Greek term for civil war). Thucydides adheres to the Greek condemnation of *stasis* as a disease of the polis, and when he comes to the civil war of Corcyra in 427 in book three, he takes the time to analyze the pernicious effects of a process that introduces division into the ideally indivisible unity which is the body politic. I am hypothesizing that, in order to obscure the fault of the democracy beneath the error of the Athenian masses, it was necessary for him to deny at all cost the political character of the murder of Hipparchus.

In defiance of the national recollection of the Athenians, the historian went in search of the truth. And, naturally, he found it: the murder of Hipparchus? a love story.

Before examining the consequences of this discovery, let us make one detour, returning to the personality of Aristogeiton, the man of mature years to whom the narrative gives precedence over Harmodios. Thucydides makes mention of the fact that he was a citizen of the "middle rank." Aristogeiton then belonged to the middle class, the incarnation of political wisdom which was charged with preventing the unleashing of *stasis*, on pain of being anihilated through the inevitable divisiveness that would tear the city apart.[29] Transgressing the neutrality implied by his position, he headed a conspiracy: the motive that drove him to it must therefore have been compelling: briefly, one of those passions which in

Thucydides determine in the final analysis the nature of man. Just as the "true cause" of the Peloponnesian War is not to be sought in economics or politics, but in the powerful psychological factor that is fear,[30] the impulse behind Aristogeiton's rebellion must have been stronger than any political conviction. A passion. The craziest of all, the one that leads to all paroxysms: love. In a world in which ephebes are loved by their elders, it is Aristogeiton, the man of mature years, who knows the sufferings of love. On this basis Thucydides reverses the received Athenian version to give the initiative to the latter. Aristogeiton loves Harmodios; Hipparchus would come between the lover and his beloved; Aristogeiton rebels. "Thus the origin (*arkhê*) of the conspiracy and reckless undertaking arose out of the suffering of love (*di' erôtikên lupên*), born of the momentary panic of Harmodios and Aristogeiton."

The phrase "momentary panic" should not mislead us: it is the writer's art to conclude the narrative on the very argument which gave it rise. In the workshop of the historian, we may assume that things happened in quite a different order, and that Thucydides started from this phrase which turned up in the course of his inquiry, when he finally perceived the *arkhê* of the rebellion. The archaeology of an irrational act ends with the discovery of *erôs*. Now the story can begin, in which Thucydides, at whatever the cost, brings into the daylight of *logos* the secret hidden behind Athenian national tradition.

And without further delay, the story begins.

The Secret of the Story

In fact the bold deed of Aristogeiton and Harmodios arose out of an amorous coincidence. In recounting this story in detail, I will demonstrate (*apophanô*) that [. . .] the Athenians [. . .] are inaccurate.

An "amorous coincidence" is a chance encounter on the terrain of love. But chance has little to do with Aristogeiton and Harmodios encountering Hipparchus and fatally wounding him in book six, where, overturning the earlier version of the murder outlined in book one, Thucydides resolutely dislocates chance from the act itself toward its origin. Chance assigns the roles much earlier, around the beautiful Harmodios. Everything is in place from that moment: the logic of *erôs* does the rest, and the affair depends on the narrative, which follows step by step its implacable necessity.

This step-by-step narrative in Thucydides is termed *diêgeisthai epi pleon*: to relate in detail, or rather "to relate at greater length." At greater length? Greater than one expects and greater, no doubt, than the reader, surprised by the content of the story, will find appropriate.[31] Since the production of the secret is intended to disturb a few well-established certainties, preparing the reader for the unheard-of character of the narrative is not a bad idea. And so that all will understand that the procedure is exceptional, Thucydides reserves the appellation *diêgeisthai* for this section of the narrative, unique in his work, and borrowed perhaps from forensic speeches and their rhetoric of truth.[32] Everything is in place for the reporting of a murder of passion.

Thus follows the story of a wounded love that ends in murder, and it is perhaps not too surprising that the establishment of the point of truth which is proposed in book one—the real identity of the tyrant—should be henceforward subordinated to the narrative, to which it no longer seems connected except as a digression within a digression.[33] This displacement of the kernel of truth is remarkable: was it not concerning the identity of the tyrant that Athenian tradition was revealed as pure imagination? But there is something more urgent or more fundamental in book six than the mere establishment of this point, and that is the challenging of a witness. It is a simple scenario: it is only necessary to confront, before the tribunal of historical conscience, the memory of the democracy and this love which it knows nothing about or has refused to acknowledge.[34] The Tyrannoktones were not heroes. Only lovers, whose anger and hatred led them to lose all presence of mind.

Aristogeiton and Harmodios: a lover, a beloved. A homosexual couple in which, according to Greek love, the passive role belongs to the ephebe. Aristogeiton takes the initiative, all the initiatives, while Hipparchus makes advances and initiates his vengeance, and Harmodios in the story is always in the position of object. Object of love, object of attack, a beautiful object desired and insulted through the younger sister who is his female double, and who, having suffered injury, disappears from the narrative the moment the humiliation has reached Harmodios.[35] This is the truth that Thucydides wishes to unveil, convinced that his narrative will invalidate the politicized *akoê* which, even to "others," the Athenians represented as the true story of the murder of Hipparchus.

It is this conviction which should be taken seriously, this project which should be examined, instead of the affair's being treated as banal as per the scholarly tradition, unanimously and with rather suspicious eagerness. (Why insist on the erotic aspect of the story? It has been sufficiently established, with Thucydides as guarantor. Stamped "all clear" and filed away.) But if the historian, to judge from from his *diêgeisthai*, anticipated a certain shock, such an expectation merits investigation, regardless of the actual result of the truth-operation; in this case, semi-success or semi-failure. Success from the point of view of historiographical literature, in which the Thucydidean version became authoritative;[36] probable failure as far as concerns the Athenians, who do not seem to have diminished their veneration for the Tyrannoktones in any way in the fourth century.[37] Measuring the actual effect one might object, as some have done, that there is nothing in the homosexual love of an older man for an adolescent or in the amorous caprices of a tyrant that would scandalize the Greek conscience;[38] this is the reason historians have simply added the information to the file, while the Athenians did not see anything in it to warrant a modification of their behavior. There remain to be accounted for, however, Thucydides' expectations of a completely different reception of his narrative. Even more inadequate is the attitude, widespread among modern Greek historians, which consists in projecting Thucydidean truth from the end of the fifth century onto the ancient origin of the tyrant-killer saga, maintaining that the Athenians always saw this couple as an *erômenos* and an *erastês*,[39] as if the Athenian *akoê* had to be in accord with itself from the beginning. Because Thucydides is regarded as telling the truth in all things, one forgets that he gives this truth the structure of a revelation—or a denunciation[40]— and one proposes, as if self-evident, a knowledge unrecognized (repressed?) in the collective conscience of Athens whose evidence the historical text would impose, against the grain and more than a century after the event.

To guard against the realist temptation that sees the revelation of truth as a faithful rendering of the events of the year 514, one might perhaps wish to know more about what grants the historian the unique privilege of knowing the secret of the affair. But on this point the text is entirely mute, leaving readers with the task of formulating their own hypotheses, if they so desire. The tradition of a *genos* sedulously maintained from one generation to the next, preserved against the democratic vulgate and suddenly emerging into the daylight of the narrative? Perhaps, but it is concerning the tyranny of Hippias, and only concerning this question, that Thucydides claims for himself an *akoê* more precise than any other. A pure construction governed by probability,[41] or by the desire to find at all costs another meaning in the murder? The hypothesis must be put forward. This is how Thucydides' construction is endlessly constructed upon.

Although having already engaged in the practice of construction, I prefer to return once more to the text, and the modalities of its articulation with the rest of the work. One fact merits attention: in six chapters in book six—five, if one brackets the one that deals exclusively with Hippias and the power he possessed—derivatives of the word *erôs* occur five times. In the context of a love story, there would be nothing remarkable about this in any author other than Thucydides. But love—the word, and even more the phenomenon—is remarkably absent from the Thucydidean historical universe. In the remainder of the work there are only four other occurrences of *erôs* and its derivatives among the eight books,[42] two of which occur once again in book six, which is indeed concerned with love, since it is dominated by the passionate impulse that compelled the Athenians, under the influence of the youth and rhetoric of Alcibiades, to covet Sicily and its riches.[43] Seven occurrences in book six, two in the seven books remaining: the imbalance is patent. There is no doubt that the year 415, whose recital Thucydides interrupts in order to reconstruct the history of an old murder which was dictated by passion, is governed by emotion.[44] But because only the *erôs* of the Tyrannoktones is understood, far from any figurative sense, in its sexual meaning, its exposition tends yet again to appear exceptional within the historical text.

Exceptional is the emergence of *erôs* in the author who gives the least possible space (without Harmodios and Aristogeiton I would have wanted to write no space) to the question—moreover, a very Greek question—of sex. Exceptional too is the function it is assigned, that of punctuating the narrative in the form of a revelation in which Thucydides undertakes to substitute the truth, the whole truth, for a collective error. Certainly the recurrence of the word "love" is desirable in a narrative that takes the place of a demonstration: when proofs are lacking, repetition can produce conviction. Thus the establishment of the truth occurs directly at the level of narrative framework, which is reduced to the successive stages of erotic intrigue ("The bold deed arose out of an amorous coincidence [. . .]. Aristogeiton was the lover of Harmodios [. . .], excessively wounded in love, he conspired [. . .], in a paroxysm of enraged love, they killed him [. . .], thus out of the suffering of love [. . .]").

My hypothesis is that the repetition is supposed to be sufficient to convince the reader of the truth of the story. This invites reflection on the figure of the anonymous recipient, discreetly invoked in the outline of methodology and designated thoughout the book by the indefinite pronoun (the reader: *tis*, "someone," or even "one"; without form, but alone supposed capable of responding in all justice to the exhortations of the text).

No doubt we should see in the repetition of derivatives of the word *erôs* only one of the many resources of *écriture* inevitably used to win over the reader. To read Thucydides as the historian intends, one has to submit to the authority of his own reflection, which basically comes down to sacrificing pleasure for the sake of comprehension. In other words, sacrificing the charm of listening to the discipline of reading.[45] And here more than elsewhere, submission is necessary if one wishes to accord the unveiling of the truth the reception the text expects: having adopted the postulates of the historian as his or her own, only the faithful reader knows that, for a historical proceeding, *erôs* is no acceptable resort. It is to such a reader, and to no other—neither professional historians, his competitors, nor Athenians, his co-citizens so little concerned with ex-actitude—that Thucydides destines a revelation which must surprise in order to rectify.

But it is possible that *erôs* cannot be translated onto the page with impunity. Because it concerns hearing as much as writing, because it has an echo-like effect within these passages, repetition could surreptitiously reintroduce something of *akoê* into historical writing. I can imagine a faithful reader who, confronted with the repetitive structure of the text, is concerned about the nature of the support that this tale of love and murder requires: should the rectification of error demand that writing go so far as to transgress rules it has so conspicuously enacted for the reader's edification? And however committed one may be to the intellectual pre-cepts set out once and for all in the methodological outline of book one, how could one not be puzzled by the sudden bursting onto the scene of an element which, once the parenthesis of archaic history is closed, will not reappear in the structure of the *Peloponnesian War*?

I confess to being puzzled, rereading this text albeit neutralized by generations of readers who have found in it nothing but philological problems. And to wondering if, by establishing his text on the border between writing and hearing, Thucydides was not seeking to obscure, beneath the charm of the story, an operation that would consist of finally expelling *erôs* from the present, by assigning it a determining role within the long-elapsed period of tyranny.

This would mean that he accomplished two operations in one. The first consisted of depriving the old murder of any political signification, and the second was intended to make love retreat into the past, in order to return with greater serenity to the history of the war, which had stumbled over the year 415 and the emotional impulse of the *dêmos*. But the distinction between the two operations must be understood as originating only in the linear temporality of the analysis of the text. In its overdetermination, Thucydides' account knew only the one, which became merged with the narrative itself.

Two operations in one, and the single project of extracting the present from the grip of the past. Demythifying the heroicism of the Tyrannoktones ought to free the Athenian polis from any excessive veneration of ancient exploits, while pushing *erôs* back to the time of the Peisistratids expunges, provisionally, signs of political irrationality from the narrative. In any case Thucydides is the inventor of this past *erôs*.

Such are the risks and surprises of the Archaeology. Engagement in an enterprise of rectification; contradiction of the memory of one's contemporaries; revelation of the truth, rescued from ignorance or oblivion, reconstructed and perhaps even simply constructed; the confounding of tradition, caught in the act of misapprehension. And the discovery of *erôs*, which, as in a cosmogony, invades as an explanatory principle the austere prose of historical argumentation.

Reconstructing, counter to the tradition, a stretch of Athenian memory—one of the earliest "historical" memories of the polis; attacking the revered image of the liberators of Athens, the memory of its heroes; in the radicality of his project, the enterprise of Thucydides reminds me of the terms in which Freud presents his construction of an

Egyptian Moses. No doubt this association has led me to insist, some-times more than I should have, on the Athenian destination of the text; but although I may have had to complicate the hypothesis along the way, to admit that the historian was less intent on bringing revelation to the Athenians than on denouncing to the world the culpable negligence of his co-citizens in the matter of history, nevertheless I do not believe that the trail should be rejected. One of the most opaque elements in the thought-world of the *Peloponnesian War* is the way the author has of being Athenian, regardless of his identity as Athenian citizen which the historical genre demands he record by way of signature, giving the book its opening words.[46]

Therefore I find it pertinent that the conjunction of Athens and *erôs* is made in Thucydides, and also that its moment was the past. Athens, the very *locus* of ambivalence for the historian; love, this outlaw from historical discourse; the past, so much smaller than the present (and par-ticularly this period, both somber and highly charged with significance, encompassing the last years of the tyranny—an Athenian version of the period evoked in the outline of methodology "which takes on a mythic charcter by virtue of its antiquity"[47]): there is no doubt that at the meet-ing point between these three suspicious elements a meaningful overde-termination is at work. And it is gratifying that the discovery of *erôs* is linked to the archaeological enterprise which the historian undertakes solely with a view to freeing the thinking of the present from everything that inhibits its freedom of development: the past, in the first place, but also sexual love, and sedition set up as a model.

But already the construction has begun which aims at reconstituting what is at stake in the narrative: in other words, what precedes the nar-rative, or at least the writing of it. Faithful to his practice, not to say his ethic, of closing all access roads leading to the workshop of the historian, Thucydides begins writing the history of Harmodios and Aristogeiton (rediscovered? reinvented? we cannot know) only when any too-visible traces of the the scaffolding of intelligibility have been removed.

There will be those who find it regrettable, accustomed by modernity to frequent a mode of thought which, like that of Freud constructing the murder of an Egyptian Moses, would not omit to take its own opera-tions as object. One might also find it rewarding to respond to the chal-lenge of a work that hides its secrets of fabrication. Thus have I been led by a passage in Thucydides to an inquiry on the construction of history.

CHAPTER 7

Why Greek Mothers
Supposedly Imitate the Earth

A generic phrase is repeated as if it were self-evident by historians and anthropologists of religion—from Bachofen and Dieterich to Jean-Pierre Vernant[1]—concerning Greek representations of maternity: "It is not the earth which imitates women, but, as Plato says, women who imitate the earth." Or even more succinctly: "The Greeks thought that women imitated the earth."

That such a remark, in itself surprising despite its claiming the authority of Plato, should create unanimity is intriguing, and I would contend that the argument from authority is not sufficient by itself to account for such agreement, and that one cannot repeat this affirmation as self-evident truth without anticipating some enormous imaginary benefits.

Perhaps in borrowing a phrase from the *Menexenus* one aims at efficiency, seeing there, condensed into a few words, the totality of what the history of religion articulates between the figure of the Earth Mother and the agricultural metaphors of marriage, in which women are a field to be worked.[2] Fine, but with the reservation—habitually "forgotten"—that Platonic issues of *mimêsis*, with all their intricacies, always raise more questions than they resolve. But considering the difficulties inherent in Platonic *mimêsis*, one must not dismiss as negligible quantities either the textual deep-rootedness or the authorship of a phrase which Hellenists interminably borrow from one another, to the point of forgetting that it is a quotation, and affording it the status of an immemorial Greek truth.

My hypothesis is the reverse: the error common to all the users of this text consists, precisely because they wish to *use* it, in reducing it to

83

a statement, instead of taking the time to read it, in its entirety and within the actual context and development of its arguments.

We must not, however, overestimate the demystifying effect of such a project: returning the phrase of the *Menexenus* to its author and to its text does not mean that one nourishes the illusion, by "restoring" its Platonic integrity, of putting an end to the uses and abuses which have made it a *topos*. And should we really speak, as I have done, of a communal *error* on the part of the scholarly tradition? Nothing is less certain, because it is possible that those who *want* to use this phrase in the service of their own discipleship to the Earth Mother know in a roundabout way what they are doing; they know at least that using this phrase protects them from what they do not wish to say at any price.

Patience, however! To begin with I will pretend to be convinced that one can proceed in a counterdirection to the highly authoritative tradition, and to believe that it is sufficient to really *read* the text in order to gainsay its use in the service of something other than itself.

First it is necessary to put it in context, and in the context of this context. This is the moment in the funeral oration given by Socrates for the requisite elaboration on Athenian autochthony. Here it is stated that the autochthonous citizens of Athens are raised "not, like others, by a stepmother, but by a mother—the territory they inhabit," and that now that they are dead and buried, they rest "in the familial places [translating this phrase (*en oikeiois topois*) I can never help thinking of the *heimliche Orte* of the female body in Freud's "The 'Uncanny' "[3]] which gave them birth, nourished and cared for them." Whence it becomes necessary to address an encomium to this mother, and if the reader has not identified the Platonic funeral oration as a pastiche[4] in which every statement, taken too far and pushed to the limits of its own logic, self-destructs, and has forgotten that in the *Republic* the maternity of the earth has to do with the "noble lie" directed toward citizens,[5] he or she may be impressed by this enthusiasm for Attica, authentic mother of all Athenians. Now we come to the second part of the encomium, which I translate as literally as possible:

> In the distant past when all the earth produced and fostered animals of every kind, wild and domesticated,[6] in this period our own land showed that she was barren and pure of savage wild animals (*sic*), but that from among the animals she chose and engendered for her own use man, who in intelligence surpassed the others, and alone believed in justice and the

gods. Now there is strong evidence in favor of the argument that it was her, our land, who brought forth the ancestors of these dead and our own. This is that everything which gives birth possesses nourishment appropriate to what it gives birth to, by which a woman also reveals whether or not she has really given birth (she is feigning having given birth if she does not possess sources of nourishment for the child). This is exactly what our land also, who is at the same time our mother, furnishes as sufficient proof of her having engendered men: for first and alone at that time she bore the fruit of wheat and barley for human food, by which the human race is best and most beautifully nourished, because she really did produce this animal herself. Now such evidence should more readily be accepted on behalf of the earth than of women: it is not the earth which imitated women in conception and generation, but women the earth.

(Menexenus 237d3–238a5)

Read it again, and it resembles—intentionally, but in the end perhaps geniunely[7]—a syllogism whose conclusion ("our land created man") is present from the beginning.

In the first place we have one of those poor divisions that are mocked by Plato in the *Statesman*:[8] Athens and everybody else, or more precisely "the whole earth" as opposed to "our land." The former was productive rather in the way that a field produces vegetables, although the products were animals, wild and domesticated; the latter, already engaged in reproduction (who needs women after this?), engendered man. Were there no human beings outside Attica? So we must suppose for the time of origin. Subverting the autochthonous discourse which knows only males (*andres*), sons of the land of Attica and practically citizens already, Plato substitutes a myth of the origin of humankind, albeit one rooted in the soil of Athens.

Now there must be proof, proof that "our land gave birth (*eteken*)." This is already taken care of with the verb *tiktô*, for those who know how to read it. Since *tiktô* designates above all human reproduction—compare the objection of the rationalist Xouthos to autochthonous belief in the *Ion: ou pedon tiktei tekna*, "it is not the soil that gives birth to children"[9]—one should understand that the meaning of this text on the maternity of the earth contradicts the lesson that has just been laboriously relayed:[10] beneath the dogma of parthenogenesis, the text refers to sexual reproduction.

Is it surprising that the heralded proof introduces the female, who alone permits the argument to be sustained? No doubt precautions were taken to conceal the point: the neuter substantive *pan to tekon* ("everything which gives birth") aims at generalizing, and above all desexualizing, birth, in a text where feminines are overabundant. The word *gunê* appears to be introduced only as a supplementary example ("a woman *also*"). Even more remarkable is the identification of that nourishment which the female produces as irrefutable proof[11] that she has really given birth; is this not—deliberately perhaps—to court masculine absolutism which in the *Eumenides* leads Apollo to refuse the mother the name of *tokeus* on the grounds that she is only nursing the seed within her which the father has planted?[12] In fact, far removed from all those Greek dreams of purely paternal heredity, this passage in the *Menexenus* makes no allusion to a father, not even as a mere "sower." It is true that in autochthonous myths the sower is not necessarily a father: the Theban Spartoi were never the sons of Kadmos the Sower, and the Athenians were barely the sons of Hephaistos whose desire fertilized the soil; but just as traditional is the discourse which opposes the woman-furrow, domesticated and civilized by the agriculture of marriage, and the solitary births of the all-fertile Earth.[13] From this angle, well represented by the declarations of the Aeschylean Apollo, the sower is on the contrary the active principle and name-giver,[14] confronting an inert field that receives the seed "as a stranger (f.) a stranger (m.)." In the insistent silence which the *Menexenus* observes on the subject of any (male) engenderer, should we see the sign of a revalorization of the role of the mother? This would certainly not be the sole indicator of such an operation in Plato.[15] But it must be acknowledged that the very absence of any "agricultural" vocabulary in the phrase concerning the female deprives of all legitimacy the use to which historians of religion put the *Menexenus*.

The First Man, or How to Do without Women

Under the auspices of *trophê* (nourishment), the argument, whose articulations are as parodically underlined as ever, passes from the female to the earth as though nothing had happened: "our land also, who is at the same time our mother, furnishes . . . sufficient proof . . . " It is the Eleusinian ear of barley, nourishment appropriate to humankind, which now bears witness to the land of Attica having *really* given birth to man. And what is more, before any appearance of humankind elsewhere on earth. The soil of Athens as *prôtos heuretês* (first inventor) of man? More even: absolute *arkhê* of humankind. *Exit* woman: she is decidedly no more than supplementary, and at no time does she receive the name *mêtêr*, which is reserved for the earth and forms an expression with *gê*. In such a well-supported demonstration, what reader (if suspicion has not already prompted him or her to be wary) would dare remark that, like *gunê, gê* was introduced by *kai* ("the land also . . . "), and wonder which of the two, the earth or woman, in the end dominates the other? But already the text labors to obscure the questions it has raised, and the educational lesson takes over: the earth "first and alone" . . .

The die is cast; from the anteriority of *gê te kai mêtêr*, we may conclude from now on that the earth is exemplary. And relegated to second rank, woman is reduced to the resources of imitation. It is still possible that some suspicion remains as to the demonstrability of the line of argument; we need only be aware that, as if to have woman more easily forgotten once divested of her pretensions to the title of mother, it was necessary to distance her definitively with a statement that nothing in the passage really supports: "such evidence should more readily be accepted on behalf of the earth than of women." Why? Doubtless by pure authoritative argument, since no other explanation is given. And the argument hastens to its conclusion: "it is not the earth which imitated women, . . . but women the earth."

To recapitulate: glorification of the Athenian Earth Mother is obligatory in a funeral oration, and Plato conspicuously complies with the rules of the genre, while in the rest of the Platonic corpus the Earth Mother enjoys only the purely instrumental status of a useful lie or a seductive *muthos*.[16] I would therefore maintain that in giving imitation the last word, Plato provides for those who would read it a sure indication that this is indeed the real, philosophical lesson of the passage in the *Menexenus*, in which woman is dispossessed of any primordial link to maternity—autochthony *oblige!*[17]—only after having supported an essential point in the argument. The drastic simplifications inflicted on this dual-meaning text become all the more obvious when one extracts from it the sentence on *mimêsis* in order to come to the rescue of the archetypal maternity of the earth.

It should also be noted that, because of its approximate character, the way the expression is quoted typically denatures the letter of the text. Repeating "women imitate the earth," one commits a twofold sin through inattention to the text: by truncating the quotation one avoids having to take account of the first part of the phrase, where the negative cast strongly resembles a denial;[18] and by resorting to the present tense, one thinks one is imposing the atemporal and repetitive law of imitation. But the verb *memimêtai* is not present-tense; it is a perfect, which, as often in Plato, expresses an event whose consequences endure, yet is still a *past* event.[19] This event is undoubtedly *arkhê*, origin itself, which along with the maternity of the soil of Attica has set the record for good: the anteriority of the earth once established, woman would always occupy the position of imitator. But we know that in the context of imitation, it is usually rivalry that Plato is suggesting. And thus simply transported back to its origins, the rivalry between woman and the earth for the title of all-powerful genetrix arises once again.

It remains to understand how and why the tradition came to be founded on such an inattention to the text, not to speak of deliberate avoidance or rejection. Reconstructing the "how" would presuppose a long and patient investigation of the totality of the classical tradition, which I will not here attempt.[20] It is the "why" of this affair that interests me here. Or, in other terms, the question of advantages: what might be the advantages to the Greek tradition mocked by Plato, of the statement that the earliest confinements were those of the Earth? And what advantages do the history and anthropology of Greek religion reap even now from the incantational repetition of a formula that vouchsafes woman to imitation?

As for the advantages to Greek thought, I have returned to the question several times. And in default of "answers," I have gradually formed varied and sometimes contradictory hypotheses, all sharing something necessarily Greek.

The first, and simplest, has to do with what one gains by materializing woman. Just as the earth woman is a creature paralyzed, inert, and passive according to Semonides of Amorgos,[21] so is it probable that by reducing woman to the imitation of the earth, one assigns her a completely material existence, which predisposes her toward playing the role of pure receptacle and yielding action and soul to the male without a fight. "Material maternity"[22] on the one hand, fertile and productive force of the spiritual principle on the other: from the Apollo of Aeschylus to the speculations of Bachofen—to name only one—what a satisfying bipartition! Simple, but of a simplicity which did not satisfy the Greeks alone. . . .

The second hypothesis, very Greek, has to do with the operation of conceptualizing origin without women; that is before woman, this supplement, appeared. In Hesiod men must first separate from the gods before they may receive the "beautiful evil"; those who believed themselves to be the human race (anthrôpoi)[23] painfully discovered their status as sexual beings (andres). Before, there was a Golden Age; with or without gods, but belonging to themselves, the same with the same; after, the bitter taste of a male existence and the necessary subjection to marriage. Moreover in this type of discourse it is necessary to pinpoint when indeterminacy begins, in order to postulate from the beginning—a beginning expandable at will—not only the earth in its solitary self-sufficiency as in the Menexenus, but males also; just what Plato rejects. But some Greeks will reconcile the Hesiodic model with Platonic discourse: when Plutarch adopts the expression from the Menexenus,[24] he includes it in an argument on the archaeology of generation in which woman is declared second, and with her her womb; in fact the arkhê happened without her, because no living being can be engendered ex nihilo, and the male may quite naturally step into this role. Only a progenitor is necessary; the earth will do the rest:

> It is probable that the first birth took place through the force and self-sufficiency of the engenderer, *directly and without intermediary from the earth*, and that it did not require the organs, envelopes, and vessels now produced by nature as expedients in creatures which give birth, to compensate for their weakness.

Given that Plato, taking representations of autochthony a step further, prefers to endow the earth in the beginning with pregnancy and generation (kuêsis kai gennêsis), while in Plutarch nothing could take place without the earth being fertilized by the masculine principle of the engenderer (toû gennôntos), the gulf between the two discourses is not negligible. But in terms of female maternity, the result is very much the same: in both cases, and whether it is for the sake of assigning them to a primordial earth or an earth already passive and fertilized by a sower, what mothers must be deprived of if they are to be separated from origin is pregnancy and reproduction, which Greek men nevertheless considered both natural and also the most civic-minded of female duties. Might there be doubts concerning the natural character of such a "nature"? This is suggested in the Plutarch text, which assigns *phusis* the manufacturing of the womb in the name of *mêkhanê*: in the name of expedience.

One more step and I arrive at my third hypothesis, in the form of a question, and one more unanswerable than ever. Is woman natural? No easy task, ultimately, to decide whether the anxiety of Greek men vis-à-vis women is based on what is natural in their "nature," or on its purely artificial character. Nevertheless I suggest that it is the constant overfantasizing of the artificial dimension of women that necessitates the sudden, emergency restoration of a maternal nature to mothers. No tragedy so stridently proclaims the attachment of "the race of women" to their progeny than that of the eponymous Medea, sorceress and murderer of her sons. For the better appropriation of maternity, making a fiction out of women is an imaginative solution highly prized by *andres*. Then out of fear that they might really be fictive, one hastens to imagine them as completely maternal, but the insistence with which the myth credits the best mother with guilty impulses[25] is reminiscent of the first construction: woman as "machine."

Mothers Have No Names

Considered from the starting point of this endlessly renewed alternation between the natural and the artificial, the earth appears to be a kind of haven for the imagination: less equivocal than mothers, therefore more reliable. She bore and nourishes what she produced. Perhaps in the course of reading one becomes aware that the *Menexenus* distinguishes between two female figures, of which only the first truly deserves the name of mother, if the latter is not reserved for the earth: she who has really given birth, and she who has in some fashion procured herself a child (the verb *hupoballomai* suggests substitution or deceit) and raises it as her own, without being able to give it nourishment. Doubtless, in the reasoning behind this rationale, such an opposition is aimed only at nudging the earth in the right direction before finally giving it the advantage over woman. But it is probable that this distinction also spoke directly to the Greek reader, whose fears and certainties it renewed. One has only to think of Aristophanic comedy, in which women are by definition suspected of concealing or making false claims about their children, to be convinced that we have here an obsession, whose power of amusement derives from one's identifying it within oneself. The poet occasionally complicates the question by imagining himself in the situation of the single mother whose child is raised by another woman; his first comedy was a child which, as a virgin, he could not give birth to, and which, exposed and "supposed" by another woman, was nourished and raised by Athenian spectators.[26] But the feminine metaphor only emphasizes all the more how among men (the poet, his stand-in, the citizens) everything always ends well. It is altogether different among men and women, where the controlling factor is the *idée fixe* that the "mother" of a child might in fact not be, in which case the name of the father becomes a mockery, thus dissociated from its blood.[27] *Mater semper incerta?* A Greek way of absolving the father from all inquiry, by casting suspicion on the mother.[28]

Such a configuration obviously has no provision for the—inadmissible, unthinkable—case of the mother who cannot feed her child. True? False? Before such a choice, the "syllogism of maternity" founders irretrievably. At the same time it is possible that such a figure is envisaged at some level in the *Menexenus*. Let us introduce one more sentence into the passage in question, which the very logic of the text necessitated: between the discussion of imitation and the *meta de touto* ("after all this") which ushers in a new theme, the soil of Athens is praised for not having been "avaricious of its own fruit," for having even "benefited others."[29] Certainly this sentence could be interpreted as an allusion to the ear of wheat celebrated in the Eleusinian Mysteries; but following on the question of *mimêsis*, such a declaration suggests that the same cannot be said concerning women. If this "fruit," food proper to humans, is indeed wheat, it follows that praising the generosity of *gê* amounts to inversely suspecting mothers of avarice: could they grudge their own children the very milk which they should produce for them? Unless one is to understand that the real fruit of Athenian soil is man, in which case the text goes so far as to suggest a tendency among women to withhold maternity. The accusation takes shape.

A hard lot, that of the Greek male, forced to depend for the perpetuation of his name on a mere copy, a fake. Thus Euripides' Hippolytus speaks of "counterfeit" and reproaches Zeus for having set "the race of women" among men like a contingent of colonists.[30] Everything is falsified in and through women, beginning with the credibility that lingers about the name, the sweet name, of mother.

Whence the nostalgia for the righteous *Gê Mêtêr*, a very common nostalgia: it isn't only the Greeks and Bachofen who insistently repeat the old adage by virtue of which "the earth produces its fruits, which is why you must call Gaia *Mother*."[31] I would not swear that those historians of Greek religion who try to originate everything in the Earth Mother are not still pursuing the same phantom. The Earth is the One, sole incontestable mother, while the feminine, caught up in a process of imitation, is always multiple. To speak of human *genetrices* one says: mothers.

What critical reading of the passage in the *Menexenus* will ever succeed in ridding us of the habit of repeating that "in pregnancy and generation, it is not the earth that imitates women, but women the earth"? I doubt that any could succeed, so great is the extent to which this phrase, beyond its specifically Greek applications, may still evoke echoes within us. Echoes such as the negation that gives it its structure for a start (it is *not* the earth . . .),: if it is true that the example Freud gives of negation ("My mother, it is*n't* her"[32]) has led us, though repetition, to associate negativized utterance ever more closely with the question of motherhood.

There are other reasons which suggest that Hellenists will continue to be attached to this phrase for some time to come. Reasons which originate just as well from the *Menexenus* (after all, is this text sufficiently fortified against the first-degree interpretation which it has repeatedly spawned?[33]) as from the structure of the problem "of imitation," or from the obscurities inherent in the figure of the mother.

I will give some of these reasons,[34] for the sake of ensuring the greatest possible range to the debate.

Blame should no doubt be ascribed in the first instance to the obscure desire of the author, whose writing, with its deceptive encoding, permits a ceaseless quarrel of interpretations, primary against secondary. I am aware that at first, and perhaps at second reading it is not easy to find one's bearings, either in the Greek sonority of the phrase, where only *memimêtai* manages to escape the galactic assonances[35] (*ou gar gê gunaika memimêtai kuêsei kai gennêsei alla gunê gên*), or in the construction of the argument, where, in the absence of any masculine element, the feminines *earth, woman,* and *mother* tend to interrelate at the very moment when they are supposed to render themselves distinct.

In terms of imitation, the terrain is hardly less encumbered, and without embarking once again on the question of *mimêsis*,[36] one runs the risk of being caught in the glutinous configuration of the debate on art and nature (which of the two imitates the other?), a way of broaching once more that of the natural and the artificial in woman. Sometimes this type of debate leads to categorical decisiveness, to the affirmation, for example, that "[the imagination] will weary of conceiving rather than that nature will weary of supplying,"[37] and in fact the *Menexenus* loudly proclaims that the affair has been decided from the start. But sliding *mimêsis* into a negative statement ("it isn't *the earth* which *imitates*"), amounts to, aided by the propositional order, putting the earth in the position of first subject of the mimetic activity, and even if woman is quickly substituted for the earth in the subject role, for every somewhat demanding reader the evil is done: female imitation is but secondary and derivative compared to original Imitation, briefly reinforced by negation, and with which only the earth is secretly credited.

At the same time, inattention to the letter of the text probably arises from the most powerful of necessities. Why do specialists in Greek religion register only the official, instructional version? Because in all situations it is for the human to imitate the divine, and mortals can only copy the labors of the earth, or rather of the Earth, since the history of religions has permanently endowed *gê* with a capital letter, unlike Plato, who never gave one to Athenian soil. A reassuring trope of "scientific" thought, analogy functions in the right direction.

But there is more than one *because*. If women must imitate the earth, it is *because* the opposite would be dangerous, and must be proscribed. What could a woman be who forces the earth to imitate her, other than a witch?[38] (We know, even if the Greeks didn't, that witches are destined for the stake.) Most important, because mothers have no Name, maternity evades reflection, so that motherhood must be established elsewhere, outside itself, as if something must be made of this fleeting evidence. Established in the solid and the immutable, of which Hesiodic

Gaia, "Broad-chested earth, solid foundation of all forever,"[39] is the very paradigm; or in a *phusis*, regardless if, in the end, the price to be paid for this nature is that its contents be *mimêsis*, as long as the all-too-fragile title of mother be assured of being established by repetition, every time a woman gives birth.

CHAPTER 8

From Plato to Bachofen
and Beyond

According to historians of Greek religion, the case is closed: the Greeks considered the maternity of women to derive from the original maternity of the Earth, because they thought "woman imitates the earth."

Even if this statement must be accorded a privileged position in the constructions of historians of religion, the Earth Mother is still originally a Greek idea, and the *Greek* configuration of this question must be examined. Over and above the assembling of convergent facts of thought and cult, this implies an attempt to distinguish the discourses, sometimes dissonant, attached to this subject,[1] in order to determine the conditions and applications of such a figure. Naturally I do not intend to mount such a program, and I will limit my examination to the analysis of arguments that repeatedly surface, in both ancient and modern sources, from the use, explicit or no, that is made of the passage in the *Menexenus* when it is said that "woman imitates the earth."

Among modern historians of Greece, such a declaration generally heralds or concludes considerations on Greek marriage as metaphorical plowing and the very real festival of the Thesmophoria, attested in almost all poleis as a fertility rite. Two typical lines of thought, therefore, whose substance will be briefly recapitulated.

Woman, a Field to Be Plowed

In support of the statement that in marriage woman is a field to be plowed by man, three proofs are generally offered, always the same and always interrelated: the institutional betrothal formula as reconstituted in a comedy of Menander, certain literary formulations, characterized as "metaphorical," of this reciprocal identity between marriage and plowing, and a text of Plutarch stating that the most sacred kind of labor (plowing) in Athens is conjugal labor (plowing). Whence it is concluded that, in her procreative function, "Woman [. . .] is now identified [. . .] with a field."[2]

At the center of this collection is the word *arotos*, glossed in Chantraine's *Dictionnaire étymologique* as "plowing, plowing-season; wheat-field, harvest; figuratively, procreation of children, children." But when the father of the betrothed solemnly declares to his future son-in-law that he gives him his daughter as an *arotos* for legitimate children, is "figuratively" really the correct term? Literary instances of such a figure, all belonging, as we shall see, to poetic language, prompt me rather to recall the particular *topos* of the "metaphor without metaphor."[3] For every passage such as that in *Oedipus Rex* which compares in parallel formation *aroton gês* and *gunaikôn paidas*, harvests of the earth and children of women, how many more abrupt formulations are there, such as that in the *Cratylus* where it is suggested that the name of the virgin Artemis comes from her hatred for the *plowing* of men *in* women?[4] There is also the use of the word *aroura*, both in Plato and in tragedy, as the most appropriate term for designating woman or womb as "female field"— womb and woman amounting to the same thing, by virtue of a recurrent metonymy.[5] Between woman as field and the sexual act as agricultural activity,[6] there appears to be perfect coherence, and many more such instances can be provided.

At this point it is perfectly natural, they say, for historians and anthropologists of Greek religion to evoke the Thesmophoria, whose ritual program has no other aim than the reinforcing of the analogy between the fertile field and the female body.[7] To this end certain dissonant characteristics, automatically displayed by a ritual ensemble so complex[8] that the meaning of the festival is fully apprehensible in its indissociably agrarian and sexual dimension, are wiped out. Three basic elements then are retained: the rapport between this autumn ceremony and its sowings, whose rites, celebrated by women, are supposed to ensure fertility; the overt tension between the chaste seclusion of wives and the crude sexuality of the symbols they manipulate and the dialogue they exchange; and finally, from the "primitivism" of a festival in which women "imitate the old way of life,"[9] the easy deduction of its immemorial origin—neolithic at least. And all this for the greater glory of civic marriage, since only the legitimate wives of citizens celebrate the festival.

All clear, then? All too clear, actually. Modeling my version on standard lines of thought, I have carefully, imitatively, purged it of all shadowy areas.

Thus in considering terms originating from the same root as *arotos*, it is important to emphasize that the total coherence of the metaphorical field is more postulated by modern scholars than effectively verified. To write that "marriage is a plowing (*arotos*) in which woman is the furrow (*aroura*), man is the laborer (*arotêr*)"[10] certainly creates unarguable coherence, but poetic language never uses the metaphor in all its registers, and the tragedians tend to designate the male more often as "sower" than as "plowman."[11] Without lingering over the theme of the sower, one must conclude that it is the association of woman and field, and that alone, which is the determining factor. Examined close up, things are most complicated concerning the Thesmophoria. If one ignores the preexisting categories within the ritual complex, it proves impossible to reduce everything to agricultural symbolism—as also to dismiss it completely.[12] Other questions then arise: if Demeter cannot simply be reduced to the Earth Mother,[13] and if the Thesmophoria resembles a "matrilineal"[14] festival under the auspices of an inseparable Demeter and Kore, why this insistence on the civic legitimacy of *wives* when men are out of the picture, or at least as problematic as Bachofen's "sower," who, according to the logic of the *jus soli*, disappears in the furrow which he has fertilized?[15] As if the political dimension of the festival, on which all interpreters agree, confirms civic marriages in their validity only at the price of a temporary dissolution of family and the conjugal tie. We are far from the tranquil certitudes of conjugal "plowing" and the unequivocal identification of woman with the earth.

It remains to examine more thoroughly the nature of this close, even intimate relationship which is so often hypothesized between woman and the earth. Metaphor? Analogy? Assimilation? As if these three rhetorical figures melt into one another, those who study this relationship seem often to use them interchangeably. The reader who is in search of rigorous distinctions has the greatest difficulty in discerning the rules of coherent differentiation between assimilation, metaphor, and analogy.[16] So that even in Bachofen, who formulated the question, going

as far as deriving identification/indifferentiation of woman and the earth
by denying that agricultural figures are simply "ways of speaking,"[17] the
signifier seems to me irreversibly unstable. Hence the same page of *Das
Mutterrecht* reveals an irreducible oscillation between equivalence and
comparison, and woman, from one sentence to the next, is said to *represent* the earth and *to be* terrestrial matter itself.[18]

Amid all these formulations how can one decide, given that the relationship between woman and the earth seems to have less to do with
an operation of thought isolable in the singularity of its process than with
these basic affinities, immutable and also termed archetypal because articulation between the terms cannot be precisely determined? It is here
that the *Menexenus*, with its sentence about imitation, offers a comfort-
able alternate solution, and there is unanimous agreement to avoid difficult questions (which, as Bachofen clearly saw, are much more than a
simple matter of terminology) by declaring with one voice that woman
imitates the earth.[19] Even though, as is generally forgotten, the Platonic
question of *mimêsis*—rarely simple—raises more difficult questions than
it resolves.

But in order to deal with inherent difficulties of Platonic *mimêsis*, it is
important to take into account the context and the author of a phrase
which Hellenists borrow from one another interminably, to the point of
forgetting that it is a quotation. It would no doubt be instructive, and a
bit overwhelming, to systematically set out both the spectrum of degrees
of omission and the list of interpretations which are based on this phrase.
Having little taste for collecting curiosities, I will limit myself here to the
mention of a few exemplary or particularly striking constructions.

There are those who do attribute the phrase to Plato, while giving it
content that the passage in the *Menexenus* seems at pains to avoid:
"woman, to cite the formula of Plato, 'imitates' the earth by receiving
within her the seed which the male has made to penetrate";[20] but the
male is singularly absent from the Platonic version. There are also those
who think that they have found in the *Menexenus* the idea that the earth
is the first woman.[21] And those who distort the quotation for the sake of
a highly personalized meaning, as when Jane Harrison uses it to accompany a chapter of her *Prolegomena to the Study of Greek Religion* devoted
to the "Making of a Goddess," as well as those who, quoting at second-
hand, attribute to Plato remarks he would have great difficulty recog-

nizing as his own.[22] And all those in great numbers who attribute the Platonic paternity of the formula to chance: Ludwig Preller, for whom the philosopher is expressing himself "en passant," Albrecht Dieterich, who sees it as the simple enunciation of a popular belief, and finally André Motte, to whom it falls to set down what his predecessors merely left understood: an immemorial truth whose form alone, almost accidently, is Platonic:[23]

> For the rest, the remarkable formula of the *Menexenus may be disengaged from the limiting context* of the argument it serves. It is *inherited from a distant past,* and is an adequate *translation* of *the Earth-Woman identity* which arose spontaneously, at all levels of ancient consciousness, like *a truth which goes without saying* and requires no justification. (Emphasis added)

What I maintain here is the exact opposite: the cardinal error, common to all the users of this text, because they desire only to *use* it, consists in reducing it to a single sentence, instead of reading it in its ensemble and according to the development of its argument.

History of an Omission

Before I embark on a history of the utilization of the *Menexenus,* I will hazard a hypothesis, proposing to identify in Bachofen's *Mutterrecht* one of the essential stages of "omission."

To my knowledge the first citation of the phrase from the *Menexenus* in *Mutterrecht* arises quite indirectly: in Latin, and at second-hand since Bachofen quotes the celebrated Renaissance jurist Cujacius, who refers to Plato. This takes place in a passage devoted to the link between marriage and agriculture—here we are again—both of which are referred to a right belonging to the mother that Bachofen deduces from formulas with which Roman jurists characterized the *jus naturale,* as opposed to the *jus civile,* the right of the city that belongs to the father. In order to establish this "*jus naturale* of material creation in which woman is the *solum* and the father is comparable to the sower [. . .] Roman jurists connect the *fructus praedii* and the *partus ancillae* [. . .]. *Mater enim est similis solo,* remarks Cujacius on this point, *non solum simile matri, ut Plato in Epitaphio.*"[24] Plato, captured in Latin translation. If Bachofen did not possess the immense erudition his work demonstrates, one might think that he knew the *Menexenus* phrase solely from Cujacius' citation.

The second citation, occurring in the chapter on Athens, is used to support the affirmation of the superiority of the spiritual principle incarnated by Zeus over maternal right and chthonic religion, which go hand in hand. Here we learn that for woman, who is "the earth itself" and the "material principle," as for the earth, the words of Apollo reducing the mother to the status of nurse are in force: "In the *Menexenus,* Plato, and also Plutarch after him, literally say the following: 'It is not the earth which imitates woman, but woman who imitates the earth, and so for all animals of the female sex [. . .].' "[25]

I halt the quotation here, because the text of Plutarch has already impinged on that of the *Menexenus,* and in fact Bachofen, who proceeds with innumerable references to Plutarch, has cited Plato only through an excerpt from the *Table-Talk,* which intersects with the *Menexenus* precisely where we have chosen to see the conclusion of the theme of earth and woman: "Because it is not, says Plato, the earth that imitates woman, but woman who imitates (*mimeitai*) the earth."[26]

Is it to Plutarch then that the tradition owes the present conjugation of imitation? It might well have originated with Cujacius, supposing there are no other intermediaries. But as far as the modern tradition of historians and anthropologists of religion is concerned, it is perfectly possible that it is to *Plutarch as cited by Bachofen.* Bachofen insists on the timeless present of the law of imitation, while the treatment in the *Table-Talk,* before arriving at Plato, has dealt at length with the question of the origin of generation (*arkhê tês geneseos*), still designated as "first generation" (*prôtê genesis*), which will eventually be revealed in highly canonical fashion to have taken place "thanks to the power of the engenderer, directly and without intermediary on the part of the earth." A tradition, then, more rooted in Bachofen than in Plutarch, not to speak of Plato.

But that is not all. If I am right to consider Bachofen as a source—one source, naturally—of the phrase in question, a series of omissions follows: that of the name of Bachofen itself (it is as if his work, too, quickly appropriated by opposing but overtly political currents of thought, is not a reputable source, and therefore Bachofen is not cited[27]); then the name of Plutarch, whom Bachofen's remarks turn into a pure continuation of Plato. And it is not certain that, from one end of the chain of borrowings to the other, the users of the phrase are all aware that they are really citing Bachofen citing Plutarch, and not Plato. If we add the "omission," already mentioned, of reading the *Menexenus*, the series is complete.

But we haven't finished with Bachofen. The phrase, still present tense, makes at least a third appearance in *Mutterrecht*, on the subject of agriculture and marriage in the chapter on Egypt: "Agriculture is the prototype of the conjugal union of man and woman. It isn't the earth which imitates woman, but woman who imitates the earth."[28] And Bachofen continues, without the merest reference to Plato. The silence cannot be attributed to a lack of acquaintance with the *Menexenus*, cited many times in different contexts in *Das Mutterrecht*.[29] There is a fundamental reason for this: for Bachofen, as for many of his successors, the phrase has become the anonymous expression of a truth indistinguishable from origin itself. Doubly "original," because it has to do with the *arkhê* of which it comes.

Here I interrupt what can only be an exemplary fragment of the history of a citation. I have, moreover, no project in mind other than proposing these reflections on *how* for consideration. How a tradition is built up, with everybody repeating everybody else and generally forgetting that repetition has occurred, and therefore not being concerned with finding out how the automatism has come about. But also how one uses and abuses texts, and the danger that lurks in careless extraction from a work as elaborate as Plato's, of a "truth" which one thinks one can remove from Platonic jurisdiction.

I leave it to readers to reflect on the benefit—incomparable, to judge from the dossier I have just half-opened—that must arise from depriving of reference a phrase now petrified in original truth, in order to affirm that it is truly the woman who imitates the earth, and not the contrary.

CHAPTER 9

Ancient Motifs, Modern Constructions: Earth, Woman

Some lines from Bachofen's *Das Mutterrecht*:

The underlying principle of agriculture is that of a regulated union of the sexes. Mother-right belongs to both. Just as the corn in a plowed field emerges into the light of day, sprouting from the furrow opened by the plow, so does the child spring from the maternal *sporium*, the Sabine word for the female sown field, the *kêpos* [garden], whence *spurii*, the Sown, from *speirô* [sow]. So Plutarch tells us. We also owe to him the idea that the underlying principle of love is to be found in the wound; this is why Love carries arrows. It is the plow that wounds the earth, it is the *aratrum* of man which wounds the maternal breast of woman [. . .].[1]

Pathos indeed, on hand to associate the union of the sexes with the practices of agriculture, if that is really the end of story; the reiteration of the words "wound" and "wounding" suggests that things might be more complicated. Modern *pathos*, perhaps, despite the reference to Plutarch—or because of it—since in his scholarly rapport with Greco-Roman antiquity, Plutarch is already sufficiently at a remove to have to proceed by reconstruction, if not simply by construction. Nevertheless the substance of Bachofen's treatment is authentically ancient, and reading the paragraph mobilizes in the memory of the Hellenist the rubric "agricultural representations of marriage."

What the Koran expresses directly ("Your women are a [field of] labor for you. Go to your [field of] labor as you like, and work for yourselves in good time!"[2]), the Greek formula for marriage says likewise in all simplicity, when the father announces to the bridegroom: "I give you my daughter for the harvesting of legitimate children (*gnêsiôn paidôn ep' arotôi*)." Harvesting? Taking *arotos* as close as possible to its literal meaning produces "plowing productive of legitimate children."[3] References abound: tragic and philosophical texts in which *aroura* (field) is the female "field" and *arotos* is inextricably plowing and harvest, without having to pass, as in a Greek etymological dictionary, through "fertilization" as a "figurative meaning" of the word. In the etymologizing speculations of the *Cratylus*, the virgin Artemis expresses through her name the "hatred she feels toward the plowing (*aroton misêsasês*) of man in woman."[4] Different literary expressions of a thought which according to historians of religion is also expressed (is first expressed[5]) through ritual, during the celebration of the Thesmophoria, the festival of Demeter the Law-giver reserved for married women, wives of citizens in fact, who alone are qualified to honor the goddess of grain.

Literary "metaphors" verified through religious ritual: who would not be satisfied with the total picture obtained through such conjunction? Who would not henceforward state as self-evident truth that "woman *is identified* [. . .], in her procreative function, as a field"?[6] Once stacked up in mutual support, texts and rites are conceived of as illustrating a founding principle, or at least a universally Greek principle, which Plato would have expressed as "woman imitates the earth." And specialists fall over each other quoting a line from Plato in permanent isolation from its context, which allows one to ignore the philosophical traps concealed in a passage where hidden meaning contradicts explicit message.[7]

It will be clear that I incline toward the opinion that such an operation is problematic, in that it brings together the heterogeneous as it would the scattered pieces of a jigsaw puzzle. At the least, the mere assumption that one can diminish the difficulty through baptizing texts and rites as "representations," entails the assumption that one has reconstituted the Greek view of marriage. If one agrees to condone categories which are somewhat vague without too much anxiety, one can be content, as I can be and have been. But there is one step that cannot be taken: that which amounts to forcibly repatriating the dissimilar into the maternal bosom of the same; this is what occurs when one gives the Hesiodic names of Pandora and Gaia to woman and the earth, and when, battening down one on top of the other, one treats Hesiod as official spokesperson of this fiction, which then becomes hardened into ideology.

Pandora, Made of Earth

The Hesiodic version of the creation of woman is twice treated by the poet; a myth, or rather a portion of a myth, concluding and crowning the story of Prometheus, with a few significant deviations from each other. It is obviously not uninteresting that the first woman, anonymous in the *Theogony*, is given a name in the *Works and Days*. But in both cases the woman as a product of craftsmanship is an artifact, if not an artifice, modeled by Hephaistos on the order of Zeus: "a fashioned maiden."[8] The text says that earth is the necessary material for this sculpting or pottery-making, and that it must be moistened with water: but it says no more, and there is no reason to do violence to the silences of the text in order to uncover at all costs the Earth beneath the earth.[9] Such is the gesture which, as if to reconstitute the analogy of woman and the earth, the great majority of Hesiod's readers find necessary.[10]

Since the earth creature in the *Theogony* introduces marriage and the differentiation of the sexes into the world of men, is there any need to assign to the text conclusions which it does not draw, crediting Hesiod with the idea that from now on man must labor woman as one labors a field?[11] Because in the *Works and Days* woman receives the name Pandora, is it legitimate to neglect the etymology of this name internal to the narrative in order to state that, given that "Pandora" is one of the names of the Earth Mother, the bride who is so named is both woman and earth?[12] I do not believe so. Rather than being at pains to systematically reestablish a unity which one imagines lost, but which may have never existed, it would be better to take note of the differences—some are abysmal, and I would hazard that most of them are—and make use of them as such, as strategic emplacements or observation points for the analysis of a tradition in all its complexity. In other words, I would like to appropriate the terms used by Freud to distance himself from the unifying tendency of Lou Andreas-Salomé: "The unity of this world seems to me to go without saying, or deserve no more than mention. What interests me is the separation and classification (*Scheidung und Gliederung*) of what otherwise would be lost in a featureless mass."[13]

Certainly in the struggle with the force of original desire (which is also the desire for unity), nothing is bound to hold good to the end and under all circumstances. Did Freud himself always achieve this? It merits investigation, but that is another story which would lead us too far astray. Let us return to our earth woman. Because our era has once again learned to listen to polyphonic music, it sees itself as attentive to the diversity of voices, and I support a call to reading practices that are respectful of "separation": beside Pandora the universal giver, I would also argue for the maintainance of the singularity of the Hesiodic figure who receives from all and gives nothing, coherent with its completely exteriorized existence which hardly predisposes it toward fertility.[14]

This by no means implies that one must avoid any *rapprochement* between the account in Hesiod and occurrences of the divine epithet. As long as one does not forget the lessons of dissimilarity; in which case there will be no reduction of the poem to representations which undeniably constitute its context, but which it has obviously rejected or denied in order to define its own trajectory. Otherwise, if resistance to multiplicity is really too strong, it will indeed be necessary to yield to the desire to unify and to construct systems without hiatus, unassailable but immobile. One must choose.

One must choose: privilege the dissonances and follow, with every myth, the narrative framework which creates its specificity, or choose unity and construct a discourse which is logical and of great power. Here every effort is made—and has already been made, through highways and byways—to opt for the former, which considers the agricultural fiction of marriage, whatever its reality in institutional discourse, as completely inadequate for rendering a full account of the myths of Hesiod. But the latter, which postulates the identity of woman and the earth, lacks neither ambition nor legitimate intuitions, and has long since earned its place. Let me merely suggest that, in the unfailing perfection of its all-encompassing elaborations, it is productive of quasi-myths, which ideally deserve to be studied for themselves; their organization—let us avoid the word "structure," too easily discredited by the prevailing winds—affords a pure intellectual pleasure equal to that of the narratives themselves.

It is here, where construction becomes delirious with reason, that we return to Bachofen, and his establishment of agriculture as the very starting-ground for the principle of maternity.

Gaia and "Gaia," or the Conjugal Agriculture of les modernes

We begin with a highly constructed argument in the Egyptian chapter of *Das Mutterrecht*:

> We have demonstrated then the link between justice and material motherhood for two stages of life: the lower or Aphroditean-hetairic stage, and the higher or cereal-marriage stage. The first corresponds to unregulated swamp-procreation, the second to ordered agriculture. During these two cultural stages it is the life of nature which is model and measure of the human condition. Nature has reared Justice. Agriculture is the prototype of the conjugal union of man and woman. It is not the earth which imitates woman, but woman who imitates the earth. Marriage was seen by the ancients as an agrarian relationship, and borrowed its entire judicial terminology from the circumstances of agriculture. Note the expression *ep' arotôi paidôn*, as well as *aroun, speirein, geôrgein* in connection with the male act, and the names Gaia and Gaius in the marriage formula *ubi tu Gaius, ibi ego Gaia* [. . .]. All this has more than metaphorical significance; it is the reflection of a fundamental idea which sees agriculture as a model for human marriage.[15]

In order to better identify the pieces of the puzzle, let us examine the composition and development of this passage.

—Two stages of the earliest history of mankind, two degrees of culture, both fashioned by nature. In the eyes of the jurist Bachofen therefore, the law is the most important product of culture, nursed by nature in its infancy. This implies that if the law is essentially that of marriage, agriculture is its prototype. Nothing, so far, which cannot be imposed a priori.

—Next, minus even the punctuation to indicate quotation, Plato's phrase concerning the imitation of the earth by woman is inserted in the passage like an anonymous assertion of truth; this is a means of tacitly providing oneself with Greek support, even while concealing the local connection beneath a general law. In fact this phrase is pivotal to the passage: it introduces the idea that judicial terminology is borrowed from agriculture—and from agricultural *acts*, since more than vocabulary is at stake. The Platonic imitation has been redirected; the language of justice is for Bachofen a "reflection" of Idea.

—It is true that this direct borrowing is expressed in words or locutions. The harvest as the ultimate aim of Greek marriage; "ways of speaking" (*Redensarten*) which, both in tragedy and in Plato, indicate generation through agricultural procedures; finally the Roman formula sanctioning marriage.

—In conclusion, after a few other examples, just so many tokens tossed into the file on conjugal agriculture, there is the statement that it is less a matter of pictorial turns-of-phrase than the straightforward and authentic expression of the *Grundidee* developed throughout the paragraph, which functions as an *analogon* to the book as a whole.

We are already acquainted with the Greek materials of this construction, beginning with the inevitable phrase in the *Menexenus*, which scholarship may be citing or plagiarizing from Bachofen without stopping to acknowledge its debt to a work all too easily appropriated by opposing political views and hence, according to the academic pruderies of Hellenism, discreditable.

Let us turn to the Roman material, to the names that according to Bachofen constitute the traditional formula of marriage: "Where you are Gaius, I am Gaia." A way of expressing that the man—the masculine—is the giver of form and meaning to his wife, whose generic name is a feminine facsimile of the husband's.[16] Or a way of declaring, in the words of Plutarch's gloss: "Where you are lord and master of the house, I am lady and mistress of the house."[17] Whether such a formula preserves the memory of a woman, a Gaia Caecilia who was an exemplary wife,[18] or whether it was erroneously produced by generalizing from an example leaves Bachofen indifferent.[19] As a Cratylus-type philologist,[20] little concerned with ancient explications of Gaius and Gaia, he sees much more than convention in these names: nature, as always, expressing itself directly, or Idea, self-expressed, to be understood in its original purity.

Bachofen is convinced that there is something original in Gaia, although he has had to proceed by construction around the name of the wife in order to arrive at nature.

Let us go back to the beginning. For the reader, everything begins with an enigmatic sentence in the first pages of the chapter devoted to Lycia: "*Gê* and *gunê* or Gaia appear to be on an equal footing with each other."[21]

There is no point in rereading again and again what is obvious: in a sentence of Greek provenance, here is Gaia (whom I read in Greek, like the Hesiodic name of the Earth Mother) beside *gunê*, like the most adequate of synonyms, next to *gê*. Gaia, another name of *gunê*? I registered uncomprehendingly the seeming anomaly.

The second appearance of Gaia which, for me, was the moment of intuition, coincided with the opening pages of the Athenian chapter. Commenting on the myth of the dispossession of the women of Athens,[22] Bachofen concludes: "As long as they possessed the name *Athênaiai*, they were true citizens. Later they became simply wives of citizens. Later the woman said: *ubi tu Gaius, ibi ego Gaia*. According to ancient law it should be the man who says: *ubi tu Gaia, ibi ego Gaius*."[23]

Abruptly, Bachofen binds Athenian women to a Roman formula; at the same time he originates the "primitive" formula, forgotten in the inexorable progression of history toward father-right, in which Gaia is the model for Gaius. Suddenly, illumination: if one moves thus from Athens to Rome, it is because the original Gaia is Greek, just as throughout the book the religion of the Earth Mother is Greek; but since law is by definition Roman,[24] it is from the final formula, expressed in Latin and dominated by the motif of the bridegroom, that, through the overlapping of Gaia by *Gaia*, of the Roman bride by Greek Earth, Bachofen derives—he would say "uncovers"—the primitive formula which has disappeared, like a philologist reconstructing an earlier stage of language or a historian of religion hypothesizing an *Urmythos*.

I was impressed by what I considered to be my intuition. Alas! On reading further I had to conclude that Bachofen himself, with some delay certainly, yet with unmistakable clarity, provided the key to the riddle: "In the marriage formula *ubi tu Gaius, ibi ego Gaia*, the two genders [or the two sexes: *Geschlechter*] are denominated from the same root *gaîa*."[25]

The Greek *gaîa* becomes the (religious) "root" of the (juristic) names Gaius and Gaia. The next occurrence, which we started from, juxtaposes the Greek marriage formula, which concerns plowing, with the Roman formula, where out of the dissimilar Bachofen derives the same, since Gaia—now it is unmistakable!—is distantly related to the earth and to the time when Gaius was merely a masculine doublet and dominated by the motif of the woman/mother.

At the moment of strategic articulation, then, we have a little etymology, closer to the Greek practice of naturalizing the meaning of
proper names than to the science modern philologists designate by this
name.[26] In the last occurrence of Gaia, which is in the Egyptian chapter,
the mythopoeic imagination of Bachofen happily gathers together all the
key words and all the languages of the book: "*Gamos* derives from *gê* just
as *gunê* does, just as *ga* and Gaius, Gaia, *Gatte* (husband), *Gattin* (wife) are
designations which belong to earth-matter penetrated by Eros."[27]

In the *Cratylus*, Plato associates only *gonê*, generation, with *gunê*
(414a). Bachofen could not bring himself to imprison woman in sexual
reproduction in this way;[28] for the coherence of his elaboration, Earth
would have had to give its name originally to both woman and marriage.
Thus the derivation *gê* > *gunê* was already functioning in the Athenian
chapter.[29] The most surprising, given that Bachofen is not obsessed by
the Indo-European linguistic model,[30] is the integration of the German
words for husband and wife into the genealogy of words derived from
gê. It is true that the German language has already made a legitimate appearance in the etymological excursus of the Athenian chapter, where
Frauenzimmer and *Erde* were connected to two words for earth.[31] But—
need we repeat—these are present constructions, directed toward the
present and for the use of the present. Such is the modern practice of
myth, as constant as it is constantly denied.

It remains to observe that in Bachofen, "Gaia" designates only the
Roman bride, carefully distinguished graphically from the word *gaia*—
always written in Greek, necessarily for the earth of the Greeks—while
the name of the earth goddess regularly receives the transcription
"Gaea."[32] So that in reading the Lycian chapter I should have identified
Gaia, from its first occurrence, as the Roman word for wife. An error,
certainly. But at least it stimulated my imagination by directing it toward
the hypothesis explicitly formulated later in the text.

Gaea and *gaia* transcribing the same word whether we give it a capital letter or not, it is the name Gaia that is important; for Gaia, generic
Roman *woman*, Bachofen postulates a derivation from a compound like
gunê-gê,[33] which gives woman and the earth in the order that informs the
conception of their relationship before any construction takes place.
Even if the *Menexenus* conspicuously proclaims the opposite,[34] even if

Bachofen derives *gunê* from *gê* and Gaia from *gaia*, it is not possible to continue to ignore the wording, always hidden beneath ancient and modern constructions, of the true statement concerning woman and the earth. To formulate it in my own way:

If indeed one must imitate the other (but is this inevitable? Cf. Hesiod, who takes pains to distinguish them), *it is the earth which imitates woman*,[35] and in no wise the reverse.

It is a common rejection of this statement which explains the curious consensus among readers of Hesiod to "forget" the artificiality of Pandora, made of earth, not stipulated as fertile. One doubts that Bachofen was the last to do so.[36] As for the goddess Gaia, because she must be absolutely first and one hundred percent fertile, there is a general tendency to forget the Hesiodic version in the *Theogony*: that she proceeds immediately to give birth to a partner "equal to herself, who was able to cover her entirely" (126–127), as if already parthenogenesis was a burden right from the start. And that through his insatiable and savage ardor this companion, still covering her, pushes his children back into the bowels of the Earth, who is thus encumbered, smothered, and crippled in her fertility (154–160; 176–178). Bachofen, discreet on the subject of Hesiod, eventually makes allusion to this affair only at the precise moment when Kronos, attacking Ouranos, "accomplishes the wish of Gaia."[37]

So necessary is it that women be like the earth, and that the Earth be untiringly, naturally, and joyously fertile. An old story, but one with which, I suggest, *les modernes* have not finished.

CHAPTER 10

The Return of the Excluded

> This heterogeneity and the law of contamination between the complete
> other of this heterogeneity and its regular re-appropriation [. . .], this is
> what has concerned me the most in my reading, especially my reading of
> the Greeks.

The reader will no doubt have recognized the voice of Derrida, recently on the subject of "Nous autres Grecs."[1]

I begin with this statement because this Derridian concern has accompanied me throughout the pendulum swing which has repeatedly
brought me back from Greek tragedy or historiography to Plato. The
subject then is Plato, along with "Pharmacy" and "Chôra." Plato again,
perhaps.[2] But undeniably Plato, for it is Plato I have read with Derrida.

Plato: because after Derrida it is difficult to leave Platonism un-
touched. But also because it is just as difficult to ignore the fact that in
the end Platonism renews itself, that it is destined to renew itself endlessly, by virtue of the modalities of its inscription in the text,[3] on the in-
visible, ever-transgressed frontier that defines the place, all the places, all
the motifs of the question of place, in Plato.

In my view the central concern is between *khôra* and *khôris* in Plato.
Between *khôra*, neither palpable nor intelligible, and therefore a principle
of indecision, and *khôris*, which separates and isolates. It so happens—but
this is not at all accidental—that *khôris* is found in etymological dictionar-
ies *sub verbo khôra*,[4] which already suggests that the game will be unending,
and yet which does not authorize any reader, even Heidegger,[5] to read
khôra in Plato as "that which separates," but always as that which receives;

and the tension between *dekhomai* and *khôris*, such as is exploited in the *Phaedrus* for example, between the soul which sees the beautiful object, receives it, and is overcome, and the separated soul which is overcome with sorrow,[6] will be considered as constitutive of the Platonic view of place.

Outside Plato, *khôra* is the territory of the city, with firmly closed borders protected by the remote spaces of the *eskhatia*. But in the civic *khôra* in the *Menexenus*, the *Republic*, or the *Timaeus* we find the stranger, sometimes in the form of those autochthones who say that they were born there, from the earth itself.

How then has the stranger entered? He was "sent on his way,"[7] but he returned in the signifier. This is the movement whose effect I make every effort, with every reading of a Platonic dialogue, to track down. This is the operation, or movement, I am speaking of here.

It has been remarked that either one gets rid of a thing or one should get rid of it, but the words have taken over—metaphor, it may be argued, but Derrida has taught us to work on what, for my part, I call "metaphor without metaphor."[8]

What does one send on its way? Myth, women, the body, *métis*[9] also (the list is certainly not finite). And all this returns, woven into the dialogue like the place itself—moving and yet fixed—of the text.

This might take place—the simplest case—in a sentence, for example a certain sentence in the *Laws* concerning the women of Sparta who, unlike the women of other city-states, do not weave. The text describes the Lacedaemonian women as "freed from wool-working, and therefore *weaving* (*diaplekein*) a life wholly devoted to exercise" (*Laws* 7.806a2–4).

This might also develop over the course of a dialogue such as the *Phaedo*, which is nothing but a long adieu to the body, because one apparently becomes "blind of soul by fixing one's eyes on things," and by straining to "touch" sensations (*Phaedo* 99e). As if corporeality is driven out merely to be enshrined in the heart of the soul. . . .

Women, the body. . . . I have already had occasion to mention the feminine which is disappropriated, reappropriated, because only women can associate *erôs* and parturition, and David Halperin has written significantly on the Diotima of the *Symposium*.[10] Here then I will speak neither of women nor of the feminine. But I would like to say a few more words on the *return of the body* in the *Phaedo*, because the *Phaedo* is aimed explicitly at relating the separation of body and soul to *khôris*, to the point that this dialogue, as an expounding of Platonism, is somewhat disdained by our modernity.

And yet. . . . No doubt the aim is to "proceed toward each thing by thought alone, without in the act of thinking turning to sight or to any other sense, but, through thought alone and unadulterated (*eilikrinêi têi dianoiai*), to take up the hunt for beings, each of which exists alone and unadulterated (*eilikrinês*), and this after having as much as possible rid oneself of one's eyes, ears, and body, since that is what disturbs the soul" (*Phaedo* 65e–66a). Nevertheless the statement of separation in the *Phaedo*, to the extent that the formulation is developed, begins with the body: "apart from the soul, rid of it, *the body exists by itself*, and the soul apart, rid of body, is by itself [. . .]" (64c).

If we are truly concerned here with unmixed purity (*eilikrinês*, see below), why does *touch*, rivaling sight, gradually become the privileged signifier of the soul? Why is it that, whether it be intoxicated by the body to the point of vertigo or whether, weightless, it launches itself in the direction of what is pure, it should be said to be *in contact* (*ephaptomenê Phaedo* 79c–d)? And why is the relationship to the intelligible one of contact, as if we were dealing with the perceptible? If the soul has body "metaphorically," is it not its fragility that is apparent, like it or not, in the signifier?[11]

This verb *ephaptomai* intrigued me, and I followed its trail in the *Theaetetus*, where it is in effect in the service of the soul that never ceases to "enter into contact," as if this operation were characteristic of its identity, and also in the *Sophist*, where it was necessary to acknowledge that the same verb expresses material gesture in its provocative glorification of materiality.[12] Heraclitus was right to privilege the dynamic of contact (*sunapsies*: everything and not everything);[13] but it is true that *sunapsies* in fact constitutes the very text of Heraclitus. On the other hand *ephaptomai* is, as they say, *in* Plato, which also makes possible our never seeing that the soul possesses body, since what is signified is not there.

Let us look at the first lines of "Plato's Pharmacy":

A text is a text only if it hides, at first glance, at first coming, the law of its composition and the rule governing its game. Moreover a text remains forever unlocatable.[14]

The *Phaedo*, if one really reads it, effectively conceals the difficulty inherent in thinking of separation outside any thematic of contamination. It has even concealed the soul in the cold body of Socrates (*psukhomena*: 118a2, 5); doctors, readers of the *Phaedo* themselves, have failed to reveal that in order to kill Socrates, the course of the hemlock must not cease in the middle of his body, but rather proceed as far as the head, to better contaminate the soul.[15] They kept quiet so that Socrates' soul could become separate, and this is why the *Phaedo* is the foundation of Platonism: because the signifier passes for being only a signifier.

I am interested therefore in the extra twist which is the Platonic signifier, in what it constantly displays the better to conceal. It displays body, contact, *écriture*, or stranger in order to make belief in soul, separation, *logos*, or autochthony, more creditable, the trick being to make out of *logos, in extremis*, a good *écriture*,[16] an inscription of truth, to give the soul a sense of touch like its very own gesture, or to produce autochthones in the workshop of a craftsman designated Earth Mother—ready to chalk all this up to metaphor, so that it passes and one passes over it. I wonder if in Plato the trick is not in the end *syntax*, which permits some otherness to subsist in the text as such, but modalized, even neutralized, given that once linked together—and the style is *sumplokê*—sensitive words, caught in the articulation, are present for and against themselves. Apropos of syntax in the *Sophist*, for example:

> That therefore [. . .] one says: lion, stag, horse, and all the other words which designate the subjects doing the actions, here [. . .] is a series from which no discourse results; because, [. . .] here [. . .] the given sounds indicate neither action nor inaction, nor existence, whether of a being or a nonbeing, since verbs are not added to the nouns. Then as soon as the articulation has been made, immediately the *prôtê sumplokê* becomes discourse.
>
> *Sophist* 262b–c)

To turn back to the passage of the *Phaedo* already cited, if the trick is to conceal series beneath articulation, it consists perhaps in writing the following: "*apart from* the *soul, rid* of it, the *body* exists by itself, and the *soul apart, rid* of *body*, is by itself" where the same sequence *soul-rid-body* encloses (but also: is enclosed in) two opposing modalities of separation.

If there are in Plato subtexts which are *signs*, like *pharmakon*[17] or *khôra*, I would suggest that in Platonic texts it is the sur-text which bears the mark of orthodoxy. Syntactic against semantic, the struggle between the authorized sur-text of Platonism and the shifting subtext of word-signs is no doubt an unequal one, and I understand why Derrida refuses to translate the signifiers he isolates, keeping, as far as the whole is concerned, to the use of conventional translations, while indicating that that is what they are. For my part, however, I would argue that one should always *translate* Plato over again, even if this is to "overline" the text, so that by being in view and overmuch in view in its syntactic structure, the sur-text leads the blinded gaze away from its most obvious articulation, toward the one that undermines it. For this reason, to try to reveal the excluded, returned and well-hidden in the dialogues, I will systematically translate the bits of Plato which I cite.

If I now take leave of myth, trickery, woman, and the body, if *écriture* fades into the background, as a variant of the adaptation or inscribing of citizens into their territory, it is for a reason. In order to achieve the return of the excluded, I have chosen to orient myself within the Platonic discourse the philosopher borrows from the orthodoxy of the city of Athens, a discourse that explicitly excludes the other, all others; and by so doing I hope to show how, by introducing subtexts which operate on it internally, Plato sees to it that it retains some of the other.

An Athenian Abroad

From scrupulous attention to the work of autochthony in the text of Plato, one reaps the benefit of being able to examine some of the articulations of the "long discourse on hospitality, war, the excluded from the polis, and the place of the stranger in philosophy," whose necessity Derrida observes.[18]

"The stranger in philosophy"?[19] This naturally recalls the situation which in dialogues such as the *Sophist* or the *Statesman* is occupied by a protagonist designated insistently as stranger. But I also think, preferentially, of the stranger in the *Laws*. This stranger is unusual for having come from Athens, for being an Athenian in Crete, and, thanks to this displacement, apparently miraculously free from the morbid inflammation which is "Athens" in Athens for an Athenian. An Athenian stranger in Crete,[20] the Crete that its inhabitants love with a particular intimacy, since contrary to the general Greek practice they refer to their country not as their "fatherland" (*patris*), but as their "motherland" (*matris*) (*Republic* 10.575d). Land of the mother, land of "before" or the "already past,"[21] old without question, where, however, a new colony is to be established in which the protection of strangers is a sacred duty, placed as in the *Laws* under the authority of Zeus Xenios (5.729e–730a).

Once again it is necessary to understand the meaning of "stranger."
An "other Greek," certainly, in the language of Plato's contemporaries;
"Greek" or "Barbarian" indiscriminately, if the stranger of the *Laws* ac-
cepts the "methodical rejection of segregation" between Greeks and
Barbarians the *Statesman* solemnly suggests.[22]

The stranger in Plato: an instrument of heterogeneity for dissolving
deeply embedded opinions.[23] May his nameless figure help me to combat the prestige of the Same, in order to better view the Platonic strategy of autochthony. This highly Platonic invocation is not exaggerated,
because it concerns a question I have continuously touched upon and
put off at the same time, since I wrote *The Children of Athena*, when I
had to recognize that "my regret—its name is Plato."[24] But although I
may have more than once rejected the temptation to deal with a question entitled "Platonic Autochthonies," it is possible that a return voyage through "Pharmacy" and "Chôra" might finally give me the
strength to break the enchantment. Let us see.

Platonic autochthonies, then.

From the *Republic* to the *Sophist* and from the *Menexenus* to the
Timaeus, the motif of autochthones recurs: multiform, and, to say the
least, enigmatic. In its ensemble one would place it between the fable in
the *Sophist* in which adherents of matter are called (in opposition to the
Friends of Forms) "autochthones" (247c) and "sons of the earth" (*gêgeneis:*
248c), and the "noble lie" of the *Republic*, whose content is certainly a
myth of autochthony, but which as a "myth" (*muthos*) provides civil ed-
ucation with a model (*tupos*: 2.377b, 379a) aimed at creating an impression in the minds of the citizenry. The fact that this useful fiction, forged
by legislators who were political surgeons (3.389b, 407e), is explicitly cat-
egorized as *pharmakon*,[25] suggests the size of the stakes involving autochthony in any attempt to express sameness in a regime of *différance*. Focusing on the Greek conformity among these elements, one might
add—taking nothing away from the work of alterity—that in both the
Sophist and the *Republic* the myth, which one would expect to be Athenian first and foremost as far as the Athenian Plato is concerned, is displaced from Athens in order to take on its Theban form. A composite and
complex form evidently, since the Theban myth associates autochthony
with the city's foundation (obviously primordial, since well before it was
the city of Oedipus, Thebes was the city of Kadmos and the Spartoi); a
form ostensibly non-Athenian, at least in tragedy, where Thebes is the ar-

chetype of an anti-Athens.[26] It may be an autochthony of the Sown which characterizes the materialists of the *Sophist* (247c), but the presentation of the "noble lie" as a "Phoenician tale" (3.414c) refers explicitly to Kadmos the Barbarian[27]—one must not forget in this instance, that the purple letters engraved on stones originated according to the Greeks from the *phoinikêia grammata*: Phoenician is the writing, and Phoenician also the inscription of the foreign colonizer in the furrows of the earth of Thebes. Likewise the useful lie of the *Laws*, in ascribing the birth of armed hoplites where the teeth were sown under the heading of "Sidonian *mythologêma*" (*Laws* 2.663e), associates autochthony and the remote origin of the founder, thus reunifying the two sides of the Theban Cycle.

Is this all then in Plato which renders autochthony foreign to itself? Not yet, since we must take account of those operations that the Earth, their mother, accomplishes to form the citizens of the *Republic* in her breast, nourishing them as befits a mother, but also molding them plastically (*plattesthai*), as the gods fashion the races of men in Hesiod: as befits a demiurge. In the exercise of this function the earth is justifiably described as working "artisanally" (*dêmiourgoumenê*: 3.414e 1).[28]

It still remains, under the heading of this "same which is not identical, but the *différance* as passage, deviating and equivocal, of a different to an other, of one term of the opposition to the other,"[29] to note the essential: *mêtêr kai trophos khôra*, "*khôra*, mother and nurse of citizens."[30] Forgive me if I lack the courage to tackle this now: the mother's time will come. For the moment, I hasten to rejoin the chapter, well known to me, on Athenian autochthony, as if to assure myself that there persists alongside the same *en différance*, the same, unbroached.

Now to Athenian autochthony then, in the *Menexenus*, the *Timaeus*, and the *Critias*.

Between the *khôris* and *khôra mêtêr*, between the most canonically positioned opposition of the same and others and the maternity of *khôra* understood as Attica, between the Plato of Platonism and the Plato of Derrida: such is the program which in the *Menexenus* reigns over the theme of autochthony. I translate as closely as possible:

The origin of our ancestors is not that of arrivals,[31] nor were their descendants made Metics (*metoikountas*) thereby, established in this land as immigrants; rather they were autochthones, living and dwelling (*oikountas*) authentically in their own fatherland, and nourished not by a stepmother like others, but by a mother, the earth where they lived (*oikoun*); and, now that they are dead, they lie in the own places (*en oikeiois topois*)[32] of her who gave them birth, nourished, and took care of them. (237b–c)

First appears separation: there are the others—and the "elsewhere" (*allothen*) from which by definition, even when they are at home, they are eternally from—and Athenians, whose relationship to the land is characterized by *oikeion*, which let us for the moment translate as "own" (although family and intimacy are also concerned). All the more arresting a contrast in that it seems reinforced by that of *metoikein* (to reside as a Metic, by definition the fate of others) and that of *oikein* (to live in one's own land.)

Since we are on the subject of separation, I will adduce a second theme in which the Athenian autochthone, identified with the genuine Greek, is characterized in the *Menexenus* by his hatred of the Barbarian—here we are certainly far from the *Statesman*. Again I translate:

So true is it that the freedom and nobility of our city are firm and sound, inimical as it is by nature to the Barbarian, because we are purely Greeks (*eilikrinôs*), uncontaminated by the Barbarians. For there is neither Pelops nor Kadmos, neither Aegyptos nor Danaos, nor many others, who, Barbarian by nature but Greek by convention, live (*sunoikousin*) with us; but it is we Greeks who live (*oikoumen*) without Barbarian contamination, whence our city is infused with pure hatred against foreign kind. (245c–d)

The matter is clear (even too much so!): no Kadmos in Athens. And imperturbably the rhetoric hurls down proofs of purity and authenticity against the alterity of foreign kind (*allotria phusis*), and mobilizes Athenian *oikein* against cohabitation. The *metoikein* of resident aliens, the *sunoikein* of foreign colonizers. Those fake Greeks.

But it so happens that thus hyperbolized, the opposition reveals its weaknesses—or rather its focal points, in those places where an excess of determination obscures it or renders it opaque.

Paternity, Women, and the Mother

First of all there is the *eilikrinôs*, "purely," of "purely Greek." In Plato this adverb is generally used of radical separation—separation due to wishful thinking, perhaps, but which would be seen to be agentive—between body and soul, for example. But although the meaning of the adverb may seem transparent, the morphology of the word is much less so. There is little to say concerning the second element, the one that bears the essential weight: from the verb *krinô*, it is triage, distinction, decision. But what do we do with *eili-*? Philologists ponder a connection to *helios*, "sun." This would give the adjective *eilikrinês* meaning (very, canonically Plato), "distinguished in the sun." A metaphysical version, certainly appropriate to Platonism and one which would not surprise Derrida, in the shortcut it presupposes between metaphor and conceptual discriminator. But another hypothesis connects *eili-* to the verb *eilô* ("turn (tr.), revolve"), the metaphor being according to Chantraine "that of grain or meal separated in a sieve which is turned."[33] For distinguishing à la Aristophanes the wheat from the chaff, the adverb *eilikrinôs* is admirably suited.[34] As long as it is not allowed to resonate in proximity to the verb *eiliggiaô*, which signifies disorientation:[35] disorientation of the soul intoxicated by the body in the *Phaedo*, disorientation of the Heraclitans of the *Cratylus*, carried away by the flux which they set in motion and which set their heads spinning, disorientation visited by philosophy on all those who knew not how to prepare themselves.[36] A dangerous proximity, then, that of *eiliggiaô*, for an agent of separation like *eilikrinôs*. . . . Perhaps in fact one must mentally restore to *eilikrinôs* the turning movement of the sieve that separates. But one must control the movement: it must not infect the mind in search of clear-cut oppositions with the staggers, or it will be lost. I like to think that Plato knew the risks, perhaps played with the contiguity, and used *eilikrinôs* consciously and deliberately.

But to those interested in points of *différance* in Platonic motifs of autochthony, I suggest focusing on the verb *oikein* and its compounds, recurrent in the two *Menexenus* passages. It is wise not to allow any ontological representation of dwelling (Heideggerian, for example) which implies a basic connection to being. Greek dwelling—*oikein*—is so far removed from any natural embedding in the earth as to provide the key word in an examination of the Greek vocabulary of colonization.[37]

The dissonance in the *Menexenus* is undoubtedly discreet. It is not the aorist *oikêsai* meaning "colonize" which is used, and the verb *oikein* is conjugated in the present (and in the first person plural: we Athenians live . . .). But we shouldn't relax too quickly: the considerations that the harmless present form *oikein* inspires in the philologist are indeed troubling, merely implying *residence*, which often entails noncitizenship. To quote the accepted legal meaning, it is reserved "especially for the Metic, notably at Athens, in the sense of being domiciled at."[38] Does this have to do with the noun *oikêsis*? Here we will summon the words of Aristotle in the *Politics* to the rescue: in no case can the "fact of residence" define citizenship, split as it is among citizen, Metic, and slave.[39]

"Resident" autochthones in their own land? Things are getting complicated. The verb *oikein* governs two types of objects, the indirect (the most common), by which one dwells *en polei, en khôrai* as a resident, and the direct (*oikô khôran* or *polin*), which means "residence full-time and with full rights."[40] But adherents of the Same should not get too excited: an Isocrates on the subject of Athenian autochthony might employ the latter construction ("we *inhabit our city* . . . "),[41] but *oikein en* is the phrase which Plato uses in the *Menexenus*. Not content with repeating it in the space of three lines ("dwelling *in* their fatherland, nourished by the earth *in which* they dwell"), Plato insists upon it, and as if to underscore the oxymoron which is residence in a fatherland, he states emphatically: *tôi onti*, truly. Although there is no doubt that to Athenian ears, and even more generally to Greek ones, *oikein*, already destabilized by being so close to *metoikein*, which it is supposed to oppose, has no need to be ironically sustained in its identity as a borrowing. To make sure that the insinuation is not overlooked, the operation is repeated a little further on, somewhat differently, for in seeming to contrast with *sunoikousin* ("they dwell with"), and used absolutely ("it is we who inhabit"), *oikein* sounds a highly ambiguous note. Fans of cut-and-dried oppositions should resign themselves to the fact that the only legitimate location for the verb *oikein* is not within a motif on autochthonous citizens, but, as in the *Funeral Oration* of Lysias, in a statement on "others," those who are to colonize foreign territory.[42] It is true that as readers of Derrida we are sensitive to the destiny in Plato of "that which has no as such"— game, writing, and now dwelling-place—and which is in "a constant process of disappearance." Because we know that dwelling cannot, in terms of Plato's text, be affirmed without being thereby denied, we acknowledge the logic whereby, in its effort to appropriate *oikein* as a good example of "ideological confiscation,"[43] autochthonous discourse comes to deny the Greek reception of dwelling, and denies itself in the same movement. But how can we escape the conclusion that the notion of dwelling renders autochthones fragile?

We should not rush to conclude that there is a general and concerted operation of back-pedaling or reversal, from the positive to the negative. Rather the text labors to undo the didactic opposition of *allotrion* and *oikeion*: as much as one insists on the ambiguities of *oikein*, is it not finally the "own" which one undermines, uprooting *oikeion* from its safe-guarding proximity—however enviously underscored in motifs of au-tochthony—to *oikia*, dwelling-place? Here I would open up a sideline to suggest that a more general law has *oikein* and *oikêsis* in Plato working to expatriate just what these words are supposed to instantiate. This is true of the soul in the *Phaedo* destined to "reside" in Hades, and which, even though endowed with a "pure residency," occupies it in the manner of a colonization as if even for the soul *oikein* has no natural place, but only endless establishments in "foreign" territory,[44] provisionary encampments that are distinct from the serene appropriateness which matches the *ousia* in the *Phaedrus* with the place it "possesses" (*ekhei* 247d1) as its own.

What does belong then to autochthones? The prologue to the *Timaeus* poses the question in a new guise, although as an Athenian (even a less than desirable one), inseparably philosopher and politician, Critias is considered to enjoy this "belonging to one's own place, polit-ically and residentially" with which Socrates, from the nonplace that is characteristically his, credits his interlocutors, not without duplicity.[45]

In fact it is the most canonical version of the myth of autochthony that provides Critias' account with its protagonists—Athena, Gê, and Hephaistos (23d–e)—and its locations. With, however, this unexpected detail, sufficiently important to be repeated in the same sentence: that the goddess "established" Athenians on her territory (*katôikisen* 24c4, d2) as one populates a colony, as in Hippolytus' imprecations against the "race of women," Zeus is supposed to have "established" women as for-eign colonists among men.[46] They are therefore "residents" (*oikeite de nun*), and it is foundation and population (*katoikizon tas khôras, kai ka-toikisantes*, 109b6) that repeatedly occur in the *Critias*, where Athena and Hephaistos "make" the autochthones (*empoiêsantes*, 109d1).

The use of such language in an autochthonous context is an anomaly that hardly needs emphasizing.[47] Faced with these technician and colo-nizer gods, it is better to accept once and for all that in a number of Pla-tonic texts a polis worthy of the name, far from being a given, must be founded, and founded in alterity. The polis of the *Republic*, for example, which must be established somewhere where importation is possible (2.370e), and that of the *Laws*, explicitly described as a colony (*apoikia* 3.702c; *katoikizô*, 3.702c, e; 4.707e, 708a, b) after book four has unveiled the long history of the successive foundations of humanity, and whose jurisdiction will be largely borrowed from the Other (*heterothen*), without its foreign character (*xenikon*) being considered for one instant an impediment to its proper functioning in the city of the Magnesians. He who envisions the polis in its essence would be an *oikistês*, then, before being deemed legislator or statesman, and the founding of the city of the *Laws* requires (this is actually the conclusion of the dialogue [12.969]) restraining the stranger from Athens, preventing him from pursuing his journey. Foundation and colonization are one and the same, and the philologist intervenes opportunely with the statement that of all classical prose-writers, Plato boasts the greatest number of occurrences of the verb *katoikizô*, far ahead of Thucydides: forty-four for the philosopher, twenty-one for the historian—a significant difference.[48]

Reading Plato necessitates constant attention to the twists and (re)turns of the excluded within the framework of meaning in the text, and so we are reminded by this Athenian chapter; a tacit rule, yet as compelling as the explicitly formulated rules of Platonism (that of the *meletê thanatou*, for example). Through the colonizing act of the gods, ancient Athens—supposedly the city of the Same—is eternally displaced, distanced from itself; dare I say "Platonized"? The self is established as an other: this is the important news which the other Greek Plato conceals at the Greek core of Platonism. True, the operation has its limits, which are those of *Greek* modalities of thought; the self is also *established*, thus deriving from a logic which is ultimately classical in a Greek context. The *Timaeus* is also marked by the intractable radicality, i.e., absence of name or location,[49] which characterizes Vedic texts, for example, and Derrida will no doubt continue to use it to justify himself to the Greeks, "hated"—I quote, knowing it must be taken *cum grano salis!*—and enthralling.[50]

This might resemble a leave-taking, except that "the mother Remain(s)"—especially since "Remain(s) is always said of the mother."[51] There remains, then, the fact that up to now I have passed over the mother in silence, and that this might fairly be objected to.[52] Particularly because in the discourse of autochthony, especially in its Platonic version, the mother is named again and again, even when an overly philosophical reader thinks he can identify only the father.[53] It is the mother who should be heard in Athenian pronouncements on *khôra*, as when the *Menexenus* states concerning citizens who died in combat, that having been "nourished not by a stepmother like others, but by the *khôra* where they live as if by a mother," they rightly repose in the "intimate places" (*oikeioi topoi*) of their "parent."[54]

But the mother is not all repose.[55] How are we to regard the maternity of the earth when it is credited with fashioning the *gêgeneis*, in its primordial creativity, by joining the other to the other? A passage in the *Statesman* invites this question, although without ensuring the sexual reproduction of humans a status other than that of *mimêma* of this original production, certainly more artisanal than "natural":[56] in place of the Same to be imitated, an operation of heterogeneous assembly is always taking place in the depths of her whom the *Statesman* does not designate as mother, but to whom the *Republic* accords this title.[57]

The mother, decidedly, is not all repose—another illusion gone west; but true, Derrida warned us of this. From "The Pharmacy" to "Chôra" by way of *Glas*, he has repeated the odd statement that the mother is apart, always an outsider, at any rate rendered dissymmetrical[58]—one has only to think of the dissymmetrical expression *mêtêr kai patris* in the official rhetoric of autochthony—absent from itself like *khôra*,[59] to which no determination, beginning with the femininity of the mother or nurse, can be rightfully attributed.[60] There is much to dream on, but much also to work on, starting from what Derrida actually says of *khôra*: that it is "of a virginity radically rebellious against all anthropomorphism," to the extent that Plato himself, in "comparing" it to a mother (or to a nurse) risks betraying this repugnance, or better yet, this indifference to incarnation, which he yet sets up as radically remote from feminine apparitions of the goddess Gê in the imagery of the Greeks.[61]

Yet the matter is still more complicated than suggested above. It also happens that, inversely, the comparison aims at protecting the distance of the mother rather than threatening her. When the noble lie of the *Republic* advises citizens that, having arisen from the earth, they must treat their *khôra* "like a mother" (3.414e3), can we really understand something other than anthropomorphism in this *hôs peri mêtros?* We need only emphasize the "like," which distances the mother from the determining and determined instance that is evidently, for Greek citizens, the territory of their city—*khôra*. Then one appreciates the attention afforded by the text to correcting a first utterance which is basically anthropomorphic ("being a mother, the earth gave them birth," *hê gê autous mêtêr ousa anêken*: 414e2–3), thus protecting *mêtêr* from an overly brutal identification.

"Save the mother?" Here I must go back to my earlier reading of the celebrated passage of the *Menexenus* (237d1–238a) on woman, imitator of the earth.[62] Pointing out that *tiktein*, "give birth," a key word in the passage, could be applied only to human reproduction, I read the text as contradicting in advance the final denial ("It isn't the earth which imitates woman, but woman the earth"). Under the disconcerting light of the returns of the stranger I will attempt another reading, suggesting that if it is absurd to say with the Athenians that the earth "gives birth," it is perhaps because secretly the earth is really a mother, and that the mother "is certainly not a woman."[63] But we must indicate everything that separates mother, indifferent, undifferentiated, and elusive, from what in the programmatic themes of the *Republic* and the *Laws* is meant by the plural "mothers." Because mothers are human mothers in their multiplicity, disappropriated engenderers of their progeny yet eternally free from the care of their own, and to whom the polis in its wholly functional benevolence gave an entire generation to comfort and nourish. *These* are mothers. And then one of them would be *the* mother, one only, or so one imagines, formless perhaps like the Erda of the *Ring* produced by Patrice Chéreau,[64] and who regularly consents to the Earth being taken for her.

The *mêtêr* who is not a woman, women who are not the mother; autochthones fashioned by a craftsman divinity or established like a founding colony; a stranger from Athens. And Socrates the *atopos*; alone, because he has no place, in not being caught in the movement which, from *khôra* in the *Timaeus* to the civic *khôra*, uproots all places from themselves. A movement which is general, but at the same time insubstantial, which one might easily overlook.

It is altogether there, but altogether other, because the *there* has slipped on the self. Altogether there, but altogether other? Such an optimistic (or grandiloquent if you prefer) utterance must be corrected on the fly, by slipping in "a little." It is altogether there, and altogether has become a little—just a little—imperceptibly, altogether other. A little shaky. It is up to the reader to follow the stranger, without pinning him down too quickly as in the end of the *Laws*, in his endless return toward the other roots of the same.

CHAPTER II

Democracy Put to the Test
of the Stranger (Athens, Paris)

To cut right to the heart of the matter, a page from Moses Finley regarding the debate—poorly begun, but annoyingly recurrent—which confronts "modernists" and historians of ancient Greece on the subject of Athenian democracy:

> I have in the past been found "guilty of a certain romanticizing of Athe-
> nian government" and of misusing the term "democracy" because the
> *dêmos* was a narrow minority that excluded women, slaves and members
> of the subject-states in the fifth-century empire. It does not seem to me
> that a structural historical analysis of Greek (or any other) politics *in their
> own terms* either warrants such criticism or requires a litany of explicit
> moral condemnation. It is easy to score points over a dead society, more
> difficult and more rewarding to examine what they were trying to do,
> how they went about it, the extent to which they succeeded or failed, and
> why. The two kinds of consideration cannot be conflated without the
> risk, indeed the probability, of getting them both wrong. In both Athens
> and Rome the citizen-bodies were minorities exploiting large numbers of
> men, free and slave. It still remains to explain why both were pragmati-
> cally successful and politically stable for long periods, why in both there
> was a constant tension between élite leaders and the populace, including
> the peasantry; yet why one retained and even enlarged popular participa-
> tion, while the other persistently contained it within narrow limits. One
> may disapprove of either or both societies heartily: the problem of expla-
> nation does not disappear because of that.[1]

We assume that in order to formulate these criticisms Finley's critics, hailing from "political science" and "social science" departments in American universities, must be completely unaware (pretend to be completely unaware?) of the minimal knowledge of Antiquity required of a student of history. They would have done better to collect some information on what an ancient city is, before hastening to "blame" Athens. Or rather to blame Finley, guilty of doing his job—this profession of historian which, like Marc Bloch,[2] he defined first and foremost in terms of the need to understand.

Not that historians themselves are permanently sheltered from the compulsion to praise and blame. However great the desire for the truth which impels them, is it powerful enough to keep them at a distance from their own judgments and personal choices? This we may doubt. At least one can define the historian as one who makes his or her own judgments and choices, when the time comes, in full cognizance of the facts: he or she does not shrink from naming as "democracy" the regime that invented the word while living off the labor of slaves, having understood that in ancient Greece, slavery alone made the liberty of the citizenry structurally possible. Once the structure was in place, which in itself deserves neither praise nor blame, there are few specialists on ancient Greece who in the political domain circumscribed by the Greeks, could guard themselves at every moment from registering their preferences among oligarchs and democrats: the first giving the citizenry its narrowest definition, the second opening it up as much, it seems, as a Greek polis could envisage.

Athenian Democracy, the Historian, and the Present

Now we embark on a relationship of constant oscillation between our present and the very past past which the historian of Antiquity has chosen as his or her object. The question of "comparison"—on condition that one compares something comparable—now comes to the fore, or better yet, the question of analogy between a certain segment of the past and a certain sequence in the present. Finley constantly compares the old and the contemporary (as, for example, in *Democracy Ancient and Modern*), yet throughout his work he claims that it is to better reject analogy and accord the "ancient city" its uniqueness.[3]

Is there no other route than endlessly explaining the past through the past, and a society in its own terms, and only thus? For my part I would hesitate to hold myself to such a line, so strict as to practically prevent one—specificity "*oblige!*"—from translating the (Greek) words in which the Greeks related their experience. And I confess I cannot conceive of how a historian engrossed in his or her subject could avoid, when that subject is democracy, regularly confronting it with the concerns of the present,[4] after having taken the necessary time required for a historical analysis of Athenian democracy in its singularity. Thus I felt something akin to jubilation when I read Jules Isaac's *The Oligarchs;*[5] in his account of the two oligarchic episodes at the end of the fifth century in Athens, the historian illuminates side by side both the oligarchic governments and the early years of the Vichy regime.

A Greek example will illustrate my proposition: the arrest and execution of certain Metics by the Thirty. Mentioned in Xenophon and described in detail by Lysias, who witnessed it, the episode is significant for Isaac, who hardly need force the issue for the reader to understand (if the least bit alert and mindful of 1942 France), beneath the topical Athenian term "Metics" and transposed into the rhetoric of a Maurras, "Jews."[6] But one can also read Isaac and keep to the Athens of 404, observing that in contrast to the oligarchs, democracy gave rights to the Metics and protected them by laying out their responsibilities.

Now we are come to the heart of it, which is Athenian democracy and strangers—democracy in the face of strangers.

It was apropos of Greek democracy, condemned as a "narrow minority" when it always described itself (and was always attacked by the oligarchs as) the regime of the greatest number—of the majority,—that Finley was criticized; and it was on the subject of Athens that he claimed the primacy of understanding. But as every historian of Antiquity knows, the objection of the nonspecialist confronting Athens with the "exclusion" of slaves, women, and foreigners is recurrent. Will answering, as one must in order to clarify the debate, that the exclusion was different for each of these categories—structural for the slaves, political but not social for women and foreigners—convince the objector? Perhaps, if he or she is historically minded and does not insist that democracy be born completely transparent to itself, from the outset.[7] But historians themselves are aware that, reflecting on the tendency of Athenian democracy to think of itself in the form of an aristocracy or in an aristocratic language,[8] it sometimes seems as if the regime of the "the greatest number" does not achieve the peaceful overlapping of self with self with which they would like to be able to credit it, in the name of a logic perhaps unseasonably modern.

Unseasonably modern? In reality, nothing is less certain. In the grand days of Athenian democracy its opponents did not hesitate to credit the *dêmos* with full consciousness of the extent of its power. And I will try to show that from the classical period, democracy in Athens never ceased to be conceived of by the oligarchs not so much as a failure—here no doubt is the modern point of view, formulated with hindsight—as an overstepping of its canonical definition, ready then to include if not women (which even the French Revolution will leave beyond the bounds of citizenship), at least Metics, even slaves. But let us not anticipate, even if it is important to observe right now that the oligarchs who credited Athenian democracy with unsuspected virtualities of integration, lent it a great deal more than adversaries of today's democracy, when they, like the National Front, use ancient Athens as an original model of discrimination.

Without further delay, then, the question of strangers in the city.

Strangers in the City: The Fact, the Idea

Such a question is enigmatic seen from today's point of view, and the historian of Antiquity knows this full well, having more than once been summoned to explain this city of Athens wherein, if one was not born a citizen, one had little chance of becoming one. Thus under the heading "Benefits of Autochthony" I wanted to show how, even while comforting Athenians with the assurance of being of pure stock, the autochthonous idea was not a racist ideology. An analysis of the Athenian citizen's identity has also permitted me to observe that it was probably better to be an Athenian Metic than an immigrant in 1990s France.[9]

It is clear that Athenian citizenship is not a thing to be taken lightly. Aristophanes was merely in tune with the people when he made every demagogue in sight a "stranger" of obscure origin, even though this was completely contrary to the actual political choices that were made. Rigor was enshrined in the institutions presiding over the status of the citizen. We know that whoever was denounced in the demes as non-

Athenian could appeal to a tribunal of the polis, at the risk, if the judgment of the deme's assembly was confirmed by the civil judges, of losing his citizenship and even his freedom. Sold as a slave, the dispossessed Athenian could contemplate at leisure the rigor in matters of citizenship of those he had considered his fellow citizens.

Inversely, the condition of a foreigner declared as such was protected from the moment when, residing permanently in Attic territory, he received the title of Metic. Praising the merits of the city of Athens, Pericles had good reason to contrast its characteristic openness with the expulsions of strangers which were a property of the Spartans.[10] It is true that a Metic was subject to a personal tax, could not take legal action but had to have an Athenian "patron" do it for him, could not acquire land, and had no political rights; it is also true that the murder of a Metic was classified as only involuntary homicide or manslaughter, yet significant that it was still recognized as a form of homicide. It is also significant that a Metic could, under certain conditions, be exempted from the special tax. Moreover, what becomes of his radical "political exclusion" when we know that in 415 one of the *hetaireiai* implicated in the political unrest had a Metic at its head? Finally these resident strangers, subjected as were wealthy citizens to the required generosities known as liturgies, were hardly liable to complain, for through this constraint, like that of the war tax and service in the army, they acquired limited but incontestable integration into the city. As for Athenian democracy, it had need of Metics for the many services they rendered the citizen-body, and in no wise was it content merely to tolerate their presence. It actively encouraged it. In a word, "the *polis* of the citizens could not exist without the presence of strangers."[11]

But it must be added that as regards citizenship, Athenian democracy did not always enforce such rigor with equal firmness throughout its existence. To take a good century of the democracy's history, from the reforms of Cleisthenes in 508 to the return of the *dêmos* after the dictatorship of the Thirty in the last years of the fifth century, several fluctuations may be observed which would certainly contradict the impression of linearity one is quick to receive by comparing the Cleisthenian opening-up of the political spectrum with the very strict redefinition of citizenship by the restored democracy. I am not going to offer a detailed examination of these fluctuations, which certainly cannot be reduced to the decree of Pericles in 451–450 which redefined citizenship along stricter lines,[12] and though I stick to the two extremities of this temporal sequence, the stakes are clearly visible in both, despite the different stands.

Cleisthenian reform then, as described in Aristotle's *Politics* under "civic right acquired after a constitutional change:" "[. . .] as did Cleisthenes in Athens after the expulsion of the tyrants; for he incorporated many strangers and Metic slaves into the tribes."[13]

Whatever the reservations Aristotle formulated regarding such a "fabrication" of citizenship, the philosopher gave the essential: *in the beginning* (in the earliest period of the democracy), *political* integration. And in the same author's *Athenian Constitution*, he mentions the "new citizens" whom Cleisthenes "mixed" in with the people "in order to have more people participating in civic rights." Things begin, then, under the sign of openness.

At the other end it is the desire for closure that predominates. But once again, this does not signify an ineluctable evolution, from "generosity" to "avarice," since the period under consideration was divided in deliberately symbolic fashion between two "tyrant"-overthrows, not to mention any of the multiple stages which constitute the process in its complexity.

After the fall of the Thirty Tyrants and the restoration of democracy, two politicians are in confrontation although officially allied: Thrasybulos, who reassembled the exiled democrats at the fort of Phyle in the northern confines of Attica and then led them to Piraeus, reputedly more democratic than the city of Athens itself, held by the oligarchs and their partisans. It was then from Piraeus that, after the defeat of the oligarchs and various other vicissitudes, he finally brought them back to the city to make a solemn and triumphal entrance. And Archinos, who was also said to be at Phyle. The first, a hardened democrat, the second—a moderate; but Paul Cloché, author of a recognized work on the democratic restoration, considers the latter, not unreasonably, to be a "moderate aristocrat." Shortly after the battle of Munichia, in which the democratic forces defeated the Athenians based in the city, Thrasybulos, according to Xenophon, promised *isoteleia* (fiscal equality, i.e., tax exemption) to all the non-Athenian combatants in his army, "even if they were mere strangers"—which means: if they weren't even Metics.[14] What happened next is not recorded by the historian, but in any case Aristotle says much more, not only concerning *isoteleia* for Metics and foreigners, but also concerning a decree of Thrasybulos giving citizenship to everyone from Piraeus, "of whom some were clearly slaves."[15] Enter Archinos, a good politician says Aristotle (meaning good at chipping away sharp corners), who attacks the decree on the basis of illegality. Under threat of direst prosecution, Thrasybulos withdraws his proposition, and honest men breathe a sigh of relief.

We know the sequel: that even the Metics received for the most part merely symbolic recompense for their adherence to democracy, and Lysias, who participated at Piraeus, a staunch partisan of democracy, only *isoteleia*, when he had nearly become an Athenian citizen. But it is true that he dared attack the memory of Theramenes, praised to the skies by "moderates" like Archinos for, despite being one of the Thirty, having opposed Critias, proponent of strong-arm tactics. In opposition to the more hardline oligarchs, who distributed among themselves the property of Metics who had been executed and called for a drastic reduction of the civic body, Theramenes argued for a more discrete reduction, which would reserve citizenship "for those moderates who are able to defend the city with their horse or shield."[16]

In short, in 403 Thrasybulos tried to act like another Cleisthenes,[17] but Archinos restrained him in the name of those moderates who had openly acclaimed the "constitution of Cleisthenes"[18] during the oligarchic episode of 411, in which they participated, as if by enlarging the scope of citizenship from the outset, the founder of democracy had actually closed it for the future as early as 508. One appreciates the nuance. And one should not credit Archinos with opinions that are overly democratic. . . .

In Xenophon's version Theramenes, defending himself against the attacks of Critias, declares "never to have ceased from making war on those who think that good (*kalên*) democracy is impossible without slaves, and those who out of wretchedness sell their country for a drachma, sharing in government."[19] There is no doubt that the final periphrasis applies to the poor, those whose census category is that of the *thêtes*, serfs, who provide democracy with its broad foundation and who are the first to be excluded from full citizenship by the oligarchic powers-that-be. As for the mention of slaves, it appears quite likely that Xenophon, reconstructing the oligarch's speech against his rival Critias after the fact, slipped it in as a tacit allusion to the arguments, beyond the text, of Archinos against Thrasybulos.

There was then at least one democrat to hold such a view, purely circumstantially besides: democracy regained, according to Thrasybulos, should reward those who served it well. But it also happens that oligarchs attribute similar intentions to all democracies at all times; therefore they push the analysis of the detested regime well beyond the strict definition which guarantees its stability. Democracy then becomes ideologically unbalanced—politically this is merely good strategy—and is henceforward supposed to encompass all noncitizens. If this was Theramenes' strategy, defending himself before an audience of diehard oligarchs, it wasn't bad. But it is the overall problem that interests me, because it is here that we come upon strangers once again.

This begins in the second half of the fifth century, with an anonymous Athenian oligarch whose satirical pamphlet was mistakenly incorporated into the Xenophontic corpus.[20] Nothing, according to this personage, permits one to socially distinguish slaves and Metics from the ordinary people in Athens (just as badly dressed and educated); hence the impunity enjoyed by the former. Especially since slaves row in the ships just like citizens: how could the latter make themselves feared by the former? And he insists on equality of speech (*isêgoria*) which in a democratic city obtains between the free and the enslaved, between citizens and Metics, "because the polis needs Metics, owing to the many jobs that need doing and also the fleet. This is why, for Metics also, we have established equality of speech."[21]

Slyly, the author of this text uses the purely political term *isêgoria* to designate the exchange among equals which was a marked characteristic of Athenian life. It does the trick. But if there is a trick involved, it must derive from a highly elaborated construction in which Athenian democracy is conceived as wholly conscious of itself,[22] governed down to the smallest details of everyday life by a purely political project. As if to be a logically minded oligarch meant to construct a more coherent democracy—could I say more modern?—than the Athenian regime ever really was.

Could we say that the oligarchs were clairvoyant, that they saw a possible extension of democracy? Or that they simply misrepresented in order to criticize more easily? In the first hypothesis, the political adversary *sees* (this is what makes an authentic adversary) everything which is not visible to the partisan; under the circumstances he sees that democracy—here is perhaps one of the transhistorical components of this political form—is only virtually thinkable, never completed, and always to come. I confess to inclining toward this hypothesis, even knowing that slavery for some was the condition of liberty for others, even if I was able to show that autochthonous ideology tended to present strangers as "wooden patches" even in their own city,[23] in Athens above all. In the second hypothesis, which is perhaps more likely, one insists on the purely oligarchic—or at least aristocratic—character of this image of Greek democracy. But must one really choose? After all, hatred makes one see, before it mobilizes the imagination.

Adversaries of democracy were certainly not all visionaries, but they knew "their" democracy well and knew that a climate of liberty induced political satisfaction.[24] It is Plato's reflections on the extravagances of liberty that are most illuminating. There one discovers that, as in Pseudo-Xenophon, the germ of all laxity is in egalitarian excess; but this time the list of relationships contaminated by democratic equality seems exhaustive, as one successively encounters the relationship between father and son, Metic (stranger, even) and citizen, young and old, teachers and pupils, and, the summit of all conception, between the free and the enslaved, between men and women—this last form of equality receiving the appellation *isonomia* ("equal participation"), just as completely political as that of *isêgoria*, discussed above.[25] That Plato goes on to see manifestations of this unbridled liberty in animals is an indication that criticism is dominant in this ironical passage; but it is just as true that all the pairs called to bear witness to the democratic penchant for erasing hierarchies which the philosopher wishes to uphold, are, here and there in the dialogues, important operators in the Platonic text, and it is of relevance to my hypothesis that that of Metic and citizen adjoins that most crucial of father and son.

We must proceed: one may well hesitate between the two hypotheses mentioned, but it is incontestable that this discourse on democracy envisages the roundup of all "exclusions," and more precisely for what interests us here, that of the dissymmetry between citizen and stranger.

Other times, other strategies. To better discredit Athenian democracy among the Greeks, its adversaries credited it with the tendency to be excessive that for modern democrats characterizes the very essence of democracy. Contemporary adversaries of democracy on the other hand exalt the intransigent closure of a Greek democracy according to their own lights, a model they try to turn against the current partisans of a democratic regime.

Which brings me to a most burning contemporary issue. Is there a potential relationship between Athenian democracy and the question of the integration or exclusion of immigrants in France in the 1990s? An affirmative answer is possible if one chooses to analyze the work of Cleisthenes as a foundational integration of strangers into the city.[26] The National Front responds equally in the affirmative, but in order to disqualify from the outset any contemporary prospect of integration; this way they reap the routing of their adversaries as a benefit of the operation. To this end the theoreticians of the party estimate it better not to encumber themselves unduly with rigorous historical analyses and, without considering the structure of a Greek city of Antiquity, to clamor that Western tradition begins with discrimination.

Finley was decidedly right: nothing should ever excuse the historian from *explaining*. This is why I chose to pursue—lengthily perhaps—the preceding Greek odyssey in its entirety, without evading opacities and difficulties, and without concession to *idées reçues*. And with the hope that the reader will perceive everything that, in reference to Greek practices of the classical era, made Athenian democracy a regime of openness, which it is not wise to consider—and still less to use—without taking account of the distance that, in the face of Antiquity, is necessarily ours.

No doubt precautions were conspicuously taken in the discourse of the National Front to hide behind the authority of a recognized historian. For thereby everything is permitted in the practice of "history," from trickery to force by way of deliberate omission.

Twenty-Five Centuries of Tradition?

On May 2, 1990, during a session of the National Assembly devoted, according to the *Journal Officiel*, to the struggle against racism, anti-Semitism, and xenophobia, the lone representative of the National Front in the Assembly, Marie-France Stirbois, delivered a speech on ancient Greece on the occasion of an exceptional proceeding of inadmissability presented by her party.[27] Or more precisely on "the first democracies, the true democracies," characterized by their knowledge of "necessary discrimination" between strangers and citizens (p. 910). The sophistication of the lecture and the abundance of information it exhibited seemed designed to present this information as a history lesson.

For whom remains to be seen.

This lesson, which to judge by their reactions one could well imagine as useful in terms of general culture for a good number of the deputies, did not have the unique aim of raising the cultural level of the Assembly, especially since under the circumstances—an evening session which promised to be lengthy—those present were not up for long discourses on ancient Greece. Therefore it is open to doubt whether the real target of the speech was the deputies: it was less a matter of convincing these whom the past apparently did not greatly concern than of occupying the floor in the name of the National Front, credited on this occasion with all the external signs of culture. The gap between the learned tone of the lecture and the much more colloquial style of Marie-France Stirbois' contributions to the debates suggests that the speaker was not the author of what she had merely to read, which was in fact assembled by a member of the Science Council of her party (later in the evening a deputy brought up the name of M. Le Gallou [p. 935]). One surmises that this "speech" did not encounter its sole intended audience in the Assembly. I view it as a multipurpose text whose scientific— therefore authoritative—character was directed toward the intellectual accreditation of the position of the National Front on immigration and immigrants in the France of the 1990s. It is in this light, to the extent that it is an indirect yet effective intervention in the French politico-intellectual debate, that I treat the text as a document which merits detailed examination from within my own field of expertise.

The strategy is clear: it consists of staking a claim just where the Left assumes it is on home ground. Athens invented democracy; "you make constant reference in your report to the legislators of 1789" (p. 909); but these "were inspired by thinkers who derived their political ideal from the precepts of ancient Greece"; yet the ancient Greeks preached discrimination between foreigners and citizens; therefore you are caught in self-contradiction. These are the broad lines of reasoning repeated ad nauseam in the speech.

A cunning strategy certainly, even perverse: mounted against contemporary adherents of democracy, Athenian democracy is seen as providing the National Front with the authority of "twenty-five centuries of judicial and political tradition" (p. 909–910). Hence it is called to testify against itself—we will see how the speech does exactly this—that throughout Antiquity law and political philosophy proclaim with one voice the radical exclusion of strangers. Let us imagine a recipient who knows nothing of ancient Greece: how could he fail to conclude that Greek democracy was exactly what the speech says it was, a regime of discrimination? This would be effective; and perhaps particularly so if some well-intentioned individual were to arrive to complicate things with a basic, straightforward question after a quick read-through: "Was ancient Greece of the extreme Right?"[28] I would like to claim that it is never too late for the historian, even if false problems arrive to complicate his or her task additionally, to reestablish the primacy of the necessity to understand, by submitting to a critical reading constructions which claim to be history.

A little historiography to start with—nothing is more effective against the temptation of hasty generalizations. A thinker of the extreme French Right in the first decades of the twentieth century, Charles Maurras certainly did not pretend to praise democracy the better to condemn it. His route was direct: he abhorred democracy, Athenian or French, and the first as a model for the second which allowed him to speak of the "French demos"; but he understood the character of the ruling idea, declaring "Democracy is not a fact. It is an idea."[29] And although his declarations concerning foreigners resemble those of the National Front,[30] at least he did not feel the need to call on Athenian democracy as reinforcement for his pronouncements. You might say that with a Maurras the dispositions are clear.

But there is nothing more underhanded than praise which aims to compromise.

Let us return to the present. Announcing an appreciation "of the dispositions taken at Athens at the height of the golden age of its democracy," the speaker knew that she would elicit protests, and in fact she got them, from the Communist benches. To which she could respond (an easy shot) "*You* always turn to democracy. To proceed" (p. 909). And cited the decree of Pericles of 451–450 which refused citizenship to "whoever was not born of two citizens." But Aristotle, who reports this, justifies the measure by "the growing number of citizens"[31] which threatened to reduce the share due to each, through the Greek principle of redistributing surplus among all group members. It is hardly surpris-

ing that this democratic explanation was not retained in the speech of
Marie-France Stirbois[32]—it is true that the Aristotle she cites here and
there is not that of the *Athenian Constitution*, who was no doubt considered too much the historian for these purposes.

But the essential wellspring of the speech is the reference, at its center, to Gustave Glotz, "member of the Institute and eminent Hellenist"
(p. 909). This is weighty intellectual backing, a little archaic perhaps, but
certain to impress the hearer, even the nonspecialist reader who could
not be expected to keep track of the highly particular uses which, without naming him again, the speaker makes of Glotz's work.

Now, since the choice concerns precisely the historian's identity as
witness for the prosecution, it is a very calculated one: what could be
cleverer on the part of a National Front theoretician than using Glotz, a
highly integrated Jew and representative of the state-supported science
of the Third Republic,[33] against the very object which engaged all his
sympathies? Glotz against Greek democracy: even "deportees in the past,
Jews, men of the left [. . .]" will be cited as defense witnesses in favor
of revisionism—defended, we note, as a likely characteristic of "all genuine historical proceedings" (p. 931). We have seen this strategy before:
Athenian democracy against democracy, Jews (or Jewish *names*[34]) against
any antirevisionist measure, Glotz against Athenian democracy.[35] Of
course between ancient Athens and the reality of Nazi extermination,
the stakes will rightly seem disproportionate. Nevertheless the aim is one
and the same: turn the other against his/her staunchest ally, and baptize
this operation in the name of historical research.

As for the content of the argument, the source is clear: *La Cité grecque*,
a classic work published in 1928 and several times reissued, from which
the author of the speech derived his inspiration, borrowing or carefully
lifting entire sentences from it. Except that, a not insignificant point (yet
one which only comparative reading will reveal), only descriptive sentences expressing facts are borrowed. For the generous and republican
interpretations of Glotz, radically opposed conclusions are substituted
("Discrimination, certainly, always discrimination" [p. 909]).

A few examples and a little *explication de texte* will make this clear.

An extract from p. 271 of *La Cité grecque*: "Within each city, foreigners had only severely limited rights, even if their condition was determined not only by law, but by treaty, even if they were permanently established in the city as Metics [. . .]"

And the version of the same sentence in the National Front speech: "One must in effect be aware that in each city foreigners could only claim rights that were strictly limited, even in fact when their condition happened to be permanently determined by treaties, even in fact when they were permanently established in the city as foreigners" (p. 909).

Let us pass over the rhetorical inflation of "even in fact when" from "even if"; this will be deemed "style." More difficult to pass over the word "claim," which, on the part of foreigners residing within another city, suggests the desire for a second citizenship besides their own, contradicting the attachment on principle manifested by the Athenian Metics toward their city of origin, which alone deserved in their eyes the name of fatherland[36] (Glotz was certainly aware of this, speaking more soberly of "having rights"). We might also add that the existence of a foreigners' "claim" implies a systematic repugnance on the part of the cities toward according these limited rights. Glotz justly recalls that they were established *by law*, yet all mention of law has disappeared from the National Front version, the better to increase the scope of the discrimination. But this is not all; speaking of missing words, there is another absence even more remarkable: the word "Metic," naturally recurrent in Glotz's technical treatment, has disappeared from the imitation. I am willing to bet that its systematic application to Jews in the 1930s has made it embarrassing, to the point that even where it would be topical its use is avoided. An excessive precaution in the elimination of traces, reminding us that the National Front boasts of not being anti-semitic.

Let us continue our exercise in comparative reading. Through the voice of Marie-France Stirbois, it is established that "although there existed rudimentary treaties for right of asylum, we must be aware that the right of pleading a case was a prerogative in principle reserved to citizens" (p. 909), which sends us back to *La Cité grecque* (p. 274): "Through these rudimentary treaties of asylum, the Greek cities learnt to conclude real treaties of private international law, *symbolai* or *symbola*. The great difficulty arose from the right to plead a court case being in principle reserved to citizens."

Already where the first formulation supposes an extra restriction, Glotz's analysis valorizes the treaties, revealing a project of imposing limits to the civic exclusivity of each local right.[37] Moving on, the special magistrate under whose jurisdiction the Metics were placed was for Glotz a "solution" to the above-mentioned "great difficulty"; in the National Front version this becomes a pure mark of discrimination, as implied by the rest of the sentence: "The old constitutional law placed them in general under the jurisdiction of a special magistrate and *a supplementary distinction was made* concerning foreigners in temporary residence" (p. 909; my italics).

Discrimination, then, "always discrimination"; the slogan finds a natural place in the rhetoric of Mme Stirbois, while Glotz's account rightly insists on Athenian concern with taking the law into account in every situation, as well as the varied role of the different categories of "foreigners"—"not to assimilate [all foreigners in temporary residence] as Metics residentially established in the territory," but not to treat Metics "as judicially of the rank of citiens" (p. 275). A simple matter of point of view? I don't believe so. To each his specific right: this is the lesson the historian draws from the facts; with the nationalist theoretician we are far from this, because the imitation has distorted the facts in the service of a systematic explanation by discrimination.

The republicanism of Glotz's choices may have led him, elsewhere in *La Cité grecque*, to some frankly anachronistic interpretations, owing to his dreaming of an Athens which would have gone beyond its natural limits (for example, concerning the citizenship given the men of Samos in 405, or when in his final flight, he suggests that without "the Macedonian phalanx [which] halted everything," Athens would have started down the road of abolition);[38] but the oligarchic extrapolations of democracy said just that, and whatever the explanation that one gives, the important point is that such a discourse might have been upheld by the Greeks.

The deliberate rejection of all historical perspective, however, is corrupt in principle, and this is what results from insisting on praising for its politics of exclusion a regime that all Greek writers, all opinions heaped together whether for praise or condemnation, considered as the constitution "most common to all." At this point therefore I must turn to the treatment reserved in the National Front speech for the Greek texts themselves.

Because one must be in command of Western political philosophy in its entirety if one declares it to be unique and unchanging for twenty-five centuries, it is the philosophical texts that are most sought after, and it is to them that I limit this brief examination.

Greek philosophers as the bards of exclusion might be surprising, even if one is not a reader of Glotz.[39] But Marie-France Stirbois insists on it: "Discrimination is inherent in our history and finds its first expression with the dawn of thought." She quotes Heraclitus that "what is opposite is useful, and it is out of struggle that the most beautiful harmony is born." But once again, the distortion occurs in the interpretation: if "know thine enemy" is indeed "an eminently political act," rather than Heraclitus it is Carl Schmitt who should be quoted, in whose thought one is hardly concerned to give "harmony" its very Greek meaning of "tension maintained in equilibrium."[40] Aristotle? He is cited initially: a passage from book five of the *Politics* on the absence of ethnic community as a civil war hazard, without its being anywhere mentioned that among the eleven causes of *stasis* listed in the same book, that one occupies only the *tenth* and penultimate position. The lifting of quotations drastically stripped of their context is a common practice, and the National Front is not alone in this; but Aristotle thus portrayed appears truncated, not to say rigged. Against mention of the Syracusans, who suffered civil war after having awarded right of the city to foreigners and mercenaries after the tyranny, we can point to the reforms of Cleisthenes, which in analogous conditions inaugurated in Athens an enduring political stability. As for the Aristotle who, in the *Politics*, repeats too often that one cannot make a city out of like elements because total homogeneity can never create a single unity, he is unknown—and with good reason—to the National Front.

Is it truly necessary to pile on the examples? There is the treatment meted out to the architect Hippodamos of Miletus, who divided urban space into three city "parties," yet who became via this made-to-measure Greece a theoretician concerned with the threat of danger from abroad (p. 909).[41] And to demonstrate conclusively that Greek thinkers "profoundly refused to consider the equality (*sic*) of citizens and strangers," the speaker also quoted the Plato of the *Laws*, even more radical, said she, for being preoccupied with the fact that "the citizens avoided contacts with foreigners" since he established his city at a distance from commercial and maritime thoroughfares. But book four of the *Laws*, which she is surely alluding to, denounces the proximity of the sea as a "brackish and debilitating neighborhood," while there is no explicit mention of foreigners, and everything has to do with "unstable and dishonest habits" or "men of all kinds" (*pantodapoi*), traditional designation for the last category of the *dêmos*.[42] Whence it appears that as with Hippodamos, it is in fact only a matter of containing citizens of the last class within limits that should not be transgressed. No question of foreigners. Rather it is forcing, or better yet falsifying, the texts to find in them at all costs the obsessive fear of the stranger, not by any means a ruling passion. On this point intellectual honesty demands the recognition that "the philosophers [admit] the necessity of the foreign element in the city for its economic life, even if they are wary on principle of unhealthy influences which might result from contact with the outside world."[43] But in this rhapsodic and repetitive disquisition, was there ever a question of some sort of honesty?

Some of the *découpage* performed on the Greek material is very crudely done. Using a single line from the text of one of the most critical of the tragedians, the *Iphigeneia* of Euripides, and out of context yet again, the speaker quotes, "it is in the order of things that Greeks command Barbarians." It is no doubt pointless to linger on the abrasive irony of Euripides when the purpose of the quotation is solely to allow Marie-France Stirbois to say that she is "much less excessive." But crudity approaches the sinister when the conclusion begins on p. 911, with the "timidity" of the "demands of the National Front," compared to the "imperatives of the classics." With a final dash of "Japanese culture" (without further explanation), and an appeal to the *Mahabharata* on behalf of the caste system applied to race, with supporting remarks by Alain Daniélou, even while emphasizing how much this audacious leap beyond Europe proves that the "National Front has open ideas," the argument concludes.

The "Greece" then to which the National Front lays claim is but a caricature of the Greece studied by historians of Antiquity. Need I state that I am speaking of *classical* Greece? And that, working on Athens, I have no intention of abandoning to the National Front the city of Cleisthenes and Thrasybulos, turning instead to seemingly more relevant and fashionable objects of study such as Hellenistic, Roman, and Christian Greece, not to mention Rome.[44] It is certainly wrong "to limit Greece [. . .] to the classical period [. . .] whose center is Athens," as we are virtuously reminded.[45] But beyond the fact that historians of Antiquity have not waited on this advice before studying other periods, or investigating Argos, Gortyna, Olbia, or Miletus in the classical period, one is wary of hasty readings that counsel the rejection of Athenian democracy. Which rejection amounts, in the end, to following the devious suggestion made to partisans of democracy by a national-populist party well versed in the adage: plant a suspicion, and something of it will always remain.

It is not that the task of the historian of classical Greece is simple, particularly if he or she is interested in matters of the present. Against those liberal thinkers who consider all politics worthy of the name to originate with Machiavelli (as if references to Antiquity in his work were not ubiquitous) or Kant even' (more secure, they reckon), the historian claims the intellectual virtues of an even more distant regard which would discover in ancient Greece some of the Greek problems of present-day democracy. But such a position does not imply that one thereby refuses to take into consideration the relays and ruptures, the actual paths of transmission—to "forget" medieval culture would be a gross error,—and the irruption of the new. If one must, on the other hand, leave something to the thinkers of the extreme Right, it is certainly the illusion, conscious or no, of a Greece where we would be born, of a permanence without discontinuity of the "Western" tradition through twenty-five centuries.

There is work to be done. For historians presently, this means combating each in his or her own field everything which is error and falsification. To do history: this is no doubt the best response to false historians who counterfeit interest only in order to disqualify its methods and its very idea. In short, to act in the domain of thought, reminding of the imprescriptible or irrevocable right of what has existed to be understood, above all, in its own time. With the hope that readers will themselves deduce that those who falsify ancient artifacts are just those who, more generally, are given to the falsification of the history of the present.[46]

Notes

Chapter 1. At Last, Born Mortal

1. Plato *Politics* 270e–271c. (These pages were written at the invitation of Yves Bonnefoy, for his *Dictionnaire des mythologies* [Paris, 1981]).

2. See J.-P. Vernant, "Work and Nature in Ancient Greece," in *Myth and Thought among the Greeks* (London/Boston, 1983).

3. C. Bérard, *Anodoi* (Neuchâtel, Rome: Institut Suisse de Rome, Bibliotheca Helvetica Romana 13, 1974): 32.

4. Hesiod *Works and Days* 145.

5. Plato *Menexenus* 238a; A. Dieterich, *Mutter Erde* (Leipzig, 1913).

6. Plato *Statesman* 269b.

7. F. Dupont, "Se reproduire ou se métamorphoser," *Topiques* 9–10 (1972): 139–160.

8. Pausanias 2.15.5; Apollodorus *Bibliotheca* 2.1.1.

9. Hesiod *Theogony* 187.

10. M. Detienne, "Dionysos mis à mort . . . ," *Annali della Scuola Normale Superiore di Pisa* 4 (1974): 1213–1216; reprinted in *Dionysos mis à mort* (Paris, 1977).

11. *Odyssey* 19.162–163.

12. Plato *Apology* 34d.

13. *Works and Days* 106–201.

14. P. Vidal-Naquet, "Plato's Myth of the *Statesman*, the Ambiguities of the Golden Age and of History," in *The Black Hunter: Forms of Thought and Forms of Society in the Greek World*, trans. Andrew Szégedy-Maszak (Baltimore, 1986), 287. Also in the same volume the chapter entitled "Land and Sacrifice in the *Odyssey*: A Study of Religious and Mythical Meanings," 15ff.

15. *Works and Days* 110, 128, 144, 158.

16. See for example *Theogony* 372, 564, 755.

17. Ibid., 879; *Homeric Hymn to Demeter* 352.

18. G. Dumézil, *Le Festin d'immortalité: Esquisse d'une étude de mythologie comparée indoeuropéenne* (Paris, 1924), xv–xvi.

19. *Etymologicum magnum*, s.v. "*Ikonion*."

20. Euripides *Suppliants* 531–536.

21. Empedocles frag. 454, ed. Bollack; Plato *Protagoras* 320d.

22. J.-P. Vernant, "Prometheus and the Technological Function," in *Myth and Thought*, 238; in the same volume see the pages devoted to the "Hesiodic myth of the races," 3ff. and 33ff.

23. *Works and Days* 108; Pindar *Nemean* 6.1f.

24. Hesiod frag. 1, ed. Merkelbach-West.

25. *Theogony* 556, and for the following, 567–570.

26. J.-P. Vernant "Le Mythe prométhéen chez Hésiode," in *Mythe et société en Grèce ancienne* (Paris, 1974), 192–193 (repub. 1992).

27. Euripides *Medea* 573–575; *Hippolytus* 618ff. For the following, *Theogony* 591, 588–589, and 592.

28. F. Frontisi-Ducroux, *Dédale: Mythologie de l'artisan en Grèce ancienne* (Paris, 1975), 73 and 102.

29. *Theogony* 572; *Works and Days* 71.

30. *Iliad* 18.417–420.

31. L. Séchan, "Pandora, l'Ève grecque," *BAGB* (April 1929): 5.

32. M. Guarducci, "Leggende dell'antica Grecia relative all'origine dell'umanità e analoghe tradizioni di altri paesi," in *Atti della Reale Accademia Nazionale dei Lincei* (1927): 379–458, and in particular 436ff.; E. Simon, "Pandora," in *Enciclopedia dell'arte antica classica e orientale* (1963) 5: 930–933.

33. Plato *Symposium* 190b. See L. Brisson, "Bisexualité et médiation en Grèce ancienne," *Nouvelle Revue de Psychanalyse* 7 (1973): 27–48.

34. "La Structure des mythes," in *Anthropologie structurale*, vol. 1 (Paris, 1958), 239.

35. See, for example, Aristophanes *Thesmophoriasuzae* 786ff.

36. Aeschylus *Seven against Thebes* 182–201. On the "race of women," cf. N. Loraux, *Children of Athena: Athenian Ideas about Citizenship and the Division between the Sexes*, trans. Caroline Levine (Princeton, 1993), 72ff.

37. Pausanias 8.1.4.

38. Thus L. Preller in *Philologus* 7 (1852): 1–60.

39. *Theogony* 563.

40. Aeschylus *Eumenides* 13.

41. *Iliad* 2.549.

42. Pausanias 2.15.5.

43. C. Lévi-Strauss, *Les Structures élémentaires de la parenté* (rev. ed., Paris, 1968), 53–54.

44. Pausanias 2.15.5, and for the following, 2.19.5.

45. Despite Plato *Menexenus* 237d7.

46. According to Pausanias 1.14.2.

47. Hesiod frag. 2, 4, 6 and 234, ed. Merkelbach-West; Acusilaus, *F. Gr. Hist.* 2, frag. 34–35; Pindar *Olympian* 9.41ff.

48. Apollonius of Rhodes *Argonautica* 3.1085–1086.

49. For example, *Iliad* 2.308ff.

50. *Metamorphoses* 1.393–394.

51. Pindar *Olympian* 9.44.

Chapter 2. The Benefits of Autochthony

1. On the Theban tradition see Francis Vian, *Les Origines de Thèbes: Cadmos et les Spartes* (Paris, 1963). (This chapter first appeared in the revue *Le Genre Humain* 3–4 [1982]: 238–253.)

2. Herodotus 2.171; the Arcadian tradition has been studied by P. Borgeaud in his *Recherches sur le dieu Pan* (Geneva, Rome: Institut Suisse de Rome, Bibliotheca Helvetica Romana 17, 1979): 41–69. See also Chapter 4, below.

3. A completely inverted order of values dominated the discourse of colonization in the nineteenth century. Then it was the invader who told the story; assigning himself the role of civilizer, he spoke of autochthonous populations with amused condescension.

4. Quotation from Emile Benveniste, "Expression indo-européenne de l'éternité," *Bulletin de la Société de Linguistique* 38 (1937): 111.

5. See Nicole Loraux, *The Invention of Athens: The Funeral Oration in the Classical City*, trans. Alan Sheridan (Cambridge, Mass., 1986).

6. See Chapter 11, below.

7. See the article by C. Mossé, "Citoyens actifs et citoyens passifs dans les cités grecques," *Revue des Études Anciennes* 81 (1979): 241–249.

8. On the reforms of Cleisthenes, the basic source is that of P. Lévêque and P. Vidal-Naquet, *Clisthène l'Athénien: Essai sur la représentation de l'espace et du temps dans la pensée politique grec de la fin du vi⁰ siècle à la mort de Platon* (Paris, 1964; rev. 1983 and 1992).

9. I developed this analysis and that of the notion of "race of women" in *Children of Athena: Athenian Ideas about Citizenship and the Division between the Sexes* (Princeton, 1993).

10. The Greek formulation of this idea (as in Aristotle, for example) speaks of generation and corruption; on the "time of men," see P. Vidal-Naquet, *The Black Hunter: Forms of Thought and Forms of Society in the Greek World*, (Baltimore, 1986), 39–60.

Chapter 3. The Politics of Myth in Athens

1. These pages were written at the invitation of Yves Bonnefoy for his *Dictionnaire des mythologies* (Paris, 1981).

2. Critias frag. 25, Diels-Kranz (DK).

3. Concerning myth in the polis see especially: M. I. Finley, *Myth and Tragedy* (New York, 1988); M. P. Nilsson, *Cults, Myths, Oracles, and Politics in Ancient Greece* (New York, 1972); J.-P. Vernant and P. Vidal-Naquet, *Mythe et tragédie en Grèce ancienne* (Paris, 1972); P. Vidal-Naquet, "Slavery and the Rule of Women in Tradition, Myth, and Utopia," in *The Black Hunter: Forms of Thought and Forms of Society in the Greek World* (Baltimore, 1986), 205–223.

4. See, for example, Apollodorus 3.14.1; St. Augustine *City of God* 18.9.

5. Aeschylus *Eumenides* 736–738.

6. Apollodorus 3.14.6.

7. H. Metzger, "Athéna soulevant de terre le nouveau-né," in *Mélanges Paul Collart* (Lausanne, 1976).

8. Jacoby, *F. Gr. Hist.*, 323a F 2 and 324 F 2.

9. See Apollodorus 3.14.1 and 6 and Pausanias 1.18.2.

10. The Berlin Cup: ARV², 1268.2. See F. Brommer, "Attische Könige," in *Mélanges Langlotz* (Bonn, 1957), 152–164.

11. See Plutarch *Life of Theseus*. On this hero cf. J.-P. Vernant, "Some Aspects of Personal Identity in Greek Religion," in *Myth and Thought among the Greeks* (London/Boston, 1983), 327–328. For Theseus in Athens: H. Herter, "Theseus der Athener," *Rheinisches Museum für Philologie* (1939): 244–286 and 289–326; H. Jeanmaire, *Couroi et courètes* (Lille-Paris, 1939), 18–21 and chapter 4: "Attika: Les origines rituelles de la geste de Thésée"; C. P. Kardara, "On Theseus and the Tyrannicides," *American Journal of Archaeology* 55

(1951): 293–300; M. P. Nilsson, "Political Propaganda in Sixth Century Athens," in *Mélanges Robinson*, vol. 2 (Saint Louis, 1953), 743–748; A. J. Podlecki, "Cimon, Skyros, and Theseus Bones," *Journal of Hellenic Studies* 71 (1971): 141–143; P. Vidal-Naquet, "An Enigma at Delphi," in *The Black Hunter*, 302–324.

12. For a few indications on Athenian myths see Marcel Detienne, "L'Olivier: Un mythe politico-religieux," in *Problèmes de la terre en Grèce ancienne* (Paris, 1973), 293–306, also in *l'Écriture d'Orphée* (Paris, 1989), 71–84; A. Ermatinger, *Die attische Autochthonensage* (Berlin, 1897); Nicole Loraux, *The Invention of Athens: The Funeral Oration in the Classical City* (Cambridge, Mass., 1986); J. Rudhardt, "Une approche de la pensée mythique: Le mythe considéré comme un langage" (1966), *Du mythe, de la religion grecque et de la compréhension d'autrui* (Geneva, 1981), 105–129 (*Revue Européenne des Sciences Sociales* 19, no. 58).

13. Euripides *Medea* 824–828.

14. Lysias *Funeral Oration* 4–5.

15. Pausanias 1.15.2.

16. Francis Vian, *La Guerre des géants* (Paris, 1952), 250.

17. Lysias *Funeral Oration* 17.

18. Plato *Menexenus* 239A.

19. Pausanias 1.14.6.

20. Euripides *Ion*271.

21. Demosthenes *Funeral Oration* 27–31.

22. Pausanias 1.1–29.

23. *Ion* 495–496.

24. Plato *Lysis* 203A–B; *Phaedrus* 227A.

25. *Phaedrus* 227A; Pausanias 1.32.6 and 37.4.

26. Nilsson, *Cults, Myths, Oracles, and Politics*, 12–15.

27. Pausanias 1.14.2; Herodotus 9.27.

28. P. Lévêque et P. Vidal-Naquet, *Clisthène l'Athénien: Essai sur la représentation de l'espace et du temps dans la pensée politique grec de la fin du vi° siècle à la mort de Platon* (Paris, 1992), 118–121.

29. "La Structure des mythes," in *Anthropologie structurale*, vol. 1 (Paris, 1958); 231.

Chapter 4. An Arcadian in Athens

1. These pages (published in 1981 in *Le Temps de la réflexion* 2: 521–528) arose from a reading of Philippe Borgeaud's *Recherches sur le dieu Pan* (Geneva, Rome: Institut Suisse de Roma, Bibliotheca Helvetica Romana 17, 1979). All parenthetical references refer to this work.

2. Herodotus 6.105–106: the herald Philippides, a citizen of Athens, who was sent to ask the Lacedaemonians' aid at the time of Marathon, encountered the god Pan on Mount Parthenion in Arcadia; the god declared himself the Athenians' friend and regretted their negligence in his regard; after the victory the Athenians established a cult to Pan.

3. See above, n. 1.

4. As a *topos* for a land which is elsewhere, Arcadia plays a role analogous to that of Scythia (cf. François Hartog, *Le Miroir d'Hérodote: Essai sur la représentation de l'autre* [Paris: 1980], 23–205), except that, unlike the Scythian elsewhere, the Arcadian is Greek.

5. Is there a notion of Arcadia which is *not* located outside the country of the "real"?

The problem of the Arcadian view of Arcadia is an important one; it is most likely that if it existed at all, it would have been a divided view, at the least.

6. Demosthenes *On the Embassy* 261.

7. Herodotus 9.26–28.

8. Text cited by Borgeaud, p. 40.

9. See P. Vidal-Naquet, "Plato's Myth of the *Statesman*, the Ambiguities of the Golden Age and of History," in *The Black Hunter: Forms of Thought and Forms of Society in the Greek World* (Baltimore, 1986), 285 301.

10. According to Plato (*Menexenus* 237e–288a), the land of Attica produced grain at the same time as man: the opposition of "the existence of milled grain" and the "existence based on acorns" recalled by Borgeaud (p. 31) parallels that of Athens and Arcadia.

Chapter 5. Glory of the Same, Prestige of the Other

1. "Autochthonous Languages" was the title of the seminar of Léon Poliakov in which I had the pleasure and honor of presenting material from this chapter (published in the review *Le Genre Humain* 21 [1990]: 115–139). With a few modifications these pages are also a reprise of a lecture given at the Facultés Universitaires Saint-Louis (Brussels) and published in the *Cahiers de l'École des Sciences Philosophiques et Religieuses* 2 (1987): 69–94.

2. Herodotus 8.144.

3. Nothing to do, however, with the central characteristic of etymology as language of the gods in Vedic thought: see C. Malamoud, *Cuire le monde: Rite et pensée dans l'Inde ancienne* (Paris, 1989), 243–249.

4. See E. Benveniste, *Vocabulaire des institutions indo-européennes, vol. 1* (Paris, 1969), 360–361 (also pp. 94 and 341).

5. *Statesman* 263d; Greeks/Barbarians: ibid., 262d–e.

6. See also Chapter 2.

7. *Politics* 3.1275b.22–25. Neither the response based on birth, implicitly rejected as unverifiable, nor that of naturalization, seen as the "fabrication" of citizens (1275b.30), could satisfy Aristotle, because in his eyes it is the question itself which is groundless: "The definition of a citizen as one born of a citizen (male or female) cannot apply to the first inhabitants or colonizers of cities" (1275b.32–34).

8. Herodotus 7.161; *Menexenus* 245c–d, with the remarks of R. Parker, "Myths of Early Athens," in *Interpretations of Greek Mythology*, ed. J. Bremmer (London, 1987), 197.

9. See N. Loraux, *The Invention of Athens: The Funeral Oration in the Classical City* (Cambridge, Mass., 1986), 145–155, and also *Children of Athena: Athenian Ideas about Citizenship and the Division between the Sexes* (Princeton, 1993).

10. Euripides *Erechtheus*, frag. 50, ed. Austin (= Lycurgus *Against Leocrates* 100), vs. 12 (*harmos ponêros*) and 13 (*logôi politês esti, tois d'ergoisin ou*). On the name, see Demosthenes *Funeral Oration* 4 (*prosagoreuomenous*), and Aristotle *Politics* 3.1275a6 (*prosêgorias*).

11. *Funeral Oration* 4; for legitimacy cf. Isocrates *Panegyricus* 24 (*gnêsios*).

12. See P. Gauthier, "Générosité romaine et avarice grecque," *Mélanges W. Seston* (Paris, 1974), 207–215.

13. In the decree of 427 according the freedom of the city to the Plateans, the clause which specifies that they can succeed neither to the hereditary (*ek genous*) priesthood nor to the archonship is explained not as a restriction on their citizenship, but as the strict ap-

plication of the law of Pericles which requires that *both* parents be Athenians. In the next generation, provided that the mother be Athenian, the problem no longer arises (see M. J. Osborne, *Naturalization in Athens*, vol. 2 [Brussels, 1982], 15, and A. Diller, *Race Mixture among the Greeks before Alexander* [Westport, Conn., 1971], 108–109.)

14. On chance: see *Politics* 3.1275a5 (*tous tugkhanontas*); on the fabrication of citizens: 1275a6 (*tous poiêtous politas*), 1275b30 (*pepoiêmenous*: Gorgias' pun rests on the official designation of magistrates as *dêmiourgoi*, in other words "craftsmen," in Larissa), 1278a31–32 (due to a lack of *gnêsioi politai*, they fabricated [*poiountai*] citizens.) See also the opposition between the citizen by birth (*genei*) and by naturalization (*poiêsei*) in Demosthenes: *Against Leptinus* 30; *Against Aristocrates* 26 and 23–24.

15. On naturalization as comparable to adoption, see F. Bourriot, *Recherches sur la nature du genos* (Paris, 1976), 212.

16. I am commenting on Isaeus 12 (*For Euphiletos*) 2: one adopts in order to have legitimate offspring, one is adopted in order to become Athenian.

17. See Benveniste, *Vocabulaire des institutions indo-européennes* 1: 327.

18. See *Panegyricus* 24 (*houtô kalôs kai gnêsiôs gegonamen*) and the verb *phuomai* in Lysias *Funeral Oration* 20, *Menexenus* 239a1–2 and Demosthenes *Funeral Oration* 4.

19. P. Chantraine, *Dictionnaire étymologique de la langue grecque* (Paris, 1968–1980), s.v. "*phulon*."

20. *Homophulos*: *Menexenus* 244a; also Thucydides 1.141.6, which refers to the understanding between *homophuloi*. *Allophulos*: among *allophuloi*, *stasis* is inevitable (see Thucydides 1.2.4 and 102.3); note also the phrase *allophulon epelthonta* designating the external invader (Thucydides 4.92.3 and 64.4), and the construct *allophulos kai polemios* (6.23.2).

21. Civil war is *emphulos* or *emphulios*: see N. Loraux, "*Oikeios polemos*: La guerra nella famiglia," *Studi Storici* 28 (1987): 5–35, n. 9–11.

22. *Politics* 2.1261a23–4 and 1263b31–35; 3.1274b39–40, 1276b40, 1277a5–6, etc.

23. Ibid., 5.1303a25–b3; this concerns colonies or poleis allowing foreigners as cofounders (*sunoikoi*) or as colonists (*epoikoi*); in each case, "the absence of a common stock contributes to instability (*stasiôtikon* [. . .] *to mê homophulon*)." As noted in Diller (*Race Mixture*, 19), this in fact applies exclusively to *Greek* populations.

24. *Politics* 4.1295b25–29; masters and slaves: 1295b21–22.

25. Hyperides *Funeral Oration* 7 develops this point (in other poleis made up of many elements, everyone has his own particular genealogy; in Athens, on the other hand, eulogizing individual lines of descent is superfluous); see also Demosthenes *Funeral Oration* 4. Do we need to be reminded that in reality many great Athenian families flattered themselves on their prestigious foreign origins, as in Herodotus 5?

26. *Menexenus* 238e–239a, whence the phrase *anômaloi politeîai*.

27. *Panathenaica* 121–124; see Loraux, "*Oikeios polemos*," 27.

28. *Epêlus*: "one who arrives, a stranger" (Chantraine, *Dictionnaire étymologique*, s.v. "*eleusomai*"); reinforced with movement: Demosthenes *Funeral Oration* 4: *tous epêludas elthontas*. See also Chapter 10, below.

29. See C. Darbo-Peschanski, "Les *Logoi* des autres dans les *Histoires* d'Hérodote," *Quaderni di Storia* 22 (1985): 105–128, as well as *Le Discours du particulier: Essai sur l'enquête hérodotéenne* (Paris, 1987), especially 113–126. On the word *autokhthôn* in Herodotus, see E. Montanari, *Il Mito dell'autoctonia: Linee di una dinamica mitico-politica ateniese* (Rome, 1981), 31–34.

30. Thucydides 1.9.2 (see also 29.3, where foreign colonists are *epêludes*.) Analogous

reasoning in Herodotus 5.65, where Kodros and Melanthos, although foreigners, become kings of Athens.

31. All these words are borrowed from the *Ion* of Euripides (813, 290, 590, 1291).

32. Herodotus 1.78 (interpretation by the Telmessians of the omen at Sardis): here the opposition is between the "child of the earth" (*gês paîda*) and the inimical stranger (*andras polemious epêludas*: Cyrus' army).

33. Tragedy readily qualifies an invader as *epêlus*: see Aeschylus *Seven against Thebes* 34, and *Persians* 243 (where Queen Atossa speaks an autochthonous language, describing the Persian army launched against Athens as *andras polemious epêludas*).

34. *Menexenus* 237b; see also at 245d the verb *sunoikein*, which is often used to denote belonging to an associated but minority community (for example Aristotle *Politics* 3.1278a 39–40, with the remarks of M. Casevitz, *Le Vocabulaire de la colonisation en grec ancien* [Paris, 1985], 201).

35. *Politics* 3.1278a35–38, quoting *Iliad* 9.648 (and 16.59); Herodotus 7.161. The etymology proposed by Wackernagel for *metanastês*, "he who lives with," agrees with Aristotle, but as Chantraine observes (*Dictionnaire étymologique*, s.v.), *meta-* seems to indicate a change of place from Homer on, and therefore *metanastês* refers to an emigrant.

36. Herodotus 2.172.

37. Ibid., 8.73.

38. Examination of the two rival models reinforces Gregory Nagy's view of the *Histories* as encoded *ainos* (*Pindar's Homer: The Lyric Possession of an Epic Past* [Baltimore, 1990]).

39. Did the Athenians feel comforted in their hostility to Thebes by the Phoenician origin of Kadmos, after the defeat at Coroneia in 447? N. H. Demand's assertion (*Thebes in the Fifth Century* [London, 1983], 53) remains unproven. More convincing is Froma Zeitlin's analysis of Thebes as a "conceptual unity," *topos* and "anti-Athens" in Athenian tragedy ("Playing the Other: Theater, Theatricality and the Feminine in Greek Drama," in *Playing the Other: Gender and Society in Classical Greek Literature* [Chicago, 1996], 341–374).

40. *Phoenissae* 638–44, with the remarks of Casevitz, *Le Vocabulaire*, 169, on the verb *katoikisai*. For the Theban myth in its entirety see F. Vian, *Les Origines de Thèbes: Cadmos et les Spartes* (Paris, 1963).

41. See Pindar *Olympian* 1.24 (same epithet in *Olympian* 9); here "Lydian" is purely laudatory.

42. One must, however, distinguish these myths of venerable origin from the tendency of cities in the Hellenistic period to search for evidence of kinship with non-Greek peoples: see D. Musti, "Sull'idea di *suggéneia* in inscrizioni greche," *Annali della Scuola Normale Superiore di Pisa* 32 (1963): 225–239.

43. Pindar *Hymns* f. 1.2, ed. Puech; *Menexenus* 245b (*sunoikousin*).

44. I'm thinking of the "beautiful shame" (*kalliston oneidos*) of Euripides in the *Phoenissae* 821.

45. Herodotus 1.171.

46. Ibid., 6.52.

47. *Pythian* 1.62–65 (*Pindothen ornumenoi*); Herodotus 8.43 (*hormêthentes*).

48. Herodotus 5.72.

49. *Pythian* 5.75 (analogous reasoning, from Tenedos to Sparta, in *Nemean* 11.33f.). The systematic use of kinship vocabulary also allows Pindar to feel at home in Aegina or in Stymphale (*Pythian* 8.99; *Olympian* 5.84).

50. Casevitz, *Le Vocabulaire*, 118–119 (on the status of the *apoikoi* in the fifth century).

51. Euripides *Bacchae* 1330–1339, 1354–1362; cf. Herodotus 5.61 and 9.42–43.

52. See Plato *Laws* III.682d–e. On Dorians and Heraclids, see, for example, M. P. Nilsson, *Cults, Myths, Oracles, and Politics in Ancient Greece* (New York, 1972), 68–72.

53. C. Duverger, on the foundation-myth of Mexico-Tenochtitlan (*L'Origine des Aztèques* [Paris, 1983], 108; see also 107–112.)

54. Aeschylus *Suppliants* 356.

55. *Metoikein*: 609. *Epêlus*: in 195 the status of *epêludes* is associated, by Danaos himself, with the condition of murderer in flight, often that of colonizing heroes; in 401, Pelasgos characterizes the strangers as *epêludas*, and it is also the word *epêlus* which, in the decree of the Argives, designates the stranger in opposition to the *enoikos* or resident (611). Note that the Danaids themselves, after invoking Zeus "of the same blood" (*Homaimôn*: 402–403), end by thanking Zeus *Xenios*, patron of hospitality.

56. In Herodotus they are a *phulê*, in Aristotle a *phratria*; see Vian, *Les Origines de Thèbes*, 216–225.

57. *Isthmian* 7.13 (*Dôrid' apoikian*); for Sparta and the Spartoi, see Vian, *Les Origines de Thèbes*, 223.

58. Vian, *Les Origines de Thèbes*, 219.

59. Herodotus 2.72. Note also 1.176, where the majority of the inhabitants of Xanthos, who claim Lycian descent, are in reality *epêludes*; "true" Lycians were not resident in Xanthos at the time of the city's destruction.

60. Thucydides 6.2.2.

61. Ibid., 1.2.5–6; the formula appears to insist on the completely artificial character of the populating of the "autochthonous" city. See also 2.36.1 (the Funeral Oration of Pericles).

62. See for example: Herodotus 1.56 (Dorians); 1.56, 5.57–61 (Thebans); 4.147 (Thera); 8.44 (Athenians); Thucydides 6.2.2 and 5 (Sicily); 6.4.5–6 (Messina). From which Aristotle deduces that the name is not a relevant criterion for a city's identity (*Politics* 3.1276b10f.).

63. See for example Herodotus 8.43; 4.147 (Theras, an emigrant from Lacedaemonia, yet still Cadmean and Phoenician).

64. My comments in parentheses, in italics. On reasoning by analogy, see Darbo-Peschanski, *Le Discours du particulier*, 148 and 150–151.

65. Thucydides 6.2–6, 1.

66. Occurrences in two relevant chapters (1.2 and 12). *Oikein* and derivatives: *oikoumenê* (2.1), *oikêtorôn* (2.3), *ôikoun* (2.5), *etoikêseis* (2.6), *apoikias* (2.6), *katôikizeto* (12.1), *ôikêsan* (12.3), *apoikias* (12.4). *Histêmi* and derivatives: *metanastaseis* (2.1), *apanistanto* (2.2); *metanistato* (12.1), *anastantes* (12.3), *anistamenê* (12.4), but also *staseis* (2.4), *astasiaston* (2.5) and *staseis* (12.2). It was A. Parry ("Thucydides' Historical Perspective," *Yale Classical Studies* 22 [1972]: 47–61, especially 52–53) who drew attention to the role of the derivatives of *histêmi* in book 1.

67. *Histêmi*: "set, place, stop, weigh, fix" (Chantraine, *Dictionnaire*, s.v.). Pindar uses the opposite strategy to Thucydides, stating that Thebes "set, erect on its heels, the Dorian colony of the Lacedaemonians" (*estasas: Isthmian* 7.13).

68. He does use the noun *stasis*; however, we know that for a Greek, beginning with Thucydides (3.82.1: *ekinêthê*), as a word for civil war (1.2.4 and 12.2) it was synonymous with *kinêsis*, movement. Such is the paradoxical destiny of the verb *histêmi*.

69. Among the many prefixes cited by Chantraine, we note, only in the Archaeology, the use of *ana-* (four times), *apo-* (once), *dia-* (once), *en-* (once), *kata-* (five times), *meta-* (twice), *sun-* (three times).

70. For an example, see Herodotus, on the Ionians: 1.145.

71. Note the preponderance of definitions of autochthony through negative comparison in funeral orations (see, for example, *Menexenus* 237b: *ouk . . . oude . . . alla . . .*, *ouk . . . hôs hoi alloi, alla . . .*); there is good reason to inquire about a positive value which is only negatively defined.

72. *Politics* 3.1257a7–8, with, for *oikêsis*, the definition of Casevitz, "the act of residing" (*Le Vocabulaire*, 82).

73. On the formula *oikeô*, see Casevitz, *Le Vocabulaire*, 75 and 87, n. 4.

74. Ibid., 76–81.

75. During the presentation of this material in Léon Poliakov's seminar, Maurice de Gandillac drew my attention, for which I thank him, to the fact that from Maurras to Brasillach, Action Française has chosen to designate Jews, like "Metics," as *occupants*. The difference is that in classical Athens, neither the purely institutional term Metic nor that of "occupant" was injurious or hostile. See also C. Mossé, "Citoyens actifs et citoyens passifs dans les cités grecques," *Revue des Études Anciennes* 81 (1979): 241–249.

76. Thucydides 2.36.1; Demosthenes *Funeral Oration* 4.

77. Euripides *Erechtheus* frag. 50, ed. Austin, v. 11; Lysias *Funeral Oration* 17 (with the opposition *ôikêsan/ekektênto*: they occupy/they possess); Hyperides *Funeral Oration* 7; see also *Menexenus* 238e (the cities of masters and slaves).

78. I am thinking of Herodotus' use of the verb *hidrumai* (8.73).

79. See Loraux, *Children of Athena*.

80. From *metoikein* to *tôi onti [. . .] oikein* and from *tôi onti [. . .] oikein* to *oikeiois topois*, it is worthwhile studying the reappropriation of the verb in the *Menexenus* 237b–c; analogous development in Isocrates *Panegyricus* 24 (from *oikoumen* to *tous oikeiotatous*).

81. On *oikeios* see Loraux, "*Oikeios polemos*," 14–17; in the same sense, Casevitz observes a preference for *oikeô* over *ktizô* in the vocabulary of colonization, once the accent is put on birth (*Le Vocabulaire*, 221–222).

82. *Republic* 3.414c; *Laws* 2.663d–664a (*to toû Sidôniou muthologêma*). Note that in the city of the *Laws*, a composite community resulting from a colonial enterprise and defined as *sunoikia*, the stranger has his place without difficulty.

83. Greed and professional cunning (shared in both cases with the Egyptians): *Republic* 4.436a2, *Laws* 5.747c4.

84. *Oikista*: *Republic* 2.379a.

85. Beyond the more or less ambivalent treatment which the *Menexenus* reserves for it, note that in the *Timaeus* autochthony is presented through the vocabulary of colonization (*katôikisen*: 24c5), and that in the *Critias* it is the result of a fabrication by the craftsmen gods Athena and Hephaistos (*empoiêsantes*: 109d1).

Chapter 6. Inquiry into the Historical Construction of a Murder

1. English translation by Katherine Jones (New York, 1955), 3. The present chapter first appeared in *L'Écrit du Temps* 10 (1985): 3–21.

2. See P. Lévêque and P. Vidal-Naquet, *Clisthène l'Athénien: Essai sur la représenta-*

tion de l'espace et du temps dans la pensée politique grec de la fin du vi^e siècle à la mort de Platon (Paris, 1992).

3. On the political connotations of the verb *harmozô* (and its derivative *harmonia*), see G. Nagy, *The Best of the Achaeans: The Making of the Hero in Archaic Greek Poetry* (Baltimore, 1979), 297–300. Harmodios and Aristogeiton are an inseparable pair: the scholia that glorify the heroes insist on using the dual, and Aristotle uses the dual (*paroxunthenta*) in the *Athenian Constitution* (18.2), whereas Thucydides uses the singular (6.56.2: *parôxuneto*) and attributes the state of paroxysm to Aristogeiton alone.

4. If, dominated by the representation of politics as pure manipulation, philological tradition sees in the celebration of the Tyrannoktones a simple ideological operation, this is because, as C. W. Fornara demonstrates in "The Cult of Harmodius and Aristogeiton" (*Philologus* 114 [1970]: 155–80), the work of historians of antiquity is influenced by Thucydidean truth.

5. 1.20.2 and 6.53–60. I refuse on principle to consider that we have here one text too many, which a final editing of the work would have resolved. Rejecting the too-easy explanation based on incompletion, I am interested in the convergence and divergence between these two means of treating the same question.

6. A. W. Gomme, A. Andrewes and K. J. Dover, *A Historical Commentary on Thucydides*, vol. 4 (Oxford, 1970), 317–318.

7. The Athenian predilection for Harmodios is expressed in a drinking song (*skolion* 11 Diehl: "Beloved Harmodios") which Aristophanes cites in the *Acharnanians* (980, 1093) as the most popular of refrains: see V. Ehrenberg, "Das Harmodioslied," *Wiener Studien* 49 (1956): 59–60, and M. Vetta, *Poesia e Simposio nella Grecia antica* (Bari, 1983), 124. Thucydides refers to it explicitly at 6.53.3. The enterprise of Aristogeiton and Harmodios: 6.54.1; dominant role of Aristogeiton: 54.3, 56.2. It is as expected that the old men of the chorus identify with the elder of the two conspirators in Aristophanes (*Lysistrata* 632f.).

8. That a young man is quickly inflamed is a *topos* in Greek thought; wisdom, the fruit of experience, on the other hand, is the province of mature men. Instead of educating his lover in the ways of moderation, Aristogeiton gives himself over to excess: 6.54.3 and 56.2.

9. Gomme, Andrewes, and Dover, *A Historical Commentary* 4: 328–329.

10. 1.22.1 and 3.

11. Thucydides and *akoê*: see M. Detienne, *L'Invention de la mythologie* (Paris, 1981), 107–111 (rev. 1992); the working of the intelligence summons the "I," but an "I" that reasons through probability (*moi dokei*, "it seems to me that"); on *tekmêria* see L. Canfora, *Totalita e selezione nella storiografia classica* (Bari, 1972), 15.

12. On *akoê* in the Archaeology see M. Simondon, *La Mémoire et l'oubli dans la pensée grecque jusqu'à la fin du v[cf12]e siècle av. J.-C.* (Paris, 1982), 266.

13. Somewhat embarrassed by the importance of this concession, Thucydides' readers have imagined a distant kinship between the historian and the family of the Peisistratids, thus legitimizing the tradition through family connection.

14. I refer to the first words of 6.60.1.

15. 1.20.1. *Basanos* is a touchstone, but also recourse to torture in an investigation; *basanizô* is to elicit speech under torture. A slave can testify only under these conditions, therefore torture guarantees the truth of his testimony; see Antiphon 1.10 and 2.3, 4. The force of the Thucydidean metaphor can be imagined.

16. Same expression in Antiphon, whom tradition sees as Thucydides' teacher (5.71).

17. *Zêtêsis, apodekhomai* (receive), *basanisai to pragma, heurein* (find) (6.53.2); *heurein* and *abasanistôs [. . .] dekhontai* (1.20.1), *zêtêsis* (1.20.3); the echo is not accidental. *Abasanistôs* is a *hapax*, as is *basanisai* in the figurative sense (in books 7 and 8 the verb has its basic meaning of torturing); *zêtêsis* reappears only in book 8 (two occurrences, one in a judicial sense). These linguistic facts are an indication that one should read the excursus of book 6 with regard to considerations of method in book 1.

18. An author of *Hellenika* possesses only ethnic identity (thus Herodotus is "of Hali-carnassus" or "of Thurii"); when, however, Thucydides appears in book 4 as a *stratêgos*, a participant in the story, his identity is expressed as customarily in the polis, through his patronymic: Thucydides, son of Oloros.

19. To borrow the expression from A. Momigliano, "L'Excursus di Tucidide in 6.54–59," *Mélanges L. Ferrero* (Turin, 1971), 32.

20. The article by I. Calabi-Limentani ("Armodio e Aristogitone, gli uccisi dal tiranno," *Acme* 29 [1976]: 9–27) emphasizes the honors accorded the Tyrannoktones, and on the basis of the decree of Demophantos (cited in Andocides *On the mysteries* 98) concludes that there was a reactualization of the cult in 410.

21. 1.20.2; cf. 6.57.2–3, where chance plays a role not in the murder of Hipparchus, whom the conspirators wished to kill first to be assured of their vengeance, but in the place where they encounter him.

22. Cf. the operations Thucydides performs in order to establish, even at the price of contradictions, that the causes of the action are not political; see M. Lang, "The Murder of Hipparchus," *Historia* 3 (1954–1955): 400–403.

23. A celebrated *skolion* (10 Diehl) credits them with having made Athens *isonomos* ("equal of rights"). In the speech which Miltiades addresses to the polemarch Kallimakhos of Aphidna to convince him to make the decision to give battle at Marathon, Harmodios and Aristogeiton are portrayed as liberators of Athens (6.109). This portrayal is also im-plicated in the Herodotean polemic which claims (6.123) that the Alcmeonids were greater liberators of Athens than Harmodios and Aristogeiton.

24. On the *skolion* 12 Diehl V 4, see Ehrenberg, "Das Harmodioslied," 66. In assim-ilating to the Tyrannoktones those who died in an attempted coup against a tyrant or in-surgent, the decree of Demophantos shows that the Athenian democracy considered the death of the latter as sufficient claim to glory; see Calabi-Limentani, "Armodio e Aris-togitone," 23–22, and the remarks of M. Ostwald, *Nomos and the Beginnings of the Athe-nian Democracy* (Oxford, 1969), 134–135.

25. Beyond Thucydides 6.53.3, see Aristophanes *Lysistrata* 1150–1156.

26. Lang, "The Murder of Hipparchus," 399–400.

27. If the use of euphemisms like *ergon* or the verb *prassein* to designate acts of civil war is, as I have suggested ("Thucydide et la sédition dans les mots," *Quaderni di storia* 23 [1986]: 95–134), a characteristic of seditious language inserted into the historical nar-rative, the presence of such euphemisms in the narration of book 6 begs the same inter-pretation.

28. *Alogistos tolma* appears only at 6.59.1 and 3.82.4 (a passage concerning seditious rhetoric); on this expression see Loraux, "Thucydide et la sédition."

29. *Stasis* destroys citizens of the middle rank (3.82.8), but they can forestall it (8.75.1; cf. 8.92.8 where old men play the same role).

30. The exposé of method ends with this declaration (1.23.6).

31. Gomme, Andrewes, and Dover, *A Historical Commentary* 4:329.

32. Judicial rhetoric: see Antiphon 1.13 (*diêgêsasthai tên alêtheian*). A rosy Platonic future awaits *diêgeisthai* (and its derivative *diêgêsis*) as the word for narrative; see *Republic* 3.392d–294b.

33. 6.54.5-7 and 55.1-4. The story of the amorous coincidence begins at 54.1 and continues at 56.1.

34. Derivatives of the word *erôs* dot the narrative: 6.54.1 (erôtikê), 54.2 (erastês), 54.3 (*erôtikôs*), 57.3 (*erôtikês*) 59.1 (*erôtikên*).

35. Which does not mean that she is superfluous, or that she is part of a mythic structure like that reconstructed by F. M. Cornford, *Thucydides Mythistoricus* (Philadelphia, 1971), 132–133.

36. Beginning with Aristotle, who gives the Thucydidean version in broad outline in the *Athenian Constitution* (18-19.1).

37. Attested in speeches such as Demosthenes' *Against Leptinos* and Hyperides' *Against Philippides* or *Funeral Oration*.

38. Gomme, Andrewes, and Dover (*A Historical Commentary* 4: 322) also believe they can confirm that Thucydides' principal revelation consists not of love, but the role of chance.

39. M. van der Valk, "On the Composition of the Attic Skolia," *Hermes* 102 (1974): 10–11, and Ehrenberg, "Das Harmodioslied," 60.

40. *Apophainô* which means "produce outside, make clear," can designate denunciation in legal terms: see Antiphon 6.9 and Lysias 21.2. But in Thucydides, *apophainô* generally means "demonstrate" by means of proofs (except when the orator is Pericles, whose performative speech needs no support).

41. According to Lang ("The Murder of Hipparchus," 599), Thucydides reasons on the basis of probability: since Hipparchus, who was not the tyrant, was killed, the reason for the murder must be private. It remains to observe that the explanation based on love is unique in Thucydides.

42. At 2.43.1 Pericles invites Athenians to become lovers (*erastas*) of the power of their city; at 3.45.5 *erôs*, along with *elpis*, figures among the psychological factors that preside over the defection of an allied city; at 6.13.1 Nicias accuses Athenians of succumbing to the bad love (*duserôs*) for what they don't have; at 6.24.3 a great love (*erôs*) of maritime expedition seizes all Athenians.

43. Devoting a chapter of *Thucydides Mythistoricus* (201–220, "Eros Tyrannus") to the *erôs* of Alcibiades, F. M. Cornford does not seem to have considered the recurrence of *erôs* in the story of the murder of Hipparchus.

44. *Epithumia* as in Plato; five occurrences of the noun, five of the verb *epithumein* in book 6: nearly half of all occurrences (ten out of twenty-two).

45. See 1.22.4.

46. By way of example, two modalities of the relationship the historian entertains toward his city: being born an Athenian, but identifying with an impartial observer who dispassionately describes the confrontation between Sparta and Athens which divided the whole Greek world in two and forced every man to choose sides; being exiled from Athens, yet devoting the last book of *The Peloponnesian War* to a precise and noncomplaisant narration of the oligarchic revolution of 411, in which he is not supposed to have been present, but which Antiphon—whose disciple he is said to be—was supposed to have masterminded.

47. Thucydides 1.21.1.

Chapter 7: Why Greek Mothers Supposedly Imitate the Earth

1. J. J. Bachofen, *Das Mutterrecht: Eine Untersuchung über die Gynaikokratie des alten Welt nach ihrer religiösen und rechtlichen Natur* (1861), ed. K. Meuli (Basel, 1948); 101, 196, 385; A. Dieterich, *Mutter Erde* (1905; Leipzig, 1913); 53; J.-P. Vernant, "Le mythe prométhéen chez Hésiode," in *Mythe et société en Grèce ancienne* (Paris, 1974), 189–90. On the use of the quotation see the next chapter. (These pages were written on the occasion of an issue devoted to "Mothers" by the *Nouvelle Revue de Psychanalyse* 45 [1992], 161–72.)

2. See Chapter 9, below.

3. S. Freud, "Das Unheimliche," *Imago* 5 (5–6) (1919); 297–324. English translation in James Strachey, ed., *Standard Edition of the Complete Psychological Works of Sigmund Freud* (London, 1953–1974) vol. 17. The adjective *oikeios*, which denotes the familial and the familiar, intimacy and possession, is involved in wordplay in the text with oikein, "inhabit" (*Menexenus* 237b6 and c1).

4. See N. Loraux, *The Invention of Athens: The Funeral Oration in the Classical City* (Cambridge, Mass., 1986), 311–327.

5. *Republic* 3.414c.

6. Why do L. Méridier (Les Belles Lettres) and L. Robin (Gallimard) translate *bota* as "plants"? *Boton* can only mean "herd animal," and *bota* and *thêria* are contrastive in this text (cf. P. Chantraine, *Dictionnaire étymologique de la langue grecque*, s.v. "*boskô*"). Refusing to translate *zôia* (237d4) as "animals" is presumably connected.

7. At least in one of the arguments which make up the proof, cited in Aristotle's *Rhetoric* ("she has given birth since she has milk") and given as a necessary condition, whence a syllogism can be drawn (1.1357b15–17).

8. Plato *Statesman* 263d.

9. Euripides *Ion* 542.

10. See N. Loraux, *Children of Athena: Athenian Ideas about Citizenship and the Division between the Sexes* (Princeton, 1993), 84 n. 71.

11. *Aluton*, says Aristotle (*Rhetoric* 1.1357b17).

12. Aeschylus *Eumenides* 658–661; see Loraux, *Children of Athena*, 120–21.

13. P. duBois, *Sowing the Body: Psychoanalysis and Ancient Representations of Women* (Chicago, 1988), 72.

14. See also Euripides *Orestes* 553.

15. The doctoral thesis of Nathalie Ernoult on the feminine in Plato (in press), insists on the basic role of the mother in Platonic thought (diss., EHESS, 1996).

16. On the deceiving *muthos* see M. Detienne, *L'Invention de la mythologie* (Paris, 1981).

17. See Loraux, *Children of Athena*, 121–22.

18. If negation does indeed consist in that "the content of a repressed image or idea can make its way into consciousness, on condition that it is negated" (Freud, "Negation," *Standard Edition* 19: 235), exactly what the Greeks do not want to think appears beneath the Platonic encoding: "It is the earth which imitates woman."

19. On this form of transitive value, and on the fact that in Plato the perfect has been "increasingly drawn into the sphere of the past," see Pierre Chantraine, *Histoire du parfait grec* (Paris, 1926), 96, 159 and 163.

20. I sketch some of the elements of this history in the following chapter.

21. In the "Iambics on Women"; see Loraux, *Children of Athena*, 91.

22. The expression is Bachofen's, *Das Mutterecht*, 385; see also 399 ("she has taken on the material function"). But it also has meaning in Freud, where paternity becomes predominant only at the price of a "dematerialization," of an "emancipation from that explicit which is material, perhaps assimilated by Freud to that explicit which is maternal, or its stubborn phantasm" (M. Moscovici, *Il est arrivé quelque chose: Approches de l'événement psychique* [Paris, 1989], 38 and 347).

23. See Loraux, *Children of Athena*, 76–77.

24. He does so in *Table-Talk* 2.3.683a.

25. See N. Loraux, *Mothers in Mourning* (Ithaca, 1998), 57–65.

26. Aristophanes *Clouds* 530–532.

27. In a system in which the name of the father is indissociable from paternal blood, in which filiation is conceived less in a legal sense than perceptually on the basis of a physical resemblance, a mother has no legitimacy beyond the procreation of sons who resemble the father; whence the motif of the "just mother" (Loraux, *Mothers in Mourning*, 71–78) as sole admissible ideal of the mother.

28. We are far from the "sensorial certitude" which characterizes the mother in Freud, albeit envisaged from the point of view of the child rather than that of the father.

29. Shall I confess? I was operating under a tacit law of my own making whereby I ignored this phrase in my *découpage* of the text, until Jean-Pierre Peter drew my attention to it "for the first time."

30. Euripides *Hippolytus* 616–617.

31. Pausanias 10.12.10, with the commentary of Bachofen, *Das Mutterrecht,* 296.

32. "Negation," 235.

33. It is not certain that an analogous question doesn't arise concerning each of the *topoi* which constitute Platonism, but this is another matter.

34. Those following were suggested to me during a presentation of these remarks before the "groupe du 30 juin" (EHESS) by Françoise Davoine, Jean-Max Gaudillière, Gilbert Grandguillaume, Yves Hersant, Myriam Pécaut, Jean-Pierre Peter, Jean-Michel Rey, and Claude Veil.

35. The galactic and the mother were magisterially put on paper by J. Derrida in *Glas* (Paris, 1974).

36. "The problem of *mimêsis* remains to be re-elaborated, beyond the opposition of nature and law, of motivation and the arbitrary, of all the ontological pairs which have made it [. . .] illegible" (ibid., 262).

37. Pascal, *Pensées*, no. 199, ed. Lafuma.

38. Thus for example the Thessalian witches, those *Pharmakides* who rather than adjusting their rhythm to the moon, impose their will upon it; cf. Aristophanes *Clouds* 749–752.

39. Hesiod *Theogony* 117.

Chapter 8. From Plato to Bachofen and Beyond

1. Some indications concerning this appear in the next chapter. (A portion of the present chapter was published in *Kentron* 9 [1993]: 45–63.)

2. J. P. Vernant, "Hestia-Hermes: The Religious Expression of Space and Movement in Ancient Greece," *Myth and Thought among the Greeks* (London/Boston 1983), 140.

3. See N. Loraux, "La métaphore sans métaphore: A propos de l'*Orestie*," *Revue Philosophique* (1990): 247–268.

4. *Oedipus Rex* 270–271; in 25–28 the complete formulation of this comparison juxtaposes, as it must (for example in formulas of imprecation), the products of women, the earth, and herd-animals; Plato *Cratylus* 406b: *aroton misêsasês ton andros en gunaiki.* The labor of man: see also Euripides *Ion* 1095: *adikon aroton.*

5. Sophocles *Trachiniae* 31–33; Euripides *Orestes* 552–554, as well as Aeschylus *Seven against Thebes* 752–754 and Sophocles *Oedipus Rex* 1265–1267 (concerning Jocasta); see also *Antigone* 569: *arôsimoi [. . .] guai*, fields to be worked. Plato *Laws* 8.839a: *aroura thêleia.*

6. Cf. the use of *geôrgein* by Aristophanes (Lysistrata 1173), with commentary by J. Taillardat, *Les Images d'Aristophane* (Paris, 1962), n. 172.

7. See P. duBois, *Sowing the Body: Psychoanalysis and Ancient Representations of Women* (Chicago, 1988), 60.

8. The festival's complexity is evident in W. Burkert's treatment in *Greek Religion*, trans. J. Raffan (Cambridge, Mass., 1985), 242–246; on the *inconsistencies* the interpretation must deal with, see the study by E. Versnel, "The Thesmophoria," in *Inconsistencies in Greek and Roman Religion*, vol. 2 (Leiden, 1992), 235–260.

9. Diodorus of Sicily 5.4.7, with the remarks of Burkert, *Greek Religion*, 244, and F. Zeitlin, "Cultic Models of the Female: Rites of Dionysus and Demeter," *Arethusa* 15 (1982): 142.

10. Vernant, "Hestia-Hermes," 140; same phrase in his "Le Mythe prométhéen chez Hésiode," *Mythe et société en Grèce ancienne* (Paris, 1974), 189–190.

11. One occurrence of *arotêr* (Euripides *Trojan Women* 135) against numerous instances of the root *speirô* (Aeschylus *Seven against Thebes* 754 and Sophocles *Trachiniae* 32–33: *speiras arouran*; Euripides *Orestes* 552–553, Plato *Laws* 8.839a), sometimes associated with forms of *aroô* (Sophocles *Oedipus Rex* 1497–1498—this is perhaps to differentiate Oedipus' action from that of Laios in the *aroura* which is Jocasta; Euripides *Phoenician Women* 18, 22). Must we along with A. Dieterich (*Mutter Erde* [1905]; [Leipzig, 1913], 46–47) hypothesize the *identity* of *speirein* and *aroun* in "the most ancient popular thought"? I am not so sure.

12. On the limits of agrarian interpretation, see Burkert, *Greek Religion*, 244–245; emphasizing the second day of the festival (*nesteia*) over the first (*anodos*), as M. Detienne has the tendency to do in *Les Jardins d'Adonis* (Paris, 1972; rev. 1989), does indeed dispense with the cumbersome thematic of fertility, although I think along with Versnel ("Thesmophoria") that one cannot get rid of it altogether.

13. As pointed out, among others, by J. E. Harrison in *Prolegomena to the Study of Greek Religion* (Cambridge, 1903), 271.

14. The expression is from Zeitlin, "Cultic Models," 140.

15. J. J. Bachofen, *Das Mutterrecht: Eine Untersuchung über die Gynaikokratie der alten Welt nach ihrer religiösen und rechtlichen Natur* (1861), ed. K. Meuli (Basel, 1948), 100.

16. This is particularly evident in duBois (*Sowing the Body*): the term "metaphor" dominates (e.g., pp. 40, 55, 57, 59, 63–64), but sometimes and for no apparent reason the word "analogy" is substituted (pp. 58–60), and it happens on occasion that one functions as a strict synonym of the other (p. 82: "the ancient metaphor, the analogy"); likewise "assimilation" and "association" occur on p. 77, while on p. 78 the same operation is described as metaphoric.

17. Bachofen, *Das Mutterrecht*, n. 15, 386; less a "way of speaking" that an "emanation of the *Grundidee.*" So also on p. 86, the Erinyes are "the expression of terrestrial, corporeal, physical life, of the tellurian being."

18. Ibid., pp. 88 and 197.

19. Such a formulation may also appear topical concerning the Thesmophoria, where the imitation of ancient times is strengthened through manipulation of the *mimêmata* of the female sexual organ. Unless one is reminded, like E. R. Dodds ("The Religion of the Ordinary Man in Classical Greece," in *The Ancient Concept of Progress and Other Essays in Greek Literature and Belief* [Oxford, 1973], 146–147), that during this festival "they tried to persuade the earth to imitate them."

20. Vernant, "Hestia-Hermes," 149 (no reference to the *Menexenus* passage); slightly different treatment and precise reference in "Le Mythe prométhéen," n. 10, 189–190.

21. C. Robert, "Pandora," *Hermes* 49 (1914): 24; see L. Preller, *Philologus* (1852): 5 ("la terre est la première mère et la première femme tout simplement parce que . . . [Plato citation]").

22. On the basis of Dodds ("The Religion of the Ordinary Man") without going back to Plato, H. P. Foley ("The Conception of Women in Athenian Drama," *Reflections of Women in Antiquity*, ed. H. P. Foley [New York, 1981], 144) states that "in the women's festival of the Thesmophoria, the women ensure birth, as Plato says, not by imitating the earth, but by making the earth imitate them."

23. Preller, *Philologus*, n. 21, 5: *wie Plato sich gelegentlich ausdrückt*; Dieterich, *Mutter Erde*, 53; A. Motte, *Prairies et jardins de la Grèce antique* (Brussels, 1973), 82.

24. Bachofen, *Das Mutterrecht*, 101, where the reference to Cujacius is given, but not that of the *Menexenus*.

25. Ibid., p. 196.

26. Plutarch *Table-Talk* 638a.

27. Thus, surprisingly, the index in Dieterich's *Mutter Erde* has no listing under "Bachofen."

28. Bachofen, *Das Mutterrecht*, 385.

29. Ibid., 668 (feminine origin), 680 (opposition between Athenian autochthones and others), 848 (put in the mouth of a woman, the *epitaphios* is connected to the *thrênos* sung by women).

Chapter 9: Ancient Motifs, Modern Constructions: Earth, Woman

1. J. J. Bachofen, *Das Mutterrecht: Eine Untersuchung über die Gynaikokratie der alten Welt nach ihrer religiösen und rechtlichen Natur* (1861), ed. K. Meuli (Basel, 1948), 100, section 6. In the absence of any complete French translation of this work, I propose my own translations, with systematic transliteration of the words cited in Greek. (These pages, first published in *Peuples méditerranéens* 56–57 [1991]: 7–17, owe much to work on Bachofen with Yan Thomas, in the framework of a joint EHESS seminar.)

2. Surah 2, verse 223; from Blachère's translation ([Paris, 1957], 62). Masson's translation (Paris, 1967) refers to "field of labor" (*champ de labour*), Chouraqui's (Paris, 1990) to "labor" (*labour*), Berque's (Paris, 1990) to "sowing" (*semaille*). Naturally I owe this reference, bibliographically, to Gilbert Grandguillaume.

3. J. P. Vernant, "Hestia-Hermes: The Religious Expression of Space and Move-

ment in Ancient Greece," *Myth and Thought among the Greeks* (London/Boston 1983), 140.

4. Plato *Cratylus* 406b; see also Plutarch *Conjugalia praecepta* 144b; *aroura*: Aeschylus *Seven against Thebes* 754; Sophocles *Trachiniae* 31–33, *Oedipus Rex* 1257; Euripides *Orestes* 553; Plato *Laws* 8.839a.

5. On the great antiquity of the Thesmophoria, see W. Burkert, *Greek Religion*, trans. J. Raffan (Cambridge, Mass., 1985), 244–245.

6. Vernant, "Hestia-Hermes," 140 (my italics).

7. Plato *Menexenus* 237d–238a. See N. Loraux, *Children of Athena: Athenian Ideas about Citizenship and the Division between the Sexes* (Princeton, 1993), nn. 14 and 71, pp. 9 and 84.

8. Hesiod *Theogony* 513–514, and for the following, 571–572; *Works and Days* 70–71, 60–61.

9. For example P. duBois, *Sowing the Body: Psychoanalysis and Ancient Representations of Women* (Chicago, 1988); interpreting Pandora as "an attempt to appropriate to the male the powers of cultivation, reproduction, thesaurization" (p. 57) leads the author to focus her attention solely on the crown that the goddess mother wears in the *Theogony* or on the jar of the *Works and Days*, which is represented as an *analogon* of the female body, to the detriment of other indications in the text.

10. With the exception of readers (*lecteurs [et lectrices]*) who relate Earth and woman only to better accentuate the difference between the one and the other; so Jane Harrison, after positing a Pandora "rise(n) from the earth; she *is* the Earth" or "goddess [. . .] of the Earth," suggests that in Hesiod, "the great figure of the Earth-goddess, Pandora, suffered eclipse: she sank to be a beautiful, curious woman; she opened her great grave-*pithos*, she that was Mother of Life" (*Prolegomena to the Study of Greek Religion* [Cambridge, 1903]), 281, 283, 285.

11. See J. P. Vernant, "Hesiod's Myth of the Races: An Essay in Structural Analysis," in *Myth and Thought among the Greeks* (London/Boston, 1983), 19, as well as "Le Mythe prométhéen chez Hésiode," *Mythe et société en Grèce ancienne* (Paris, 1974), 189–190. The existence of a posterity is only implied in the statement that a man who has not married lacks "care for his old age" (*Theogony* 605); in the *Works and Days* there is only mention that before Pandora, humankind knew nothing of *ponos* (90–91).

12. Vernant, *Myth and Thought*, 19, and *Mythe et société*, 189–190, as well as P. Levêque, "Pandora et la terrifiante féminité," *Kernos* 1 (1988): 49–62. In a 1914 article ("Pandora," *Hermès* 49: 24) C. Robert hesitates to complete the operation.

13. S. Freud, *Correspondence with Lou Andreas-Salomé*, July 30, 1915, cited by M. Moscovici in *Il est arrivé quelque chose: Approches de l'événement psychique* (Paris, 1989), 57; for commentary, ibid. p. 82.

14. See also N. Loraux, *Children of Athena: Athenian Ideas about Citizenship and the Division between the sexes* (Princeton, 1993), 83–90.

15. Bachofen, *Das Mutterrecht*, 385–386 (section 68).

16. Among the Roman explanations of this term, note that of Quintilian (*Institutio Oratoria* 1.7.28) on the letter C, meaning Gaius and which *inversa mulierem declarat*.

17. Plutarch *Quaestiones Romanae* 271e. Note that for a *Roman* expression, Bachofen cites only the *Greek* text of Plutarch.

18. Plutarch, *Quaestiones Romanae* 271e. Festus *De verborum significatione*, ed. Lindsay (Leipzig, 1913), 85. This wife endowed with every virtue was that of Tarquinius Priscus,

and was apparently named Tanaquil (see also Pliny *Natural History* 8.48.194). But Bachofen has no reason to be impressed by such an explanation, he who in *Die Sage von Tanaquil* (Heidelberg, 1870), divines Asiatic queens and female power behind the exemplary Roman matron.

19. Cicero *Pro Murena* 12.27.

20. On Cratylism see Patrice Loraux, "L'audition de l'essence," in *Le Tempo de la pensée* (Paris, 1993), 198–218.

21. Bachofen, *Das Mutterrecht*, 88 (section 2): *gê* and *gunê* are written in Greek characters and Gaia in Roman, which is not without significance in this regard.

22. Varro in St. Augustine: see N. Loraux, *Children of Athena*, 60–61, and *The Experiences of Tiresias: The Feminine and the Greek Man* (Princeton, 1995), 187–188.

23. Bachofen, *Das Mutterrecht*, 171–172 (section 23).

24. Greek religion, Roman law: if Bachofen uses Roman law as a starting point for enumerating different forms of social organization, this law codifies the power of *fathers*, the *telos* of the construction, and serves to translate and transfix earlier states retrospectively. But in the domain of the maternal, law is merely the emanation which proceeds from a religious conception of the world (ibid., 85–86, section 1). Thus in the beginning we have religion as first connection to nature: see 29–30 (Introduction), 97 (section 5), 196 and 199–200 (section 26).

25. Bachofen, *Das Mutterrecht*, 198 (section 27: Athens). The word *gaia* is written in Greek, and I transcribe it as with all the Greek words cited by Bachofen. Need we point out that the most authoritative modern commentaries on the Roman formulation do not for one moment envisage such an etymology? Theodor Mommsen, in a publication more or less contemporary with *Mutterrecht* (*Römische Forschungen* [Berlin, 1864], 1:11–12) rejects the hypothesis of Indo-European origin (comparison with a word in Sanskrit) in order to retain only that of the derivation from the old patrician *nomen gentile Gavius*, a hypothesis taken up by E. Bickel ("Die Nomenklatur der Materfamilias vor dem Jahre 527–227," *Rheinisches Museum für philologie* 65 [1910]: 582.)

26. But not Hesiodic, since Hesiod denaturalizes the etymology of Pandora (*Works and Days* 80–82).

27. Bachofen, *Das Mutterrecht*, 390 (section 69: Egypt).

28. Which is the Platonic gesture *par excellence*; see the preceding chapter.

29. Bachofen, *Das Mutterrecht*, 197 (section 27). Bachofen also lists, among others, *gua*, "labored earth and belly of the mother," citing *Antigone* 569, *guion*, member, and the "German expression" *Frauenzimmer*.

30. Which allows him, unlike Fustel de Coulanges, to put the mother and not the father at the beginning.

31. Bachofen, *Das Mutterrecht*, 193 (section 27): *eri, era*, a word for the earth, related to Latin *terra, tera* and German *Erde*.

32. See, among others, ibid., pp. 296, 428, 430, 540, 863.

33. Ibid., p. 428: "das sterbliche Weib *(gunê-gê)*."

34. But one must always be wary of negation of the type "*it isn't* the earth *which* imitates woman, but. . . . "

35. See E. R. Dodds, "The Religion of the Ordinary Man in Classical Greece," *The Ancient Concept of Progress and Other Essays in Greek Literature and Belief* (Oxford, 1973) 146–147: "At the Thesmophoria, [women] tried to persuade the earth to imitate them."

36. Bachofen, *Das Mutterrecht*: Pandora is declared the daughter of Deucalion (pp.

750, 868), avoiding the problem, and often linked to Eve (pp. 158, 404, 589) or Harmonia (p. 225). The only passage in which Bachofen refers explicitly to Hesiod's text focuses not on her, but on the opposition of Epimetheus and Prometheus (pp. 43–38).

37. Ibid., p. 863; Bachofen prefers Gaia in her role of *Allmutter* (p. 540).

Chapter 10: The Return of the Excluded

1. J. Derrida, "Nous autres Grecs," in *Nos Grecs et leurs modernes*, ed. B. Cassin (Paris, 1992), 260. (This chapter was conceived on the occasion of the volume *Autour du travail de Jacques Derrida: Le passage des frontières* [Paris, 1994], 151–159.)

2. Which means that, as recently with E. Alliez and E. Wolff, I will "privilege" Plato (cf. Derrida, "Nous autres Grecs," p. 253); at least I will privilege it by choice, pure and simple.

3. Taking into account that "Platonism" is [. . .] one of the effects of the signed text of Plato, the effect being dominant for a long time and for obvious reasons, yet this effect is always turned against the text" (J. Derrida, "Chôra," in *Poikilia: Études offertes à Jean-Pierre Vernant* [Paris, 1987], 288.)

4. I am referring to the article "*khôra*" in Pierre Chantraine, *Dictionnaire étymologique de la langue grecque* (Paris, 1968–1980) where, after the denominative *khôreô* and its dual meaning of "contain, have a place for" (tr.)/"make room, leave" (intr.), appears the adverb and preposition *khôris*: "separately, apart, except, beyond, without."

5. M. Heidegger, *Introduction to Metaphysics* (quoted by Derrida in "Chôra," n. 2, p. 294; see also p. 268, on the "teleological retrospection" featured in this text); as well as *Qu'appelle-t-on penser?*, 174–175 (in Derrida, "Chôra," n. 5, p. 295).

6. Plato *Phaedrus* 251c–d: *hotan men oûn blepousa [. . .] dekhomenê [. . .] hotan de khôris genêtai [. . .]*.

7. On the act of "sending away," cf. "La Pharmacie de Platon," in Derrida, *La Dissémination* (Paris, 1972), 75–77 (rev. 1993).

8. N. Loraux, "La Métaphore sans métaphore: A propos de l'*Orestie*," *Revue de Philosophie* (1990): 247–268.

9. M. Detienne and J. -P. Vernant (*Les Ruses de l'intelligence: La mêtis des Grecs* [Paris, 1974] 303–304), record the condemnation, but not recurrence in the signifier.

10. N. Loraux, *The Experiences of Tiresias: The Feminine and the Greek Man* (Princeton, 1995); D. M. Halperin, "Why Is Diotima a Woman? Platonic Eros and the Figuration of Gender," *Before Sexuality: The Construction of Erotic Experience in the Ancient Greek World*, ed. D. M. Halperin, J. J. Winkler, and F. I. Zeitlin (Princeton, 1990), 257–308.

11. Commenting on the *Phaedrus* 251b–d, Giulia Sissa ("On parvient difficilement à enfanter la connaissance," AAVV, *L'Exercice du savoir et la différence des sexes* [Paris, 1991]) observes that it is "when *psukhê* remains apart" that it painfully experiences its closure (p. 41).

12. Plato *Theaetetus* 190c, 190d; *Sophist* 246a9 (in the *gigantomakhia peri tês ousias*, the sons of the earth, "being in contact [*ephaptomenoi*] with everything of this order (rocks, cliffs, etc.), agree that this alone is what produces resistance and contact [*epaphên*])."

13. Heraclitus frag. 10, ed. Diels-Krantz.

14. Derrida, "La Pharmacie de Platon," 71.

15. Loraux, *The Experiences of Tiresias*, 162–163.

16. Derrida, "La Pharmacie de Platon," 171–172, 182–183.

17. Derrida speaks of the "sign-*pharmakon*" (ibid., p. 113).

18. Derrida, "Nous autres Grecs," 267.

19. On "the problem of the stranger as philosophical enigma," now cf. H. Joly, *Études platoniciennes: La question des étrangers* (Paris, 1992) (quotation pp. 38–39).

20. According to Joly (ibid., p. 42), the stranger from Athens would be "a new way for Plato to distance himself in terms of his own city, and to journey outside it beneath this anonymity."

21. See G. Bennington and J. Derrida, *Jacques Derrida* (Paris, 1991), 193, 196.

22. *Statesman* 262c–d; on the poor division (taking Hellenic identity as a unit separate from all the rest, then lumping the other *genê*, in spite of their basic diversity, together under the term "Barbarians"); the crane as poor dialectician (263d) is paradigmatic of this error. The reference is from H. Joly, *Le Renversement platonicien: Logos, epistêmê, polis* (Paris 1974), 352; on the critical function of this text, and the fact that "a discrimination does not make a division," cf. also Joly, *Études platoniciennes*, 12–13, 63–64, 88.

23. On the increasingly important role of the stranger in the dialogues, cf. P. Vidal-Naquet "La Société platonicienne des dialogues," *La Démocratie grecque vue d'ailleurs* (Paris, 1990), 95–119, whose conclusions I do not endorse, however, as far as concerns the statement that "it is not for reasons of doctrine that Plato was compelled to open wider the register of his characters to strangers." Reasons of doctrine indeed not, but definitely reasons of *thought*—and not purely sociological reasons, in any case.

24. In the epilogue to *Children of Athena: Athenian Ideas about Citizenship and the Division between the Sexes* (Princeton, 1993), 240.

25. Plato *Republic* 3.382c (*pharmakon khrêsimon*); 3.389a and 5.459d (*en eidei pharmakou*); in 3.414b–c the word used is *mêkhanê*, as in the *Laws* 2.663e–664a.

26. Or at least of the anti-polis, as demonstrated by F. Zeitlin in "Playing the Other: Theater, Theatricality, and the Feminine in Greek Drama," *Playing the Other: Gender and Society in Classical Greek Literature* (Chicago, 1996), 341–374. For tragedy, the polis concerned is called Athens.

27. An irremediably ambivalent motif, as attested in the *Laws* (1.641c) by the reference to "Cadmean victory."

28. On the co-occurrence in Plato of *phusis* and *tekhnê* in matters of autochthony, cf. Loraux, *Children of Athena*, 125–127.

29. J. Derrida, "La Différance," *Théorie d'ensemble* (Paris, 1968), 18.

30. Plato *Republic* 3.414c.

31. The word *epêlus*, which is often translated "immigrant," properly means an "arrival" or a "(late) arrival." See Chapter 5, above.

32. One would like to be able to suggest at the same time that they are "familiar" and/or "intimate."

33. Chantraine, *Dictionnaire étymologique*, s.v. "*eilikrinês*."

34. Aristophanes *Acharnians* 507–508: "We are among ourselves today, only the pure wheat of the city, the Metics being the bran, you might say."

35. This verb occurs in Liddell and Scott under the form *iliggiaô*, but Chantraine connects *eiligiaô*, "become dizzy," with *eileô*, "wind, turn round." The element *eili-* is therefore the same in the two words.

36. Plato *Phaedo* 79c; *Cratylus* 410b7; *Republic* 3.407c; *Theaetetus* 175d.

37. M. Casevitz, *Le Vocabulaire de la colonisation en grec ancien* (Paris, 1985), part 2: 73–218.

38. Ibid., 76–77 (on the aorist, denoting a new establishment), 75 (the present theme, with a note on *oikein en* for characterizing the Metic); cf. also 83 on *oikêtôr*.

39. Aristotle *Politics* 3.1275a7–8, cited in ibid., 82, where Casevitz adds that *oikêsis*, in its legal sense, means "right of residence."

40. Casevitz, *Le Vocabulaire*, 222.

41. Isocrates *Panegyric* 24–25 (with a play on *oikein* and *oikeion*). In contrast it is *oikein en* which is used twice by Thucydides concerning Athenian autochthony: 1.2.5 (Archaeology) and 2.36.1 (Funeral Oration of Pericles).

42. Lysias *Funeral Oration* 17: *tên allotrian ôikêsan* (an aorist which Casevitz [*Le Vocabulaire*, 81] translates as "they occupied foreign soil").

43. The expression is Derrida's, "La Pharmacie de Plato," 180; the above quotation is taken from p. 181.

44. Plato *Phaedo* 108c (aorist of *oikein*), 114c (*oikizein*: cf. Casevitz, *Le Vocabulaire*, 94), and 117c (*metoikêsis*: death as change of residence; but in the *Laws* 8.850a9, *metoikêsis* denotes the condition of being a foreign resident; cf. Casevitz, *Le Vocabulaire*, 178).

45. Derrida, "Chôra," 279 (as well as 276–277).

46. Euripides *Hippolytus* 617 (*katoikisas*).

47. Cf. N. Loraux, *The Invention of Athens: The Funeral Oration in the Classical City* (Cambridge, Mass., 1986), 455, n. 172.

48. Casevitz, *Le Vocabulaire*, 167–172; likewise *oikizô* is attested twenty-five times in Plato against seven in Herodotus and twenty-one in Thucydides (ibid., 91–92).

49. Cf. C. Malamoud. "Sans lieu ni date: Note sur l'absence de fondation dans l'Inde védique," in *Tracés de fondation*, ed. M. Detienne (Louvain/Paris, 1990), especially 183–84, 186, 191.

50. Derrida, "Nous autres Grecs," 275–276.

51. Derrida, *Glas* (Lincoln, Nebraska, 1986), 115–116.

52. To follow a theme in Derrida, "La Pharmacie de Platon," 164 (see also 177).

53. See Derrida, "Chôra," 293.

54. In thus translating *tês tekous*, I am forgetting neither that Greek paternal extremism withholds from the mother the title of *tokeus* ("parent" in the sense of "engenderer": see Aeschylus *Eumenides* 658–659), nor that the Latin language has co-opted *parens* for the use of the father, far from the sphere of parturition where *parens* in law refers to the one giving birth (cf. Y. Thomas, "Le Ventre: Corps maternal, droit paternel," *Le Genre Humain* 14 [1986]: 213).

55. On the mother in Derrida, cf. Bennington and Derrida, *Jacques Derrida*, 197–198.

56. Plato *Statesman* 273e. Among the effects of the world's volte-face is reproduction, designated as *tês kuêseôs kai gennêseôs kai trophês mimêma* when the living can no longer "be born in the bosom of the earth from a *competition of foreign elements*." The notion of *mimêma* evokes the *Menexenus*, 238a4–5, but with an extra twist (which I have not taken up in Chapter 8): the *khôra* of the *Menexenus* is certainly the "true" mother, but the *Statesman* adds that this mother produces the same with the other.

57. Plato *Republic* 3.414d–e (*plattomenoi, demiourgoumenê*, but *mêtêr*).

58. For example Derrida, "Chôra," 291.

59. Cf. Derrida, "La Pharmacie de Platon," 183–184 (concerning the *Timaeus* 49a).

60. Derrida, "Chôra," 271.

61. Ibid., 269, 271.

62. See above, n. 56.

63. Derrida, *Glas*, 153.

64. For this production see P. Boulez, P. Chéreau, R. Peduzzi, and J. Schmidt, *Histoire d'un "Ring": Der Ring des Nibelungen ("L'anneau du Niebelung"), de R. Wagner,* Bayreuth 1976–1980, (Paris, 1980).

Chapter 11. Democracy Put to the Test of the Stranger (Athens, Paris)

1. M. I. Finley, *Politics in the Ancient World* (Cambridge, 1983), 84 (translated by J. Carlier as *L'Invention de la politique* [Paris, 1985] with a bibliography of critical remarks addressed to Finley). (This chapter was published by Roger-Pol Droit in *Les Grecs, les Romains et nous: L'Antiquité est-elle moderne?* [Paris, 1988], 164–88.)

2. M. Bloch, *Apologie pour l'histoire*, 7th ed. (Paris, 1974), 121 (and more generally 117–121: "To judge or to understand?")

3. A theme that may be discerned increasingly often in Finley's work; but in a 1962 article ("Athenian Demagogues," translation by J. Carlier in *Economie et Société en Grèce Ancienne* [Paris, 1984], 104–105), Finley doesn't hesitate to compare—in order to contrast, naturally—an Athenian demagogue and Winston Churchill facing the Assembly.

4. It being understood that I am talking about actions which are conscious and consciously assumed, and not about the "savage" comparison which is generally used by those who reserve the severest academic censure for the practice of analogy.

5. J. Isaac, *Les Oligarques* (Paris, 1945).

6. Xenophon *Hellenica* 2.3.21; Lysias *Against Eratosthenes* 6–7; an evident source for Isaac, *Les Oligarques*, 145.

7. See N. Loraux, "Sur la transparence démocratique," *Raison Présente* 49 (1978): 3–13.

8. N. Loraux, *The Invention of Athens: The Funeral Oration in the Classical City* (Cambridge, Mass., 1986), especially chapter 4.

9. See Chapter 2, above, and my article in *Espace Temps* 42 (1989): 17–22.

10. Thucydides 2.39.1.

11. M. Austin and P. Vidal-Naquet, *Economies et sociétés en Grèce ancienne* (Paris, 1972), 118; I refer to their excellent general account, 115–118. See also D. Whitehead, *The Ideology of the Athenian Metic* (Cambridge, 1977), 69–108.

12. But see Loraux, *The Invention of Athens*, 32–37.

13. Aristotle *Politics* 3.1275b35–37.

14. Xenophon *Hellenica* 2.3.48.

15. Aristotle *Athenian Constitution* 40.2; the tradition of Athenian orators concurs with Aristotle's account.

16. Xenophon *Hellenica* 3.3.48; the idea then is to distance from the citizenship the lowest census division, that of the *thêtai* whose only resource is their capacity for work. This way one is rid of the most democratic fraction of the *dêmos*.

17. This was seen by P. Cloché, *La Restauration démocratique à Athènes en 403 av. J.-C.* (Paris, 1915), 452.

18. Aristotle *Athenian Constitution* 29.2 adds: "[. . .] with the thought that the constitution of Cleisthenes was not really democratic, but analogous to that of Solon."

19. Xenophon *Hellenica* 2.3.48.

20. One of the many proposed identities—the oligarch Critias—was recently de-

fended, not without convincing arguments, by L. Canfora, for example in *La Démocratie comme violence*, French translation by D. Fourgous (Paris, 1989).

21. Pseudo-Xenophon *Constitution of the Athenians* 1.10.12.

22. Attested by the recurrence of the verb *gignôskô* (to know, be conscious of), and the noun *gnômê* (opinion, therefore political determination) in this text.

23. See Chapter 5, above.

24. Freedom: Xenophon *Hellenica* 3.24.25 (Critias' speech); pleasure for the users of the constitution: Isocrates *Panathenaica* 130, *Areopagitica* 70, Plato *Republic* 8.558c (pleasure, anarchy, and variety, equality apparently for equals as well as those who were not).

25. Plato *Republic* 8.562b6–563b9. Likewise Aristotle (*Politics* 6.4.1319b) speaks of the democratic anarchy of women, slaves, and children.

26. I developed this theme in June 1990 at Caen, during a congress of the International Federation of the Rights of Man which celebrated the 2,500th anniversary of the reforms of Cleisthenes.

27. "Discussion du projet de loi Jean-Claude Gayssot tendant à réprimer tout acte raciste, antisémite ou xénophobe," *Journal Officiel de la République Française*, Thursday May 3, 1990, no. 18 (1990): 907–911.

28. Title of an article that appeared in *L'Histoire* 142 (March 1991), which mentioned the Le Mans colloquium where the present chapter was presented and the speech of Marie-France Stirbois, yet without mentioning that the first was concerned with the second.

29. On Demos: an article in *Le Soleil*, April 25, 1902; on democracy: *Gazette de France*, August 24, 1902; these texts are reprinted in C. Maurras, *Dictionnaire politique et critique*, ed. P. Chardon (Paris, 1932).

30. For example: "Foreigners are those who intervene in what doesn't concern them: foreign to the country, foreign to occupation, they are the smarting wound of French labor" (*L'Action Francaise*, May 14, 1908, reprinted in the same collection with a reference to the article titled "Metic").

31. Aristotle *Athenian Constitution* 27.4.

32. On the contrary, it is the moment for the speaker to name Glotz a first and then a second time, quoting him word for word that "in the fifth century B.C. people were not in the least tempted to abuse the right they enjoyed of conferring upon foreigners the title of citizen" (*La Cité grecque* [Paris, 1928], 278, quoted in the speech at 909).

33. On Glotz see the remarks of F. Hartog in "Liberté des anciens, liberté des modernes," *Les Grecs, les Romains et nous*, 119ff.

34. There is a whole name-strategy in this speech, of which the most impressive example is a listing of murderers with North African names (p. 938), supposed to prove anti-French racism.

35. As well as, in February–March 1991, Hebrew inscriptions for the purpose of reactivating anti-Semitism, and Arabic ones for fanning the flames of anti-immigrant sentiment.

36. See the remarks of Whitehead (*The Ideology*, 33-34), on the fact that funerary epigrams denote Metics neither as Metics nor as "living in" such and such a deme, but rather by their ethnicity, which gives their original citizenship; only the *isoteleis* were exceptions to this rule, and they sported their title proudly, like a quasi-citizenship.

37. On these conventions, Glotz states in the following paragraph (p. 275) that they denote "a large and truly international spirit," adding that "foreigners could see their con-

dition ameliorated by individual and unilateral measures." Nowhere else is the distortion, which consists in substituting for these conclusions the leitmotiv of "discrimination," so manifest.

38. Glotz, *La Cité grecque*, 279 and 398.

39. For whom, after Chaeronea, "the noblest ideas [of Athens] had to take refuge in philosophical doctrines in order to have, at least indirectly, some action on human society" (ibid., 398); Glotz is doubtless thinking of Stoic *philanthrôpia*.

40. Heraclitus frag. B 8, *Les Présocratiques*, ed. J. P. Dumont (Paris, 1988); the translation used in the speech is not that of Dumont ("The opposite is useful, and the loveliest harmony is born from different things"), which, apparently, did not suit the author. On the Schmittian question of the designation of the enemy and its application by Christian Meier to Aeschylus' *Eumenides*, see N. Loraux, "La Cité grecque pense l'Un et le deux," *Mélanges Pierre Lévêque*, vol. 8 (Paris, 1995), 275–291.

41. On Hippodamos see Aristotle *Politics* 2.1267b22–1268a14, and 7.1330b24, with remarks by P. Lévêque and P. Vidal-Naquet, *Clisthène l'Athénien: Essai sur la représentation de l'espace et du temps dans la pensée politique grecque de la fin du vi⁰ siècle à la mort de Platon* (Paris, 1964, rev. 1983, 1992), 124–128.

42. See Plato *Laws* 4.705a and 707a. It might be added that at 707d, speaking of colonization and the composition of the band of colonists, Plato extols the friendship that can exist in a homogeneous group, but also recognizes that a *pantodapon genos* would perhaps be more likely to submit to new laws.

43. Austin and Vidal-Naquet, *Economies et sociétés*, 118.

44. With the stipulation that studies devoted to a close comparison between Greece and Rome must be encouraged, with no agenda other than the scholarly.

45. O. Vallet, in the *L'Histoire* article cited above, n. 28.

46. I thank all my interlocutors at the Le Man colloquium, as well as colleagues and friends who, when this work was presented at the PRI seminar "Usages modernes de l'Antiquité" (EHESS), helped me to refine these analyses.

Index

Achaeans, 55
Achilles, 55
Acropolis, the, 29, 34, 35; ashes of Theseus and, 37; Erichthonios and, 45; Pan
and, 42
adoption, 51
Aegean Sea, 37
Aegeids, the, 58, 59
Aegyptos, 50, 118
Aeschylus, 45
Aetolians, 55
Agamemnon, 55
Aglauros, 42
Agora, the, 29, 34, 35, 36. *See also khôra*
agriculture: Bachofen on, 102, 106; marriage and, 99, 101; *Menexenus* and, 86;
sex and, 96; the Thesmophoria and, 97;
women and, 83
aiôn, 17
Ajax, 37
akoê, 69–70, 79, 80
Alcibiades, 66, 79
allophulos, 52
alterity, 58, 64; the foreign and, 118; *oikeô*
and, 62; the polis and, 26, 121; the
stranger and, 48
Amazons, 33
analogy, 98
andres, 10; versus the Amazons, 33. *See
also* men
androgenous, the, 8
anthropomorphism, 123
anthrôpoi, 6, 11. *See also* men

Antiphon, 154n. 46
anti-Semitism, 134
Apollo, 5, 30, 42; in *Eumenides*, 86
Apollodorus, 11
Arcadia, 15, 50, 146n. 5; Athens and, 16,
41–46; the autochthone and, 55; Pan
and, 40–46
Archaeology, the (Thucydides), 61; the
murder of Hipparchus and, 69, 70, 81
Archinos, 130–31
Argos, 10–11, 30, 58, 150n. 55; Phoro-
neus and, 10
aristocracy, 21, 23, 57
Aristodemos, 57
Aristogeiton, 65–68, 71–77, 82, 152nn. 3,
8, 153n. 23
Aristophanes, 25
Aristotle, 49; autochthony and, 17–18;
citizenship and, 136, 147n. 7; on the
city, 17; democracy and, 130. *See also
Politics*
Arkas, 8, 14, 44, 45
arkhê, 76, 88–89. *See also* creation; origin
Artemis, 96, 103
articulation, 114
artifice, 2, 93; woman as, 7
Asia Minor, 57, 59
assimilation, 97
asylum, 138
Athena, 2, 35, 121; the Acropolis and, 42;
Athens and, 9, 29–31; creation of man
and, 5; Erichthonios and, 30–31; Hephaistos and, 24; the Panathenae and, 33

167

Danaids, the, 150n. 55
Danaos, 50, 58–59, 118, 150n. 55
death, 1, 5; reproduction and, 26; women
   and, 8
Delphi, 30, 37, 39
Demeter, 103; Earth Mother and, 97
democracy, 23, 142; Aristotle and, 130;
   Athenian, 125, 127–29, 133–35, 137;
   autochthony and, 53; Cleisthenes and,
   21; the historian of, 126–27; masculine,
   33; Maurras on, 136; the Metic and,
   128–29; militarism and, 34; murder of
   Hipparchus and, 66, 72–73, 75; National Front and, 135, 137; oligarchs
   and, 131–32; origin and, 26; Pan and,
   40
Democracy Ancient and Modern (Finley), 126
dêmos, 34; Finley on, 125; murder of Hipparchus and, 72, 81
Demosthenes, 24; on immigrants, 21
Derrida, Jacques, 111–12, 114–15, 117
Deucalion, 3, 9, 160n. 36; the Hellenic
   race and, 10; Pyrrha and, 11–12
Dictionnaire étymologique (Chantraine), 95
différance, autochthony and, 116–17, 119
Diomedes, 5
discourse: autochthonous, 48–49, 51–52,
   62–63; historical, 82; in *Sophist*, 114
discrimination, 139, 140
disorientation, 119
dissymmetry, 123
Dorians, 59; Herodotus and, 55; Sparta
   and, 15
Dryopians, 55
duality, 7
dust, 5
dwelling, 119–20. See also inhabiting;
   oikein; *oikeô*

earth, 1–3, 14; Bachofen and, 106,
   108–10; Erichthonios and, 24, 30; history of religions and, 93; *khôra* and,
   123–24; maternity and, 83, 85, 89, 95;
   in *Menexenus*, 84–85, 92, 118; the
   mother and, 86, 87, 90–92, 94, 118;
   Ovid and, 12; Pandora and, 103–5,
   159n. 10; in *Republic*, 28; women and,
   6–8, 87, 95, 98, 100–101, 159n. 10
Earth Mother, 1, 9; Athenians and, 24;
   Bachofen and, 108; Demeter and, 97;

Pandora and, 7, 104; religion and, 95.
   See also Gaia; *gê*
echo, 92, 153n. 17; Pan and, 39
écriture, 114. See also writing
eilikrinôs, 118–19
enemy, the, 54
epêlus, 54, 150n. 55, 162n. 31
ephaptomai, 113
ephebes, 76
equality, 22–23, 53; origin and, 34; Plato
   and, 133
equivalence, 98
Erechtheus, 9, 31, 37
Erichthonios: the Acropolis and, 42, 45;
   andres and, 8–9; Athena and, 30–31;
   Athenians as Erichtheids, 9–10; Athens
   and, 8, 10, 44; birth of, 14; the earth
   and, 24, 30; as founder of a *genos*, 18;
   Gê and, 2; invents politics, 45; the
   Panathenae and, 33
erôs, 76, 79, 81, 82; *écriture* and, 80
ether, 5
etymology, 47
eugeneia, 34
Eumenides (Aeschylus), 86
Euripides, 92
Eve, 161n. 36
event, 63
evil: beautiful, 6, 89; as woman, 5–6, 8, 89
excluded text, 122

fact versus democracy, 136
family, 18
father, the, 86; versus the mother, 24–25,
   91, 156n. 27
fatherland, 24–25, 49; Crete and, 115;
   militarism and, 34
females, 2, 6, 93, 96, 123; duties of,
   90; the field and, 102–3; *Menexenus*
   and, 86; Pandora and, 7–8. See also
   women
fertility, 2
field, the, 1–3; the female and, 102–3;
   marriage and, 95–96; plowing and,
   95–96; religion and, 95–96; as stranger,
   86; women as, 83
Finley, Moses, 126, 134; on the *dêmos*,
   125
fire, 5
flood, the, 11

women, 87, 110; the agricultural and, 83; versus *andres*, 6, 33; *andres* and, 90; as artifice, 7; Athenians and, 23–25; Bachofen and, 106–9; the city and, 24; creation of, 6, 104; death and, 8; the earth and, 6–8, 87, 88–93, 95, 98, 100–101, 159n. 10; as evil, 5–6, 89; *gê* and, 91–93; *genos* and, 23–25; Hephaistos and, 6; Hesiod and, 103–5; the imaginary and, 23–24; the male and, 98; in *Menexenus*, 85; *mêtêr* and, 124; Pandora and, 7–8; Pyrrha and, 12; as residents, 121; strangers and, 112; the womb and, 96
Works and Days (Hesiod), 7, 104
wound, the, 102
writing, 80. *See also écriture*

xenophobia, 20, 134
Xenophon, 131

Zeus, 9, 10, 44, 45; Deucalion and, 11; in *Theogony*, 5

MYTH AND POETICS

A series edited by

GREGORY NAGY